EX - LIBRIS

WEDDING
days

"Your words are my food, your breath is my wine. You are everything to me"
Sarah Bernhardt

400
RECIPES AND IDEAS

TO MAKE THE WEDDING OF YOUR DREAMS COME TRUE

ALEXIA ALEXIADOY

Recipes

Alexia Alexiadou

Editions

Alexia Alexiadou, Alba Editions

Editor

Vaggelis Kitsakis

Art Direction

Laura Venizelou

Photographs

Vivianna Athanassopoulou

Assistant photographer

Ageliki Petropoulaki

Styling

Anna-Maria Barouch

English Translation

Eurologos Athens

Illustrations

Theano Petridou

Layout – Films

Orion Prepress Studio

Printing

E. Daniel & Co. S.A.

Binding

Dionissis Dedes

ISBN 960-91508-6-1

Copyright © 2003 Alexia Alexiadou

13, Likovrisseos & Iroon Politechniou St., 141 23 Likovrissi, Athens, Greece

Tel.: (210) 28.56.057 – 62, Fax: (210) 28.13.455

www.bestcookbooks.gr

e-mail: aalexiadou@albaeditions.gr

1st edition: 2003

I take you as my lawful
Wedded husband;
To have and to hold from this
Day forward; for better or
Worse; for richer or poorer;
In sickness and in health;
To love and to cherish, as long
As we both shall live.

**To Have and to Hold
Traditional Christian Vow**

...to my husband Vangelis

A man who doubts his love,
can or rather should doubt all the other,
less important things.
Sigmund Freud

C O N T E N T S

Alexia Alexiadou's latest book "Cooking: a Love Affair" has contributed to her being established as one of the most successful representatives of creative contemporary Greek cuisine. "Cooking: a Love Affair" was awarded the first prize as Best Greek cookbook in all categories, at the International Cookbook Revue competition in France, which took place in December 2001. The English edition of the book has been successfully marketed in the United States, Australia, Great Britain and Canada.

Alexia Alexiadou was born in Thessaloniki, Greece and received her MBA at City University Business School of London. After working for a time in the field of finance, she gave this up to enter the world of gastronomy, thus following a long family tradition. She self-published her first book "Exotic Cuisine" in 1996, which was widely acclaimed in Greece. Her experiences from living abroad contributed to an increased familiarity with the cookery of various countries, which she tried to record, guided by her innate talent.

Mrs. Alexia Alexiadou's talent for imparting a youthful air to traditional Greek and international dishes has made her a popular contributor to several Greek magazines and newspapers. She frequently appears with her mother, Vefa Alexiadou, on Greece's popular Morning Coffee Show on ANT-1 TV. She is an active member of the IACP organization (International Association of Culinary Professionals) and often travels abroad to accumulate knowledge and inspiration. In collaboration with her mother, she has created the 20 BEST RECIPES series, which won international acclaim and the Diplome d' Honneur at the 1998 Perigueux World Cookbook Fair, and which has sold in total of 30 titles, more than 2,500,000 copies in Greece alone!

Her most recent work in collaboration with her mother is "Sunny, Mediterranean Cuisine", which also received an award at Perigueux France in 1999. This book has also received an award (Silver Ladle Award 1999) for its photography in Australia.

Alexia Alexiadou now makes her home in Athens and together with her husband Vaggelis Kitsakis they run their own publishing house. With her latest book "Wedding Days" she wishes to celebrate her seven years of marriage to her husband. The result of this wedding is the author's most perfect "masterpiece", their daughter Hara.

... A TASTE OF YOUR DREAM WEDDING

... is what I plan to offer you in the pages of my new book. All fairy tales and stories, romantic novels and movies end with the hero kneeling down, asking his heroine to marry him while offering her his eternal love vows accompanied by the little velvet box holding the precious diamond-studded proof of his love. Happy endings are just the beginning in real life. Once the proposal you've always dreamed of has become reality, you land from cloud nine into the real world, and your brain is being stormed by millions of questions, when and where, who and how, the wedding dress, the reception, the guests, the parents, the church, the bridesmaids, the invitations… Relax and get organized. With the right planning, organizing your wedding will be as exciting as the wedding day itself.

In the following pages you will discover all the small secrets and essential hints for a successful wedding, and all the useful information you need to know before you step up to the altar. The process of organizing a wedding is an interminable chain of pleasant chores, shopping, invitations and festivities. Live it to the full, it is unique and unforgettable. Don't avoid tradition, all it can bring is benefits and gifts, and will offer much joy to your parents and relatives. Invite your parents-in-law to your house, plan an engagement as glamorous as the wedding you are envisaging, treat your girlfriends to a wedding shower with homemade "low calorie" desserts, invite your close friends to the last wedding gown rehearsal and grab every chance to have a ball. The following recipes will guide you step-by-step through the correct and easy organization of the small celebrations leading to your wedding day.

In my first book "Cooking: a Love Affair", you will find tips on how to "seduce" your other half, and my advice in it is: Get cooking! The message of my new book is to celebrate your love and… Get Married!

ALEXIA ALEXIADOY

The proposal

To the groom-to-be: If romance and fantasy are the main traits of your personality, then you don't need to read this paragraph. If, however, you need a little help with such things, it's never too late to add romance to your life, now that you are thinking of proposing to your beloved.

Take special care in choosing the proposal ring. A diamond is most appropriate, as the hardness of the stone symbolizes enduring love, and as it is more expensive than gold, it seems a much firmer promise, offering greater security to the woman you love. She will be happily showing it off to friends and relatives all the time, so make sure it is the wedding ring of her dreams. A family heirloom is a very good choice as it encompasses memories, loving stories and tradition.

Invite her to a romantic dinner you've prepared by yourself. For the day of your proposal, it is romantic to choose a special date in your beloved's life, such as her birthday, the day on which you first met, Valentine's Day or New Year's Day. Keep in mind that women treasure such memories forever, and you will make a great impression just by being thoughtful. Set the table, and pour the red wine into a pitcher to breathe. Dim the lights, play some soft music and decorate the room with lit candles. Don't forget the ring to surprise her with at the end of the meal, together with the dessert or next to her espresso cup. Another good idea is to offer her the ring during a special, rich breakfast. If words are not your strong point, write your message and put it in a fortune cookie. Bewitch the woman of your dreams, because she's worth it!

Organizing the wedding

To the bride-to-be: Now that you've said "yes", it's time to get organized. Your wedding day is meant to be the best day of your life. Organizing such a big event may seem daunting, but it can be an unforgettable experience if organized correctly and methodically. The book's main chapters, together with the useful advice below, will guide you step-by-step from today to the big event. The wedding planner at the end of the book will help you arrange your activities in time, so that there is a minimum of surprises and less stress. Organizing your wedding can be as easy as saying "I do".

I. Date and Venue

The first and main thing to do after the big decision is to think about your dream wedding. You should first answer the following questions and make a note of your answers.

1. What time of year should your wedding be held? Is there a particular date that means a lot to you, Christmas, for example, or Valentine's Day, or your anniversary?

2. The number of guests and their composition: you and your beloved, a few close relatives and friends, a large number of guests (around 150 is the average number for a wedding), a society reception with a large guest list.

3. The style of the wedding: romantic or modern, classic or minimal, traditional or contemporary, formal or unpretentious.

4. Where you'd like to get married: in town or in the countryside, near home or abroad? At your place of origin or on your favorite exotic island? Tradition says that the bride should marry at her home parish.

5. Would you like to hold a religious ceremony: choose the house of worship accordingly, a remote chapel, a church in the countryside, in a big city, a cathedral, a huppah or a decorated altar in your country house? Other choices if you are holding a civil marriage ceremony: the Town Hall, courthouse, registry office, indoor or outdoor home arrangement.

6. The reception area: a house or a garden, yours, your friends' or relatives' or a rented venue? Venues: a hotel, hall, garden, estate, art gallery. Alternative areas such as boats, hotels, a deserted beach.

1. Now write down the first answers that spring to mind. Then write down alternative answers to all the above, and limit your choices. Read again carefully and ask yourself how feasible it is to combine a huge reception with a small remote church on an island far away from where you live. In order to find the ideal solution, it is a good idea to plan your

budget, as this will help you exclude certain ideas, and accept others. The next step is to distinguish between dreams and reality, without, however, having to draw away from the basic principles of the wedding of your dreams.

2. Write down the new specifications of your wedding, including the date, the size of the event, the style, the ceremony and reception venues. The above should initially be decided together with your companion, and then with the family who will be footing the bill, if this is the case, of course, and the couple is not going to undertake all the expenses. Traditionally, the bride's father pays for the wedding, a tradition that has replaced the older "institution" of giving a dowry. If you have decided who your best man and maid of honor are, it is a good idea to get their approval as to the wedding date.

3. Now you are ready to start some market research. Remember that the wedding day belongs to you and your companion, and, within reason, everyone should respect your opinion. Don't let anyone draw you away from your basic principles, such as the style of the wedding and the size of the event.

4. Make an initial list with the names of all those you would like to invite as a couple, and ask your mother and your companion's mother for similar lists.

5. Make a second list with alternative choices of church in the same style or place where you would like the wedding to be held, as well as alternative special companies that you can contact for one or all of the following:

Reception hall, catering, invitations, jeweler's for the wedding rings, wedding cake, music, transport to and from the church, dressmaker's, sugared almond case or other wedding favor specialist, wreaths and candles, event designer, florist, photographer/video.

II. The Wedding Rings

1. Order the wedding rings once you have formally set a date, so that you can have it engraved on them. Many couples prefer to engrave their engagement date and their names on the inside of the rings. Gold or platinum, as thick as you prefer, you will find a huge selection of wedding bands, both classic ones, and more modern designs studded with diamonds.

2. The simple gold band in its purity and beauty symbolizes everlasting and constant love between the couple, and it is a reminder of the promise they have made to each other. Wear the rings on your right hand when you are engaged, and on the left when you get married. In the Christian Orthodox wedding, the priest will place the rings on your fingers, and the maid of honor will change them around at the wedding. In Greece and in Russia, married people wear wedding rings on the right hand.

3. The engagement tradition says that a silver platter with sugared almonds and rice is placed on a table covered with a clean white tablecloth in the bride's home. When the groom arrives at the house, he brings the rings with him and places them on the tray, to formalize his proposal. The same tray is then carried to the church and placed on the altar during the wedding ceremony. The wedding wreaths are also placed on it for the priest to bless.

III. The Wedding Gown and the Bridesmaids

1. The only choice that you are entitled to make exactly as you want, and demand that others accept, is your wedding gown. Don't decide in a hurry. Remember that simple dresses and pastel colors may be what you like, but they are also gowns you will often wear during your married life, to parties, receptions, and friends' weddings. At your own wedding, you should stand out from your guests, so white or ivory are the best choices.

2. Pay particular attention to the train and back of your dress, as this is what your guests will be looking at during the wedding ceremony.

3. Marriage in a church is a holy religious ceremony, and must be treated with respect and reverence. Choose a dress that suits you, and is stylish and elegant, in harmony with the location. Evening dresses can be as revealing as you like, but don't treat your wedding dress as just another formal garment – think of everything it must and shall represent on the big day.

4. Rent or buy? You may only wear it once, but if you can afford it, have your wedding dress made especially. After the ceremony, store it in a beautiful antique chest in your bedroom. As the years go by, you will often look at it and reminisce. The memories evoked by an old wedding dress are often stronger than those from photographs or videos. An old Greek tradition states that the dress should be worn by three other brides after you, to reinforce your wedding. Abide by the traditions, even if you are afraid your dress might be damaged. It is nice to know that your dress has given happiness to other couples, and that it has been blessed once again.

5. Order the bridesmaids' dresses together with the wedding dress. The bridesmaids should be present for at least one fitting. If, as common in Christian Orthodox weddings, you have only very young bridesmaids, dress the little girls in organza tulle the same color as your dress. Their dresses don't have to be identical to yours, on the contrary, it is a good idea to make them different, so that the wedding dress stands out. For an elegant and ethereal presence, choose pale colors, such as mint, or ocean blue. Dress the little boys in white tuxedos. Don't deny a child the pleasure of being a bridesmaid – there is no rule saying how many children can participate. Their participation is a "blessing', and their happiness will be your joy. In the Anglosaxon tradition it is normal to have a very young flowergirl and a pageboy carrying the pillow with the rings. They are followed by the bridesmaids coupled by the young men who are called the ushers. Try to choose a flattering color for the group of young women who will attend as your bridesmaids– a brown-gold metallic taffeta or a silver-blue dark gray matte gown will highly accentuate the brightness of the bridal gown. Choose colors that match the season, brown for autumn, silver for winter, mint-green for summer and lilac for spring, colors that will match the rest of the wedding decorations, such as the flowers, centerpieces, wedding favors and wedding candles. Match their bouquets accordingly. A simple suit matching the groom's is a good choice for the ushers.

IV. The Announcements and Wedding Licenses

1. Your wedding announcement must be published in a local newspaper, at the place where the ceremony will be conducted. Publication must take place at least 15 days and up to 3 months in advance. You must mention your full names, the names of both families, the mothers' maiden names, and the location of the ceremony.

2. Obtain all necessary documents in time for getting the wedding licenses. Religious weddings take place once a license has been issued by the Bishop of the area. Interested parties go to the bride's parish priest to discuss formalities.

The following documents are required by the Greek Orthodox Church:

• A certificate that declares that none of the parties involved is remarried, issued by the home parish of each. If either of the two is divorced or a widower, a divorce or death certificate is required.

• A relationship certificate. This is issued by the bride's parish priest, with two witnesses, or by declaration of the interested parties, stating that there is no relationship between them prohibiting marriage.

• An application compiled at the same time by the bride's parish priest and signed by both parties to the wedding. For all of the above you will have to pay stamp and clergy duties.

• A cutting from the newspaper where the wedding announcement was printed.

• The license is issued by the Cathedral office, from which the couple will receive it before the wedding, and submit it to the bride's parish priest or the priest who will conduct the ceremony, if this has been requested, and the bride's parish priest grants written permission to the priest in the parish where the wedding is to take place.

• After the wedding, a wedding certificate is sent to the bride's parish priest, so that the marriage can be recorded in the Parish Registers and a copy sent to the State register for declaration of the marriage.

• Before the wedding, the couple must declare and sign the surname it wishes to be given to the children born from this union. The bride is no longer obliged to change her surname, and therefore the use of two surnames in official papers is not correct. (Source: Dimitriada Holy See)

V. The Invitations, Bonbonnières, Candles and Wreaths

1. Once you have set a date and booked the venues for the ceremony and reception, it is time to start thinking about your invitations. The choice of invitation must set the style of your wedding right from the start, and will aim to put people in the mood for your unique celebration. Think about your stationery at least six months before the wedding. Check out a variety of suppliers to see what they have to offer and request samples to check the paper quality in person. Type out your intended wording and check it thoroughly. Make sure the place names are spelt correctly, that you have included all relevant times and a phone number and/or address if you require guests to reply. Send out your invitations about two months before the big day. Usually the invitation mentions only the date and time of the ceremony, while details of the reception are mentioned on a separate evening invitation. This is not valid if all the wedding guests are to go on to the reception, and in this case you can also avoid time-consuming good-byes and wishes in the churchyard.

2. If you decide to hold a Wedding List in a store, place the relevant cards in the envelope with the invitation. The wedding invitations must be printed. When you hand in the invitations to be printed, include all other material requiring the same processing, such as envelopes and place cards for the reception. Don't post your wedding invitations; deliver them personally or by courier. Print your visiting card with your new address along with the invitations. The invitation envelope can include a small RSVP card, so that you know exactly how many guests are actually coming to the reception. Usually, a special note for your vegetarian guests to check can be placed on the RSVP cards.

3. Remember to order service cards, menus and place cards together with your invitations. The "order of service" cards reflect the importance of the occasion by guiding your guests through the sequence of events, whether your wedding is held at the church, a registry office or at home.

4. Print cards saying "thank you very much for your gift" for each of your guests, to send after the wedding. When sending out your thank-you notes after the wedding, thanking your guests for their gift and for taking part in your special day, an excellent touch is to add a photo of you with them, taken at the reception.

5. The bride is responsible for choosing the wedding favors. In Greece and in Italy it is common to offer as favors 'sugared almonds' tied together in tulle with ribbons. The number of almonds should always be odd, as it bears the symbolism of the Christian Church. Choose the favors once you have decided on the style of the wedding and the dress. You may choose a bonbonnière that matches the material and color of the wedding dress. Alternatively, it can be a small object to go with the sugared almonds and follow the style of the wedding, such as a silver pomegranate for a New Year's wedding or cinnamon sticks and spices wrapped in tulle for a wedding in the countryside. In many parts of Greece, other delicacies are offered along with the sugared almonds, such as almond biscuits, honey cakes, and other sweets, prepared by the bride or her mother. The bonbonnière is a commemorative gift for your guests, and will remind them of your wedding for a long time afterwards. Treating your guests to a wedding favor is a beautiful thought. Your guests have gathered on your wedding day to celebrate with you and make your day special, and thus you must honor them accordingly. Do not forget to acknowledge out-of-town guests, proposing a special toast to them, in order to show how grateful you are that they have traveled a long distance to support you on your special day.

6. The candles and wedding wreaths used in Orthodox Christian weddings are selected by the bride and paid for by the best man and maid of honor. The candles are always two, one for the bride and one for the groom. Choose candles that match the style of the church: For a summer wedding in the yard of a small chapel you will definitely need something simpler than for a formal ceremony in a cathedral. You will find a large variety of wreaths, made of porcelain, shiny silver, or tiny pearls. White wreaths reward the couple's virtue. Buy a pretty case to keep them in after the wedding.

7. Your obligations to your best man and maid of honor are a personal gift for each, as well as the maid of honor's special bonbonnière. The bonbonnière is usually a crystal, silver or porcelain decorative object for the home, filled with sugared almonds and decorated with tulle.

VI. The Registry

1. Before you close the envelopes and share out the invitations, make sure you have "opened" your registry. Feel comfortable about opening a registry. Gift registries are an established tradition and a convenient service to your guests. Find out your choices when you go to the relevant store. One solution is to have them deliver the gifts to your house as they receive them, or have them make a list, from which you can choose what you want to keep, exchange and have delivered.

2. Choose a store selling china, crystal and cutlery. Remember that a good set of crockery and cutlery is a life-long acquisition, and even if at the moment you think it superfluous, as your social obligations increase, you will find it indispensable.

3. For your new home you will also need kitchen utensils, such as saucepans, small appliances, coffee maker, mixer and blender, pasta and meat-grinding machine, an everyday plate and cutlery set, a wok, aprons, and all those amazing accessories that will decorate your kitchen and make working in it an amusing game of creation. Whoever takes on the chef's role, you or your companion, the kitchen must be fully equipped.

4. You will need bed linen, sheets, duvets and covers for the bed, tablecloths, kitchen towels, mats and bathroom towels.

5. Many couples choose stores selling electric and electronic appliances.

6. Don't forget to send thank-you notes to everyone who sent you a present. In this way, besides saying thank you, you are letting them know that you received their gift, and notifying them of your new address at the same time.

VII. Pre-wedding Celebrations

1. Family meeting: Your first task straight after you decide to get married, is to get the two families in touch, if they don't already know each other. Traditionally, the groom's family goes to the bride's house. The groom brings flowers, and the bride's parents offer sweets and liqueur. A much better idea is to organize a dinner party at your new home, serving light and tasty dishes that you know both families will like. The suggested menu is composed of light dishes Mediterranean-style that are both elegant and easy to prepare. To break the ice, serve ouzo as an aperitif, with some piquant Mediterranean appetizers.

2. Engagement: Usually, the engagement takes place when the two families meet, and is not followed by an official ceremony. An engagement party is a good opportunity to make a festive announcement of your intention to get married, to your friends and relatives. Usually, the engagement takes place only with relatives present, who give the bride gifts of money and jewelry. Easter or Christmas are good times for an engagement. Depending on when you decide to have your engagement party, choose the menu suggested in the relevant chapter or the Christmas banquet menu, and adjust it to the number of guests. The period of time elapsing between an engagement and a wedding is usually necessary for the couple to organize its new household. The average length of an engagement is about a year, but some couples remain engaged for much longer or much shorter periods.

3. Making the bed: The Greek and Italian tradition of making the bed has equivalents all over the world. In America they have bridal showers, where the bride's friends gather to admire the wedding dress and the new home, and bring gifts. In Greece the bed is usually made by single women. Once it is made, they then "shower" it with money, and roll a pretty baby on it three times, to bring the couple fertility and luck. Combine the "making of the bed" with an invitation to afternoon tea. Serve tasty cakes, light in calories, so that you can enjoy them without feeling guilty, as you are only a few days before the wedding. This is a good chance to show your friends the wedding dress and ring, and receive personal gifts from each of them.

4. Bachelor party: A not so foreign tradition, as in olden days, in many parts of Greece where wedding celebrations began several days before the ceremony itself, the groom used to enjoy himself with his friends, while the bride didn't sleep at home for a whole week. All these pre-celebrations took place for practical reasons more than for the amusement of the couple. Today, couples usually spend the last evening of their single lives with their personal friends, partying until the early hours of the morning. In Greece the bride and groom usually arrange the bachelor party or hen night for their friends. In Anglosaxon countries it is the friends who do the organizing, as a surprise for the bride and groom. An original idea is to arrange a couple of days on an island in Greece, or some other fun place, like Amsterdam, Paris, London or Las Vegas, in two separate groups – the bride and her friends, the groom with his. Another great idea is to treat your girlfriends to a couple of days in a beauty spa. There, instead of consuming large amounts of calories in food and alcohol, you can relax and prepare for the big event.

VIII. The Bridal Bouquet and Floral Decorations

1. The bride's bouquet may only be a small detail in the whole organizing frenzy, but it is still the most important touch. No one can imagine a bride without a bouquet, whether it is a bunch of wild anemones or the most exquisite bouquet of miniature roses. Like the Virgin Mary's lily, the bride's flowers should symbolize her virtue and innocence. The unaffected beauty of flowers attracts everyone's eyes and adds a special touch to the bride's prevailingly white outfit.

2. Besides the bouquet, you will need a lot of help from the florist you choose, as you will have to decide on the decoration of the entrance of the church and the aisle, the candles, the car taking you to the church, the hallway leading to the reception, the head-table as well as centepieces for your guests' tables, the head-wreaths for the bridesmaids and the bouquets they will be holding. Give your florist the freedom to choose the most vibrant flowers of the season. Schedule planning meetings with your florist at the ceremony and reception locations. For the reception, make sure the centerpieces are tall or short enough for your guests to be able to see each other.

3. The search for a florist should begin as early as possible. Even if you plan to arrange the flowers by yourself, it is still a good idea to consult a wedding florist who will offer you both advice and flowers that might not be readily available to you. Florists with wedding experience will be most helpful with all the small details that you may overlook, like petals for the flowergirl to scatter, pretty arrangements for the powder room, ideas for fresh floral headpieces. Instead of a florist, you may decide to hire an event organizer, who will help you conceptualize and will execute the entire wedding with exceptional flair and regard for every detail. Just remember that when organizing the wedding in your own garden, you must take into consideration all the flower and plant arrangements already existing in the garden; therefore it is a good idea to meet with the specialist on location.

4. Design your bouquet according to your own taste and character. Make sure that it is unique – different to all the other floral decorations. Don't be afraid of bold colors; a majestic bouquet of red roses or yellow chrysanthemums will accentuate the bright white color of your gown even more. Don't forget to toss it at the end of the wedding. Gather all the single women together, turn your back and toss the bouquet to them. Whoever catches it is next in line to get married.

FLOWER	DECLARES	CHARACTER
Gardenias	Joy	Calm and peaceful
Jasmine	Joy of youth	Youthful and happy
Camellias	Honesty	Elegant and sensitive
Chrysanthemums	Hope	Wishing to stand out
Daisies	Childish innocence	Gentle and close to nature
Red roses	Love	Passionate and loving
White roses	Peace	Calm and stable
Yellow roses	Power	Dynamic
Miniature roses	Innocence	Child-like
Pink roses	Romance	Romantic
Sweet peas	Youthful vigor	Youthful and happy
Anemones	Fragile beauty	Sensitive
Tulips	Eternal love	Artistic
Water lilies	Unique beauty	Peaceful and elegant
Orchids	Passion	Passionate and bright
Lilies	Virtue	Elegant and pure
Peonies	Fidelity	Bright

IX. The Bridal Carriage

1. In a sunny and hot country like Greece, where most weddings take place in the summer, an open car (convertible) is the best choice. Unless you prefer a traditional carriage with horses, very common in the Corfu slip-roads or on an island where no cars are allowed.

2. A vintage car, open-topped or not, is also a good choice. A rented limousine will take you to the church in style.

3. If you are fans of the modern lifestyle, you can choose between a jeep, a large motorbike, or a boat to bring the bride in from the sea. Adventurous brides can opt for a horse, which is traditional in many Greek mountain villages. The choice of transport must be in harmony with the whole style of the ceremony. Usually it is the task of the bride's father to accompany her to the church, therefore he is also responsible for having the car decorated on the day of the wedding.

X. Nutrition and Preparation of the Bride

1. Your wedding is a time to indulge and envelope yourself in total luxury. The more time you have to organize the happy event, the better. And this is especially significant for the bride, who will want to look her best on the big day.

2. Avoid strict weight-loss diets. The easiest way to lose weight is to stop eating bread and sweets. If you absolutely must eat something sweet, choose one of the recipes in chapter "Bridal Shower", with the indication 'light' or 'for the bride'. Stick to a healthy diet, applying the golden rule every day: Have breakfast like a king, lunch like a prince, and dinner like a pauper. A diet rich in carbohydrates and the vitamins contained in fruit and vegetables will make you feel healthy and energetic, ready to face the tiring task of organizing the wedding. Avoid bad habits and late nights, especially in the last week before the wedding.

3. Relax and do some exercise at home or at the gym. A relaxing and practical idea, in view of your wedding, is to take dancing lessons. Practice the waltz and the tango, and impress everyone on the big day.

4. Avoid caffeine, soft drinks and alcohol, as they make you nervous, have a lot of calories, play havoc with your skin and create cellulite. Drink lots of water for healthy skin and shiny hair.

5. Summer brides should remember that a very dark tan does not look good with a white wedding dress, and overpowers the effect of soft make-up – so don't spend too much time in the sun. A classically beautiful bride should have china-white skin. The most beautiful brides are those who look natural. Avoid heavy make-up in daylight. To look good in the photographs, carry powder with you in order to minimize shine.

6. However you plan to groom your hair, avoid drastic changes near the date of the wedding, as the extra stress can prove to be a nuisance. Let your hair down for a less formal event, like a wedding at the seaside. A classic upsweep is favored among brides opting for the formal wedding. Upswept styles accompanied by floral wreaths, tiaras and a veil create a princess-like effect. An upsweep adds extra height to the bride, while it attracts focus away from the head and towards the face, eyes and smile. If you are wearing a strapless dress, you may consider an upsweep with a few loose tendrils of hair around the face and neck, which will render your look quite romantic. To find the perfect style, schedule an appointment with your hairdresser at least

a month in advance. Don't forget to bring your veil, headpiece and earrings.

The ceremony

I. The Wedding Service

1. Most modern couples opt for a religious ceremony. Whatever their religion or faith, they are drawn to hold their wedding in a church, chapel or huppah in order for a higher power to bless them as a couple. People want a holy place of their own for their marriage. They feel the need for it to be sacred and for God to solidify the union. Hearing the words "What god has joined together, let no man divide" is a magical moment. Keep in mind that many religions have strict rules regarding weddings of mixed faith and therefore you must do a lot of research before deciding upon the house of worship where your wedding will be held.

2. Since marriage concerns culture and religion, you must take your families' feelings and beliefs into consideration. Ask the officiant of your church about the possibilities of performing a mixed-faith wedding where elements of your culture can also be incorporated. The effect can be memorable and highly emotional as it will touch both families.

3. Many couples choose to commemorate their wedding service with a printed program. Keep the church decorations simple and minimal as a house of worship is highly imposing as it is. Choose fresh flowers to decorate the aisle. In some churches you can ask for music especially for the ceremony, or a choir accompanied by an organ player who will play the 'Wedding March' as you walk down the aisle. Your family and maid of honor can prepare a nice speech and address your guests during the ceremony.

4. The priest can read the vows aloud or you may choose to address each other and make your own personal vows. Take extra time in choosing and memorizing the words you will say to your beloved at this sacred moment, as you will be under great stress at the time. You may choose to read them out of a piece of paper, but still make sure to practice beforehand.

II. The Greek Orthodox Wedding

For the Christian Church, weddings are an important rite. With the blessings of the Church and Divine Providence, the couple is joined in holy matrimony and becomes as one. If you don't want your wedding to remain a mystery, but seek to find answers to all the questions you have with regards to the religious ceremony and its symbolism, read the following:

1. On the table symbolizing the altar, you will see the Holy Bible, which stands for the presence of Christ at the ceremony. The rings and wreaths are placed on a silver tray. The priest receives these from Christ and places them on the fingers and heads of the bride and groom.

2. The bride and groom stand next to each other. This symbolizes the equality between the two sexes. They are equal spouses, with the same rights and obligations, under the same "scales". The bride stands to the left of the groom. The maid of honor stands next to the groom with the grooms' parents to her right. To the left of the bride stands the bestman with the brides' parents next to him.

3. The priest places the rings on the couple's fingers, and holds the engagement. This symbolizes the promise that a wedding will follow. Today, the Engagement and Wedding take place at the same time, while previously they used to be held separately, with the priest present on both occasions. However, because many engagements were broken off before the wedding, despite being blessed by the Church, it was decided that the two ceremonies should be joined.

4. During the Wedding, the priest joins the couple's hands, to indicate that their lives are joined as of that moment by God. Wreaths are placed on the bride and groom's heads. They are crowned like winning athletes. The wreaths symbolize an award for their virtue and chastity. That is also what the bride's white dress and veil symbolize. The bride and groom drink from the same glass of sweet red wine. This symbolizes their community of all moments in life. Heretoforth the couple will share every joy and every sorrow.

5. After the exchange of rings and wreaths, the couple walks around the temporary altar three times with the priest, in a parade of joy and glory, to the sound of three hymns, the first of which begins with the phrase "Isaia Choreve" (hence the popular euphemism for marriage – to "dance the Isaia").

6. The guests shower the couple with rice and rose petals. The rice is for their wedding to take roots ("rizono" in Greek), and the rose petals so that their life together is strewn with flowers.

7. The priest takes the wreaths from the bride and groom's heads and delivers them secretly into the hands of God, asking Him to keep them "unblemished, unsullied and immaculate" for eternity. (Source: Dimitriada Holy See)

The reception

The reception will be the climax of the day for you, your parents and your guests, and is the most expensive part of the wedding. You should devote a lot of time and thought to it. Divide it into five parts: a. the venue, b. catering, c. decorations, d. music, e. the wedding cake and make lists of alternative solutions for all of them.

I. Venue

1. Choosing the venue of the reception is one of the most important decisions you are called to make when organizing your wedding. Once you know where the wedding ceremony is to be held, you should do some market research with regard to the venues available in the area. Unless of course you plan to hold the reception in your house, garden or country house.

2. If you don't have your own space, there are several choices: a public location licensed for such events, a rented space or a hotel. For public places, such as squares, beaches, galleries or museums, you should remember that you need to respect the location, and a special license for music will have to be obtained. Also, you will have to transport all the equipment and food, and might discover other needs that you will have to cater for. If you choose a beach, make sure it is near a house or hotel that you can use.

3. Private rented spaces should be researched as to what they have to offer, what the cost is for extra services provided, and the possibility of being provided with a closed hall or marquee if the weather turns bad.

4. Reserve the location plenty of time in advance; don't leave it until the last minute, because you could have problems, especially in seasons when demand is high, like Christmas or summer.

II. Catering

If you are planning a wedding in your own space, you can choose to employ a professional caterer or prepare the food yourself.

Scenario A: You decide to do the catering yourself, in your own space.

1. Even if you plan to prepare the reception personally, you'll need to see professionals about the following: a. equipment (chairs, tables, buffet tables, tablecloths, chair covers, crockery and cutlery, water, wine and champagne glasses, cake services), b. professional staff (waiting and bar staff, cloakroom attendant, table usher, reception attendant, parking attendant).

2. If you plan to prepare your own menu, don't even think about cooking everything yourself, because no matter how capable you are, you need to relax on your wedding day. There are two solutions. Either someone you know does the cooking, or you hire a chef to prepare the recipes you want in your own space.

3. Home-cooked food definitely tastes better, but don't think that the cost will be much less. The menu for a successful wedding reception must be elegant, with attention to detail and correct preparation.

4. Make sure there is a full bar with alcoholic drinks, soft beverages, fruit juices, good quality red or white wine depending on the food you're serving, as well as champagne for the toasts. Don't forget the ice. There should be water and wine glasses on the tables and champagne glasses for the toasts when the cake is cut.

5. Plan how you will receive your guests. Pay extra attention to the decoration of a foyer or special entrance for the reception area where your guests will be welcomed in style. They may have to wait standing for some time, until they are shown to their tables, so it is a good idea to treat them to a glass of champagne. Serve champagne and strawberries, chocolate truffles or sweets at the entrance for a stylish reception.

6. If you make the wedding cake yourself, make sure that you have enough space for it in your refrigerator. Sufficient food storage space is an important condition for a successful reception.

7. Prepare all food that can be stored outside the fridge or in the freezer well in advance. Bread is an important part of wedding receptions, a traditional aspect of wedding preparations of the olden times when it was usually prepared all week by the bride and her girlfriends. Today, you can enjoy the tradition and bake home-made bread which you can store in the freezer until the wedding.

8. If the reception is to be held in the garden, rent a marquee, in case the weather doesn't turn out as good as you would have wanted. In the winter, you can cover up the whole garden and use special portable heaters – you can even cover up the swimming pool to make more seating space. You have endless choices.

9. Pay attention to the table arrangement. The bride and groom should sit near the center, at the best table. Their parents, the best man and maid of honor, and grandparents should sit with them. Close relatives should sit at the adjacent tables. Formal or honored guests should be given prominent positions. Don't neglect those who have traveled a long way to be at your wedding; show them that you appreciate it.

Scenario B: You decide to assign the reception to a professional caterer.

If you decide to use a professional caterer, you should be well informed and know exactly what you are going to ask for in advance. If you want them to respect you and tell you the right things, you need to have done some homework. Many of the things below also apply if the reception is being held in your own space and you are personally doing the catering.

What you must decide before you go to a caterer.

1. Do you already have somewhere to hold the reception, or do you want the caterer to provide you with a place? This is perhaps the most important question you should set yourself from the beginning. Many good caterers specializing in gourmet cooking with excellent quality and taste do not have suitable spaces for big receptions, while many beautiful rented spaces provide slightly inferior catering with regards to the quality of the food.

2. Are you planning a cocktail party, a buffet, or a seated menu? A seated meal needs more space than a buffet menu.

3. What do you plan to offer your guests upon arrival (champagne for a formal reception, ouzo for a traditional Greek feast, exotic cocktails for a beach party). Make sure you have soft drinks and fruit juice for the younger guests.

4. Account for special nutritional needs of the bride or groom or your close relatives (for example vegetarians,

fasting, people with blood diseases or on a special medical diet).

5. Ask whether they offer table, chair and buffet decorating services. If you have your own ideas, you can ask your florist or a special decorator to prepare the decorations. Some companies rent candelabra, fruit dishes, lamps and other decorations.

6. Who is going to prepare the wedding cake? A wedding cake requires special skills, so if you decide to order one, make sure you choose a specialized store.

<u>What you need to pay attention to when looking for a caterer.</u>

1. Ask for detailed information on the menus available, and find out if they can prepare inspired dishes with your budget (within reason).

2. Ask to see photos and videos from previous receptions.

3. Ask to taste the dishes they prepare.

4. Ask if they will need to use space in your kitchen. If you are holding the reception indoors, watch out for unwanted smells.

5. Ask if yours is the only reception they will be handling on the particular date.

6. Ask to meet the manager of your reception.

7. Discuss the number of guests and the extra portions they usually reserve in case of extra arrivals.

8. Discuss the table list, and whether they will provide you with a chart of the names at each table.

9. What is their policy for date changes or cancellations?

<u>Small Secrets</u>

1. You will always be charged extra for staff, and often they like to be paid straight after the reception.

2. For a cocktail party, one waiter for every ten guests is enough, while for a buffet you'll need even fewer.

3. A bartender is necessary, whether you're having a buffet or a seated meal. The number of bar attendants required will depend on the number of guests and the amount of drinks buffets set up.

4. According to savoir vivre, for a seated meal you would need one waiter for each guest, but for a budgeted cost, two waiters per table should suffice.

5. You will need chefs and chef's assistants for a seated meal, as all plates have to be prepared in a separate space and then served to the guests.

6. The bar is charged separately; there is a price for wine, a full bar, or just water and soft drinks. Make sure that you have sufficient quantities of drinks and wine to last until the very end of the wedding party.

7. Marquees and chair covers are usually charged extra. Tables, chairs, crockery, crystal, cutlery and towels are usually part of an organized caterer's basic equipment. Some, however, like to offer choices at extra cost.

8. Ask for the whole offer in writing, plus the relevant value added tax, and the terms of payment, in order to avoid misunderstandings.

9. Agree on what time the caterers and staff will leave in advance, as they tend to leave early and leave the guests without service. The same goes for the musicians, photographer and cameraman.

III. Decorations

1. Wedding reception decorations are essential to set the right mood for your celebration, while at the same time they give a very personal note to the special event. Your wedding decorations should mirror your and

your fiancé's style to the guests. Before you start making plans, check the room or garden where your reception will be held thoroughly, in order to see what is already on offer. Lighting is a major aspect you should consider. Dancing rooms look much better in softer, kinder lighting, while other areas, like a beach or garden may need extra lights so that your guests are able to enjoy their food. You will need to consult with a special lighting technician for outdoor areas.

2. Three spots in your wedding reception area require your utmost attention: the entrance hall or area, the head-table area, and the place where you will cut the wedding cake. Set up a small bar with a special treat and champagne at the entrance so that your guests begin the night on the right foot. Decorate the entrance with seasonal flowers or make a special decoration reflecting the theme of your wedding, like orange tulle and silk leaves for autumn weddings, pink and white balloons for the modern bride, lit torches set in the sand for the exotic wedding. If you cannot spend large amounts of money on a wedding event specialist, you may find inexpensive yet dramatic pieces at a party-rental supplier or a display supplier.

3. The head table must reflect the theme of your wedding, whether it is a very classic and formal Christmas reception or a less formal garden party. The head table is usually long and the couple and family sit on one side so that they can view all their guests. The centerpiece of the head table can be repeated, only in a smaller version for the rest of the tables in the reception. Flowers, candles, vases or sculptures; whatever your choice for a centerpiece, it should be very tall or quite short so that it doesn't hinder your guests' conversation. You can decorate the wedding cake table with garlands such as the ones you would use to decorate a long buffet. An excellent centerpiece for a country style wedding would be to place fresh basil and mint in small pots and arrange them in the middle of the table, accompanied by small plates filled with olive oil and olive paste. This will be a colorful, aromatic and edible centerpiece.

4. Decorate the backs of the chairs at the tables with fresh flowers, elegant bows or even balloons. Fold the napkins in a special way to create a beautiful table and place your wedding favors on each guest's plate for a nice surprise and an easy decoration. Dim the lights in the powder room or switch them off and light a few dozen tiny candles. Scatter rosepetals around them for a divine effect.

5. A major aspect to keep in mind is the weather and climate conditions predominant in the area at the time of your wedding. A large expense of the wedding decorations can occur from tenting a garden or heating a tented area. A floored marquee can also be very expensive. Whether you decorate the area on your own or employ a wedding designer, remember that the simple touches are the most elegant, and that your wedding must reflect your personal style and character.

IV. Music

1. Disc jockey, violin orchestra, jazz band, a popular singer, a rock group or a traditional music band? Whatever your style, don't forget that a variety of types of music is better than listening to the same rhythm all night.

2. In the music, be faithful to the style you have chosen. Discover the elegance in contrast, without resorting to excess. Traditional Greek music and a French menu don't match, and you can't combine a wedding in a beautiful fishing village with a rock group. A violin quartet on the beach is a pleasant surprise, as is a traditional band receiving the bride in a formal garden reception, if they give their place to an orchestra straight after. Ask the orchestra to demonstrate their repertoire, and make sure it is rich and varied.

3. If you have had lessons, start the dancing with a classic waltz. The bride and groom should "open" the dancing, and, depending on your tastes and style, you can choose anything from a classic waltz to rock or something even more modern.

V. The Wedding Cake

1. There are many traditions involving the wedding cake. In older times in Greece and Italy, they used to bake a type of sweet bread, and then break it on the bride's head symbolically after the wedding; that is why the wedding cake has been established as the bride's cake. Over the years, newly-weds have started to cut the cake together, with their hands joined together over the knife, symbolizing their unity. They feed each other with their arms linked and drink champagne from the same glass, thus declaring their dedication to one another and the fact that from now on they intend to share everything.

2. In America they have a beautiful tradition where the couple saves the top tier of the cake in the freezer for a year, to share on their first anniversary. In the UK it is kept for the christening of the first child. Also, a second cake is made for the groom, usually a chocolate one to sweeten him up.

3. The cake is cut at the beginning of the reception, and once the bride and groom

have had some champagne, each guest gets a glass. Then toasts are made by the father of the bride, the best man, and the groom, who declares his love for his wife.

4. Choosing your wedding cake is one of the most important decisions you need to make when it comes to your reception. It is one of the main focal points of the venue, as it will be served to all your guests, so you want it to look good, taste exquisite and reflect your wedding theme. Choose your wedding cake carefully. You can choose a white or ivory one with sugar paste, flowers, lace or beads (see page 239) to match your dress, or an elegant china design to match the china used at a smaller reception (see page 80). Depending on the time of year, a spring, summer or Christmas-themed cake can be selected. Make sure you make arrangements to taste the cake before the wedding day.

5. Make your own wedding cake. Don't hesitate to experiment or follow the instructions of a good cookery school. Within a short period of time, and with guidance from experts, you yourself will become an expert in preparing cakes, and the result will be homemade and very tasty.

The Wedding Day

I. The Countdown to the Aisle

1. Traditionally, the couple sleeps apart on the day before the wedding. Tradition has invented this solution, very correctly, to avoid rows due to the stress of final preparations. Wake up late and don't drink any coffee. Some fresh fruit juice with a spoonful of honey will wake you up pleasantly and fill you with energy.

2. The house should be filled with laughter and music. Invite your best friends or anyone who makes you relax and feel at ease. Naturally, on this day everyone will do everything you ask. Let yourself be pampered. Yet again, tradition has left us a practical custom, as the bride's friends are responsible for dressing and grooming her. The presence of beloved faces is both pleasant and comforting, because you know that your friends are there to sort out any problems that arise. Prepare yourself and expect all the little "tragedies", make fun of them and enjoy it; don't let anything upset you. Whatever happens, keep in mind that by the end of the day you will be married.

3. Don't forget to have a big breakfast and a light lunch. Forget whatever diet you've been on so far. Have some chocolate, which will revive and energize you.

4. Start special preparations with the experts in the morning. Do some exercises, have a bath and massage, prepare your nails and do your hair and make-up – in that order – at least 2-3 hours before the ceremony, so that you have plenty of time to put on your dress and have some photos taken before you leave for the church.

5. Be patient with the photographer, even if the hot afternoon sun or the cold winter air outside are unbearable. These photos are forever. Enjoy them and help the photographer create.

6. Remember that these moments are very moving for your parents. Thank them for their help and support in making your wedding day unique. Don't forget to have plenty of photos taken with them, so you can hand them as a lovely gift after the wedding.

7. Once you are ready, think about the favorite things you want to have with you. Remember the old saying "something old and something new, something borrowed and something blue". Your wedding dress is something new, some jewelry belonging to your grandmother can be something old, you can borrow your mother's earrings, and a good-luck bead from your best friend can be something blue.

8. Don't forget to take a crystal glass for the wine and a silver tray with sugared almonds and rice with you to the Greek church. Make sure you have little baskets with rice and rose petals ready, and ask your friends to share it out among the guests. Arrange for someone to give out the bonbonnières at the end of the ceremony. Afterwards, your guests can sign your personal wedding book, and record their wishes for the new couple.

9. Set of for the church in the decorated car, with your father. The bridesmaids can ride in the same car. The best man and maid of honor wait at the church with the groom.

10. Reach the church ontime, but once you are there, drive around it honking loudly and happily as many times as you want, so that it looks like you are the traditional quarter of an hour late.

11. Enter the church on your father's left arm. He will hand you over to the groom. Another male relative can also hand you over, such as your brother or godfather. In Jewish tradition, both parents of the bride escort her down the aisle. Once you receive your bouquet, stand to the left of the groom facing the table between you and the priest, which symbolizes the altar. During the ceremony the best man and maid of honor stand to either side of the couple, except when they are exchanging the wreaths, in which case they stand behind the couple. The groom's parents stand behind him, and yours behind you.

12. After the ceremony, you should sign the wedding register together with the best man and maid of honor and stand at the exit of the church with the parents to greet the guests.

13. Once you have greeted the last guest, have photos taken with the groom and best man and maid of honor, and make your way to the reception with the groom. As you leave, the guests will shower you with rice and rose petals.

14. At the reception, cut the cake and make the toasts before eating. At the bride's table, sit to the left of the groom, with the best man and maid of honor and the parents. After the meal, the couple starts the dancing with the music they have chosen. During the reception, go round all the tables holding a glass of champagne to greet all the guests like a good host, listen to their wishes and have photos taken. The couple is expected to be the first to leave the reception.

II. The role of the Best Man and Maid of Honor (in a Greek wedding)

1. The best man and maid of honor play an important role in the Wedding ceremony, as they accept to stand by the couple spiritually, morally and materially.

2. They stand to the left and right of the couple during the ceremony. The best man stands next to the bride, and the maid of honor next to the groom. They sit in the same places at the table at the reception.

3. They exchange the rings and wreaths three times. Note that during the change, neither the hands nor the wreaths may switch over, so that in each case the wreath returns to the head of the person that was originally wearing it. They walk around the altar during "Isaia Choreve", they drink from the same glass of red wine as the bride and groom, and sign the wedding register.

4. Their obligations include paying for the candles, the wreaths, and in some parts of Greece the bonbonnières, or half of them, after an agreement with the bride. They also pay for the officiant or registrar, organist, bell-ringers, singers and church musicians.

5. The best man and maid of honor are honored guests at all pre-wedding celebrations, such as the Engagement, Making the Bed and the bachelor party.

6. They have the right to invite some of their own friends and relations. In the parts of Greece where they pay for the bonbonnières, they can invite as many people as they like.

7. They greet the guests with the bride, take photos with her, sit at her table and are generally honored. The best man should make a toast to the newlyweds during the reception. As the best man, you should prepare your speech in time for the big day.

8. The best man and maid of honor should buy a good gift for the couple, and will in turn receive personal gifts from them, such as jewelry or a watch. Also, the bride will give the maid of honor her bonbonnières, that is a crystal or silver decorative dish for her house, containing sugared almonds and wrapped in tulle.

9. In the future, the best man and maid of honor are obliged to become the couple's first child's godparents.

III. Your Role as a Guest

1. Newlyweds are traditionally not allowed to act as best man or maid of honor, or enter a church for another wedding, for a year after their own wedding.

2. If you are invited to the wedding, RSVP the invitation and send it off as soon as possible. Another wish you must respect is the wedding list. If the bride has chosen certain stores for her list, it would make things easier for the couple if you were to choose a gift from those stores. The amount you spend on the gift should depend on how close to the couple or its parents you are.

3. Ask the hostess about the formality of the event and dress appropriately. Arrive at the ceremony at the designated time. During the reception accept the seat your hostess has prepared for you. If you are a very close friend of the couple, you may wish to make a toast after dinner. Be sure to thank your hosts at the end of the reception.

IV. The Groom

Usually everyone and everything at a wedding revolves around the bride and her desires, but according to popular Greek wisdom "the groom is shaved last". If you feel neglected, think that at least you have to do a lot less organizing and your tasks are much simpler. According to tradition, the honeymoon is the groom's gift to the bride. Usually couples plan the honeymoon together, but if you agree to undertake all the planning, devote yourselves exclusively to that. Give her a pleasant surprise with the place you book, and try to remember all the places she's always wanted to visit. Read the following list to find out what you should do.

1. Choose a ring for the proposal. You might want to use an old family heirloom. The proposal ring will last a lifetime, so your future wife must like it.

2. Decide on a date and location with the bride.

3. Help your bride with organizing the wedding of your dreams as much as you can.

4. Remember that you should listen to all her complaints patiently and be understanding about her stress.

5. Help her to compile a guest list and don't assume that your future wife knows the names of every single person you intend to invite.

6. Order and pay for the wedding rings. Don't forget to take them with you to the engagement.

7. Gather up all your humor and goodwill for the family meetings.

8. Order your suit. Choose a tuxedo and bow tie; this is the best time to wear one, and it looks much better in the photos. Don't forget a tux shirt, cufflinks, cummerband, waistcoat, suspenders and shoes. A white dinner jacket can be worn instead of black for a wedding during the summer or in a hot climate. For a daytime formal wedding choose a three-piece gray or black suit and match it with a striped tie or ascot. For an informal wedding, classic ensembles such as a navy blazer or white linen suit are popular and very stylish. Keep in mind that you should check with your bride, so that your styles don't clash. As you're going to the tailor's, have another suit made for your honeymoon.

9. Decide who will be your best man and your ushers. Don't be pressurized into choosing someone you don't really want as best man. Ideally he will be a good friend, good at keeping you calm in the run-up to the wedding and on the day itself. The boutonnière will distinguish your best man from the rest of the groomsmen, as their attire should be uniform.

10. Accompany your future wife to dancing lessons if she asks you to do so, it's not such a bad idea, and you will feel good with the round of applause after your dance.

11. Choose where you will stay on your wedding night. Make sure it is somewhere romantic and ask for breakfast in bed with champagne, strawberries and anything you know she will like.

12. Find out where you can spend your honeymoon and make your choice well in advance.

13. Book tickets, hotels, check passports, get some foreign exchange if you are going somewhere outside Europe.

14. Arrange your transport from the church.

15. Arrange lodging for guests arriving from out of town or from abroad.

16. Buy your beloved a gift at every opportunity, in order to demonstrate your love.

17. Have your bachelor party, because if you don't, you'll always wonder what that evening would be like. However, remember that holding your stag night right before your wedding day should be avoided, as you must give yourself time to recover!

18. Reassure your future wife that you were a gentleman at your bachelor party, by hugging and kissing her the next day.

19. Open bottles of champagne as often as you can to congratulate the woman of your dreams for doing all the organizing.

20. Don't treat family gatherings as just traditional customs you can't avoid. Invite your good friends to come along, turn the music up loud and take the chance to have your first party in your new home.

21. On the big day invite your best friends to dress and "shave" you. Greek tradition says that whoever gets to shave the groom must also make him a gift of money.

22. At the end of the ceremony arrange for the candles, bonbonnières and gifts brought to the church to be taken by car to your new home. You may also want to arrange for flowers to be transported from the ceremony area to the reception.

23. Arrange who will bring the bride's bouquet, and where from.

24. Make sure you get to the church on time, and be there holding the bouquet at the big moment. You and the best man should wear the traditional boutonnière.

25. During the reception, make a toast to thank the parents, the guests and the best man and maid of honor. Say a few nice words about your wife.

26. Take the garter off your bride's leg and toss it to your single friends.

27. Cross the threshold of your new home with your wife in your arms.

This is the end of our story. It started on a beautiful evening, at a romantic dinner for two, where Prince Charming knelt down and offered his beloved the ring, while murmuring vows of eternal love. With careful planning and clever solutions, our heroine has managed to have the wedding of her dreams and remain rested, calm and happy throughout. All joyful love stories and fairy tales with princes end with the phrase: And they lived happily ever after.

I would like to close this chapter by paraphrasing Simone de Beauvoir:

"Marrying the man or woman of your dreams is an art, but keeping that marriage for ever after is a full-time occupation."

I

THE PROPOSAL

"I love you simply"
by Pablo Neruda

I love you without
How, or when, or from
Where; I love you simply,
Without problems or pride;
I love you in this way
Because I don't know any other way of living.

HIS COOKING ... PROPOSAL  I.

If she's taking her time inviting you, cook for her and make the first step...

Since time immemorial, a man's marriage proposal has been accompanied by bended knees, romantic words and a diamond ring. This is what every woman expects from her beloved. If you want to be original, instead of falling on your knees, invite the woman of your dreams to a romantic meal, where you can unfold your culinary expertise. A tête-à-tête dinner at home is the most idyllic scenery for a romantic marriage proposal. After a gourmet dinner for two, when the lights are low, you are both pleasantly dizzy from the wine and chocolate is melting on your lips – that is the ideal moment to ask her to be your wife.

A man in the kitchen is very attractive and commands respect from women. Often men use many more accessories and appliances in the kitchen, from modern full-body aprons to special tools for opening wine bottles and tasting wine, and this is exciting for the woman who acknowledges her beloved's refined tastes. Most men find using a wok in the kitchen easier and preferable to saucepans, perhaps because they associate the latter with their mother's traditional cooking.

A man may spend less time in the kitchen than a woman, but often the result is a pleasant surprise, as it shows a great deal of passion and is prepared with much care and attention. Since childhood, women have been imbued with the belief that they will definitely be good at cooking, if and when they decide to turn their hand to it, while for a man, cooking is a powerful challenge.

A man's kingdom is his bar. Try the recipes that follow, and you will be surprised at how often you will have to use your favorite spirits while preparing them. The right romantic dinner will have small portions, even if that means a large succession of dishes. The correct alternation of tastes creates a challenge for the palate and fills us with euphoria. Excellent quality wine, especially when accompanied with the right food and consumed in the right quantities, is an ideal introduction to the right romantic mood.

Dessert made by a man is really a unique and unexpected surprise, the ideal "icing on the cake", especially if it is to be followed by a proposal that will affect the rest of your life. Don't even think about ready-made desserts to finish off such an important evening. On the contrary, the best opportunity to present your ring is together with your inspired masterpiece. Remember that no woman can resist chocolate and jewelry. The ring that goes with your proposal can be a shiny new jewel, or an old family heirloom. Once she's had dessert, present the ring on a bed of rose petals and open a bottle of champagne to celebrate her answer. Round off the romantic meal by serving shots of "sambucca con la mosca", that is sambucca with coffee beans, which you set fire to.

Hors d'oeuvres

Preparation time 20 minutes
Degree of Difficulty ♥

• 1 small sliced baguette or pumpernickel bread cut
  in small square slices

Crostini with caprino, pesto and sun-dried tomato
• 2oz (50g) creamy caprino cheese
• 2oz (50g) cream cheese, softened
• 1/2 teaspoon horseradish sauce
• 1/4 cup pesto sauce
• 3-4 sun-dried tomatoes, chopped

Crostini with green olive paste, cashew nuts and mint
• 1 cup green olives stuffed with red peppers
• 1/4 cup capers
• 1 tablespoon balsamic vinegar
• 3 tablespoons olive oil
• cashew nuts and sprigs of mint for garnishing

1. Slice the baguette and toast the slices in the oven.
Blend the goat's cheese with the cream cheese,
horseradish sauce and pesto sauce, until they form a
smooth mixture. Place spoonfuls of the mixture on the
bread slices and garnish with pieces of sun-dried
tomato.
2. Pulse all the ingredients for the green olive paste in
a food processor until they form a smooth mixture.
Spread the bread slices with the paste, and garnish with
cashew nuts and sprigs of fresh mint.

Chilled Cucumber Soup

Yields 4-5 portions
Preparation time 10 minutes
Degree of Difficulty ♥

- 2 large cucumbers, peeled and diced
- 1 cup yogurt
- 1 tablespoon honey
- 1 small clove garlic (optional)
- 1/4 cup chopped fresh mint
- salt and white pepper

1. Pulse all the ingredients together in a food processor until smooth. Add salt and white pepper. Place the soup in a jar with a lid, and refrigerate until cold. Can be prepared the day before. Serve cold, topped with a little black caviar and chives, if you wish.

2. Alternatively, prepare cucumber shots. Add 1/4 cup of tequila to the soup and serve in transparent shot glasses. Store the remainder in the refrigerator. An excellent cooling juice.

Pumpernickel (German wholemeal rye bread)

Yields 2 loaves

Preparation time 30 minutes + 3 hours to rise

Baking time 50 minutes

<u>Suitable for freezing</u>

Degree of Difficulty ♥♥

- 1 tablespoon active dry yeast or 1oz (40g) fresh yeast
- 1/2 cup warm water, 80°F (40°C)
- 1 tablespoon sugar
- 2 cups water
- 1/4 cup molasses
- 1/4 cup wine vinegar or cider
- 1/3 cup unsalted butter
- 2oz (50g) grated dark cooking chocolate
- 1 tablespoon instant coffee
- 3 cups all-purpose flour
- 3 cups rye or wholemeal flour
- 2 teaspoons cumin seeds
- 2 teaspoons fennel seeds
- 1 teaspoon salt
- 1 cup ground All-Bran
- 1 egg white mixed with 1 tablespoon water
- extra cumin and fennel seeds

1. Dissolve the yeast and the sugar in the tepid water. Cover and leave to stand until the yeast is foaming. Place the rest of the water, the molasses, the vinegar, butter, chocolate and coffee in a saucepan and mix over medium heat, until the chocolate and butter have melted.

2. Mix the flour, rye, seeds and salt in a bowl. Make a hole in the center and pour in the yeast, the All Bran, and the melted chocolate mixture. Stir with a spoon initially, and then knead with your hands. Place the dough on a floury surface and knead for another 10 minutes, adding as much flour as necessary to make it soft and pliable. You may knead the dough in a mixer for 10 minutes, using a dough hook.

3. Cut the dough in half and place it into two oiled bowls. Brush the surface with a little oil. Cover with cling-film and let the two pieces of dough rise for around two hours. Press them down to let the air out and knead for 1 minute. Form the pieces of dough into oblong rolls and place into 2 buttered bread molds 8x4x3" (22x10x7cm). Cover with cling-film and leave to rise for about one hour.

4. Brush the surfaces with a little egg wash and sprinkle with the extra seeds. Bake the bread at 360°F (180°C) for about 50 minutes. During the last 15 minutes, cover the bread with aluminum foil, so that it doesn't go black.

5. After you remove the loaves from the oven leave them in the molds for 15 minutes before transferring them to a rack to cool completely. Serve in slices spread with cream cheese and topped with smoked salmon, or salmon tartare. Alternatively, add 1 cup of thickly chopped walnuts to the dough. The bread will remain fresh for 1 week in a biscuit tin, or for 2 months in the freezer.

Salmon Tartare

Preparation time 20 minutes
Degree of Difficulty ♥

For two
- 2 teaspoons finely chopped chives (optional)
- 3 tablespoons finely chopped parsley
- 10 drops Tabasco sauce
- 2 green onions, finely chopped
- 2 teaspoons capers
- 7oz (200g) fresh salmon fillet
- 1/2 cup lime mayonnaise (recipe below)

For a group
- 3 teaspoons finely chopped chives (optional)
- 1/2 cup finely chopped parsley
- 30 drops Tabasco sauce
- 6 green onions, finely chopped
- 1/4 cup capers
- 1 pound (500g) fresh salmon fillet
- 1 cup lime mayonnaise (recipe below)

1. For greater ease, replace the home-made mayonnaise with equal quantity ready-made mayonnaise combined with 1 teaspoon lime zest, 2 tablespoons lemon juice and a few saffron threads, crushed. Prepare the larger dosage if you are expecting company.

2. Wash and remove the skin from the salmon fillet. Place in the freezer for 30 minutes, as it is easier to cut in small pieces when slightly frozen. Chop into 1/3-inch (1cm) cubes and place in a large clean bowl. Add the remaining ingredients and the mayonnaise and mix lightly.

3. Place the mixture in the refrigerator. Will keep for only 24 hours. Serve spoonfuls of the tartare on toasted baguette slices with parsley or dill garnish, or on pumpernickel bread slices, garnished with a little red caviar.

Lime and saffron mayonnaise sauce

Yields 3 cups
Preparation time 40 minutes
Degree of Difficulty ♥♥

- 1 cup corn oil or safflower oil
- 1 cup olive oil
- 3 large egg yolks
- 2-3 tablespoons lemon juice
- 1 teaspoon lime or lemon zest
- 1½ tablespoons Dijon mustard
- 1 teaspoon saffron threads, crushed (optional)
- salt and white pepper

1. If you have never tasted home-made mayonnaise before, the exquisite taste of this velvet aromatic sauce will come as a nice surprise. Home-made mayonnaise, as opposed to store-bought, is not a sandwich spread. Quite the opposite, it is an elegant French sauce which can be used to accompany boiled vegetables, poached fillets of fish or rich meats.

2. Place all the oil in a large measuring cup. Using a hand mixer, beat the egg yolks, juice, zest, mustard, saffron (if used), and some salt and pepper together in a large clean bowl. Continuing to beat at medium speed, add the oil very slowly in a thin, steady constant flow until all the oil is incorporated. The process will take 30-35 minutes, until you have poured all the oil into the bowl and a silky smooth, thick yellow mayonnaise sauce has formed. If the mayonnaise is too runny, add some more oil and keep on beating. Do not beat too hard, otherwise the sauce will curdle. If the mayonnaise separates, place a fresh egg into a clean bowl and slowly add the separated mayonnaise, whisking it until it emulsifies. If too thin, add a little extra oil. Will keep in the refrigerator for 1 week. Use the home-made mayonnaise as an elegant sauce in the recipe for "Lobster tail risotto".

Yields 2 portions
Preparation time 20 minutes
Degree of Difficulty ♥

- 1 cup mixed salad, cleaned
- 3/4 cup parmesan flakes
- 4 slices bresaola
- a few tender lettuce hearts
- 2 toasted bagel slices

For the dressing
- 1 small egg
- 1/2 teaspoon crushed garlic
- 2 tablespoons lemon juice
- 1 teaspoon Dijon mustard
- 1/4 cup grated parmesan
- 2 anchovy fillets
- 2/3 cup olive oil

1. Clean, wash and dry the lettuce well. Share the mixed salad between two tall glasses. Sprinkle with the parmesan flakes and top with the bresaola slices.

2. Break the egg into the food processor bowl and beat with the garlic, lemon juice, mustard, parmesan and anchovies, some salt and pepper, until the ingredients are mixed together. With the machine running add the olive oil, in the thinnest possible stream, until it becomes part of the mixture.

3. Pour the dressing over the salad in the glasses, and grate plenty of black pepper over the top. Cover the glasses with the fried bagels, having fixed the lettuce hearts into the bagel holes. You can prepare the salad in the glasses several hours in advance, without adding the dressing and bagels.

Garganelli with vodka and prosciutto crudo

Yields 2 portions
Preparation time 15 minutes
Cooking time 20 minutes
Degree of Difficulty ♥

- 8oz (250g) fresh pasta, garganelli or penne
- 3 tablespoons butter
- 1 small clove garlic
- 1 medium onion, grated
- 4 sun-dried tomatoes, chopped
- 1/3 cup vodka
- 1 teaspoon tomato paste mixed with 1/2 cup single cream
- 1 large tomato, diced
- 4oz (100g) prosciutto in thin slices or bresaola in pieces
- 1 tablespoon tiny capers
- 2 tablespoons parsley, finely chopped
- salt and freshly-ground pepper
- 2 slices of prosciutto crudo, a piece of sun-dried tomato and some chives, to garnish

1. Boil the penne in salted water until al dente, about 6 minutes for fresh pasta. Melt the butter in a large deep skillet and sauté the garlic and onion.

2. Add the sun-dried tomatoes and the penne and mix over high heat. Pour in the vodka all at once and leave to simmer for a few minutes, until it evaporates.

3. Turn down the heat, blend in the remaining ingredients and heat for 3 minutes. Take the skillet off the fire and serve the pasta in glasses, garnished with a slice of prosciutto, a little sun-dried tomato and some chives. If you wish, you can prepare the dish a few hours in advance and heat before serving.

Fragrant risotto with lobster tails and lime and saffron mayonnaise

Yields 2 portions
Preparation time 20 minutes
Refrigeration time 1-2 hours
Degree of Difficulty ♥♥

- 1/2 cup fragrant rice, basmati or jasmine
- 1/3 cup lemon juice
- 2 cups water
- 1/2 teaspoon salt
- a pinch of saffron threads (optional)
- 7oz (200g) boiled and shelled lobster tails or crayfish or prawns, cut in pieces
- 2 tablespoons melted butter
- 1/2 cup lime and saffron mayonnaise (recipe on page 23)
- salt and freshly ground pepper
- alfalfa or blanched shoots and fresh endives to garnish

1. Place the rice, lemon juice, water and salt in a small saucepan and bring to the boil. As soon as it starts to boil, lower the heat, cover the saucepan and let the rice absorb all the water. Sprinkle with some grated saffron threads if you like, and mix gently with a chopstick.
2. Oil a small square 8-inch (20-cm) tin well, and press in the rice while it is still warm. Smooth down the surface with the back of an oiled spoon. Leave it to cool, cover and store in the refrigerator for 1 or 2 hours or until the next day. Remove from the refrigerator, unmold the rice on a chopping board and cut into four even square pieces.
3. Place the rice pieces on a tray, and top each piece with the boiled seafood. Season to taste and drizzle with the melted butter. Heat for 5 minutes in a 400°F (200°C) preheated oven.
4. Serve the seafood risotto on beds of alfalfa shoots and tender fresh endives. Top with 1 or 2 tablespoons of lime and saffron mayonnaise sauce.

New York Bagels

Yields 10 bagels
Preparation time 30 minutes + 2 hours
to rise
Baking time 25 minutes
<u>Suitable for freezing</u>
Degree of Difficulty ♥♥♥

- 1¼ cups milk
- 1 teaspoon salt
- 3 tablespoons sugar
- 1/3 cup melted unsalted butter

- 1 tablespoon active dry yeast
- 1 egg, separated
- 4 cups all-purpose flour
- 1 tablespoon poppy seeds

1. Boil the milk in a small saucepan. Remove from the heat and add the salt, sugar, and butter. Mix until the butter melts and the sugar dissolves. Empty the mixture into the mixer bowl and when it cools down to 80°F (40°C), add the yeast and mix. Leave to stand until foaming. Add the egg white and beat well until combined.
2. Add as much flour as necessary, little by little, kneading with a dough hook for 10 minutes to a pliable, non-sticky dough. Cover and let the dough rise for 1 hour, or until it is twice its original size.
3. Separate into egg-sized pieces for mini bagels, or tangerine-sized pieces for larger bagels. Shape into balls and make a hole in the center with your finger, so that they look like donuts. Twist around your finger to make the hole bigger. Place the bagels in a baking pan lined with non-stick oven paper, cover, and leave to rise for 10 minutes.
4. Boil in simmering water in a large pan for 15 seconds. Remove with a slotted spoon and line a buttered baking pan with the bagels. Brush the bagels with egg yolk, beaten with a teaspoon of water, and sprinkle with poppy seeds. Bake in a 400°F (200°C) oven for 25 minutes. Consume within 2 days, or store in the freezer for up to 2 months.

Toasted Bagels

An ideal solution for slightly stale bagels. Cut the bagel into very thin slices with a sharp knife and spread on a well-oiled baking sheet. Drizzle with a little olive oil, and sprinkle with various herbs, such as oregano, brown sesame, paprika, grated garlic or even with finely chopped bacon. Bake in a 360°F (180°C) oven until golden-brown.

Honey and orange duck with asparagus and Hokkien noodles

Yields 2 portions
Preparation time 15 minutes
Cooking time 40 minutes
Degree of Difficulty ♥

- 2 skinned duck breasts (8oz/250g each)
- salt and freshly ground black pepper
- 1 tablespoon butter
- 1 small clove garlic, crushed
- 1 teaspoon grated fresh gingerroot
- 1/4 cup rice wine
- 1 teaspoon grated orange zest
- 1/4 cup soy sauce
- 1 tablespoon orange liqueur
- 2 tablespoons honey
- 1 teaspoon sesame oil
- 1 tablespoon sesame seeds
- 1/2 cup Chinese 5-spices
- 2 tablespoons, finely chopped fresh coriander

For the Garnish
- 8oz (250g) Chinese egg noodles
- 4 tablespoons soy sauce
- asparagus sautéed in butter

1. Wash and clean the duck fillets well. Remove and discard the skin if it is still on, using a sharp knife, and sprinkle the fillets with salt and pepper. Melt the butter in a large deep skillet or a wok, and stir-fry the duck fillets with the garlic and ginger. Douce with the rice wine and stir for a few minutes, until it evaporates.

2. Add the zest, soy sauce, liqueur, honey and sesame oil. Cover the wok and let the fillets simmer for 20 minutes. Sprinkle with the sesame seeds and herbs, and remove from the heat. Drain the sauce from the duck fillets and cut into very thin slices.

3. Boil the noodles for a few minutes in salted water. Drain, place in a bowl and pour over the soy sauce. Serve on plates with the duck fillets. Spoon over the sauce and sprinkle with fresh coriander. Accompany with sautéed asparagus. Alternatively, prepare the recipe with a suitable cut of meat.

Asparagus Garnish

Yields 2 portions
Preparation time 30 minutes
Degree of Difficulty ♥

- 8 fresh asparagus
- salt
- 2 tablespoons butter

1. Choose thin fresh, bright green asparagus. Until you decide to use them, they should be stored with their stems dipped in cold water, so that they remain fresh.

2. Rinse well and press the stem down with your finger until the lower part breaks off. Discard the hard part of the stem that broke off. With a potato peeler or even better, a special asparagus cutter, remove the hard outer fibers of the vegetable. The remaining asparagus will be slender and trimmed.

3. Boil the asparagus in salted water for 5 minutes, until just soft. Drain, melt the butter and sauté the vegetables in it for a few minutes, to release the aroma. Serve warm.

Yields 20 brownies
Preparation time 20 minutes
Baking time 30 minutes
Degree of Difficulty ♥♥

For the Sponge cake
- 5oz (125g) fine-quality dark cooking chocolate
- 1/2 cup unsalted butter
- 1 sachet (1 tablespoon) instant cappuccino, diluted in 1/4 cup milk
- 1/3 cup sugar
- 1/3 cup dark brown sugar
- 1 teaspoon vanilla essence
- 2 eggs, lightly beaten
- 3/4 cup self-raising flour
- 1/2 cup ground hazelnuts
- 1 square 8-inch (22cm) cake mold

For the Cream cheese icing
- 7oz (200g) cream cheese
- 1/2 cup unsalted butter
- 1⅔ cups icing sugar
- 1 teaspoon vanilla essence

For the Chocolate coating
- 1/4 cup melted unsalted butter
- 1/4 cup unsweetened cocoa powder
- 1 tablespoon instant coffee
- 2 tablespoons chocolate syrup
- 1 cup double cream
- 7oz (200g) fine-quality dark cooking chocolate, in pieces

1. Prepare the cake mixture for the brownies. In a large pan, place the first 6 ingredients and stir over medium heat, until well blended.

2. Remove from the heat and let it cool down slightly. Add the eggs, flour and hazelnuts and stir gently with a wooden spoon. Pour the batter into a well-buttered cake mold, and bake in a 350°F (175°C) oven for 30 minutes.

3. Take the cake out of the oven and let it cool in the tin. Beat all the white icing ingredients together in a food processor and spread over the cake while still in the tin. Place in the refrigerator for 1 hour.

4. Mix the melted butter with the cocoa powder, instant coffee and chocolate syrup. Heat the cream in a small saucepan, but do not let it boil. Remove from the heat and add the chocolate pieces and chocolate butter. Mix to a smooth chocolate icing, and pour over the white icing. If you wish, drizzle it over the white icing, to form nice patterns. Cut the cake into square pieces and serve for dessert. The remainder can be stored in the refrigerator and served with coffee the following morning.

Chocolate Espresso Custard

Yields 6 chocolate pots
Preparation time 10 minutes
Baking time 40 minutes
Degree of Difficulty ♥

- 1½ tablespoons instant coffee
- 1 cup milk
- 2oz (50g) chocolate pieces
- 1 egg and 1 yolk
- 1/3 cup sugar
- 2 tablespoons Baileys
- 1 tablespoon vanilla essence

1. Dissolve the coffee in the milk and pour the mixture into a small saucepan. Bring to the boil. Remove from the heat, add the chocolate, and stir until melted.
2. Beat the egg and the yolk, the sugar, liquor and vanilla essence, and add to the chocolate milk. Mix well together. Share the mixture between six oven-proof espresso cups.
3. Place the cups on a baking sheet half-filled with water. Bake in a pre-heated oven at 360°F (180°C) for 35 to 40 minutes. Serve the custard desserts warm or cold. If you wish, decorate with whipped cream. Store in the refrigerator.

Screwdriver mousse

Yields 2 portions
Preparation time 30 minutes
Degree of Difficulty ♥ ♥

- 2oz (50g) good quality cooking chocolate
- 1 tablespoon gelatine powder
- 2 egg yolks
- 1/2 cup sugar
- 3 tablespoons lime liqueur
- 1/4 cup orange juice
- 1/3 cup vodka
- 1/2 cup whipping cream
- 1 egg white

1. Melt the chocolate over very low heat, adding one teaspoon of oil. Put 2 Martini glasses in the refrigerator for 15 minutes. Pour the hot chocolate into the cold glasses with a teaspoon, to form patterns.
2. Dissolve the gelatine in 2 tablespoons water and let it swell. Beat the egg yolks with half the sugar in a small pan. Add and mix in the lime liqueur and the orange juice. Heat the mixture over low heat, whisking constantly until it starts to set. Add the gelatine and stir for 2 minutes, until it dissolves. Remove from the heat and after it has cooled slightly add and mix in the vodka. Cover and store in the refrigerator for 20 minutes.
3. Whip the cream with some vanilla essence in the mixer, until soft peaks form. Beat the egg white with the remaining sugar until it forms a stiff, glossy white mixture. Mix the gelatine mixture first with the whipped cream, and then lightly with the beaten egg white. Fill 2 to 4 Martini glasses, depending on size. Refrigerate for 2 hours, until the mousse has set. Can be prepared in advance.

HER INVITATION II.

"Prince Andrew approached with lowered eyes:
I have offered you my love since the moment I first saw you, may I have some hope?"

L. Tolstoi, War and Peace

If he is hesitant about proposing, invite him to dinner. Cook for him and bewitch him by candlelight...

Men usually make marriage proposals, but it is women who have the power to make them happen. A woman can only propose to her beloved on the 29th of February of each leap year, according to tradition. But don't be disheartened. An invitation to a romantic dinner will always be accepted by your beloved, and implies that he should do the proposing. If he doesn't appear to notice the innuendo, don't resist the temptation to make the proposal yourself, once you have "seduced" him with rare tastes, delighted him with some good wine and enchanted him with a divine chocolate dessert.

A woman with a perfectly laid table, champagne waiting on ice, a cake in the refrigerator and food cooking in the oven, may, for some, be a typical "domestic archetype of another era", but in reality, such a woman remains a rare and sought-after creature for all men.

A well-laid table, food stewing in the oven and a unique dessert may be thoughts that frighten you, but if you are well organized and follow the recipes correctly, everything will turn out smoothly. You should dedicate the final hours before the meal to your appearance, because as much as he will admire your home-cooked food, your beloved will expect to find you looking beautiful when he arrives.

Set the table elegantly. Take your grandmother's china out of the closet, iron your mother's lace tablecloth, fold the napkins in style, take extra care to clean and polish the cutlery, set only crystal glasses for wine and champagne. Although the procedures may sound old-fashioned, they suggest a woman of taste and class. Remember, this is not a casual dinner for friends.

The suggested recipes are simple and light, because a romantic meal should be neither tiresome to prepare nor heavy on spicy tastes. Start the meal with Italian bread-sticks and walnut and tahini dip. Select a light dry white wine, such as Riesling, if you choose to serve the salmon, or an excellent fruity Chardonnay or Fumet if you choose the sweet and sour duck. Serve the same wine throughout the meal, making sure that you have a wine cooler full of ice next to the table.

Serve champagne with the dessert. An original idea to serve instead of champagne is to beat some strawberries and ice in the blender and serve spoonfuls of the mixture in champagne glasses together with Italian Spumante wine.

When bringing out the cake, do it with gusto, especially if it is your anniversary or some other special occasion, like Valentine's Day. Light a candle if you want, switch off the lights and bring in the cake from the kitchen with style. If he doesn't ask you to marry him there and then, don't despair; try the sweet and sour duck next time.

Creamy Stilton Soup

Yields 2 portions
Preparation time 20 minutes
Cooking time 30 minutes
Degree of Difficulty ♥

- 1/3 cup unsalted butter or margarine
- 1 small clove garlic, minced
- 1 small onion, finely chopped
- 2 celery sticks, cleaned and chopped
- 2 medium carrots
- 2 medium potatoes
- 2 cups vegetable stock
- 1 teaspoon saffron threads
- 1/2 cup double cream
- 4oz (100g) Stilton cheese, cut in pieces
- 2 tablespoons crème fraîche, for serving

1. Melt the butter in a large pan, and lightly sauté the garlic, onion and celery. Add the carrots and potatoes, which you have cleaned and cut into pieces. Add the stock, cover the pan, and simmer the vegetables for 30 minutes. Leave to cool.

2. Transfer the vegetables and stock to the food processor bowl, add the saffron, and beat together to form a smooth purée. Place the vegetable purée in a clean pan, stir in the cream and the cheese.

3. Heat the soup on medium heat, until the cheese has melted, without letting it boil. Add salt and pepper to taste, and serve the soup in bowls, garnished with a spoonful of crème fraîche, drawing a fork on its surface to form a nice pattern. Accompany with freshly baked baguettes.

Hazelnut and Tahini Dip

- 8oz (250g) hazelnuts
- 2/3 cup tahini
- 1/3 cup freshly squeezed lemon juice
- 1/3 cup water
- 1/3 cup good quality olive oil

1. Powder the hazelnuts in your food processor. Add the tahini, salt and white pepper, lemon juice and water, and beat until frothy. Slowly and steadily add the olive oil while beating, until the mixture is smooth. Serve with breadsticks.

Mini Baguettes

Yields 9 mini baguettes
Preparation time 30 minutes + 2 hours to rise
Baking time 15 to 20 minutes
Suitable for freezing
Degree of Difficulty ♥♥

- 3 cups soft flour (not self-raising)
- 2 tablespoons active dry yeast
- 1 tablespoon sugar
- 2 teaspoons salt
- 2 tablespoons vegetable oil
- 2 cups warm water (80°F - 40°C)
- 3 cups all-purpose flour
- oregano, sun-dried tomato, walnuts, olives, for various fillings

1. Place the soft flour, yeast, sugar and salt in the food processor bowl and mix together. Add the oil and water and mix with the dough hook, until the mixture is smooth. Add the remaining flour little by little, until the dough collects about the hook. You may not need all of the flour, depending on how strong it is. Keep beating for about 8 minutes, until you obtain a pliable, non-sticky dough.

2. Oil a large bowl and place the dough inside it. Coat the surface with a little oil and cover the bowl with plastic wrap. Let the dough rise to twice its size, about 2 hours.

3. Press down to let the air out. At this stage, divide the dough into 9 small pieces, cover, and leave to rise once again. Using a small rolling pin, roll each piece of dough into an oblong sheet. Brush with a little water and sprinkle over some oregano, sun-dried tomato, finely chopped walnuts or olives, to make a variety of different baguettes. Roll each sheet into a tight roll and elongate with your fingers. Cover the rolls and let them rise. Oil a baking sheet and place the baguettes side by side, leaving some space between them, to give them room to rise.

4. Cover with plastic wrap and leave to rise for 30 minutes. Make 2-3 cuts in the bread surface with a sharp knife, and brush with a little water.

5. Bake the baguettes at 450°F (225°C) for 15 to 20 minutes, or until they are golden-brown. Leave to cool on a grid. The baguettes can be wrapped and stored in the freezer.

Pasta, Artichoke and Asparagus Salad

Yields 2 portions
Preparation time 15 minutes
Cooking time 10 minutes
Refrigeration time 1 hour
Degree of Difficulty ♥

- 6oz (200g) colored pasta shapes, farfalle, penne or other type
- 6oz (200g) fresh green asparagus
- 6oz (200g) mini canned artichokes
- salt and freshly ground black pepper

For the aromatic vinegraitte
- 1/3 cup olive oil
- 1/4 cup good quality wine vinegar
- 1 tablespoon tiny capers
- 1½ teaspoons dried oregano, crumbled
- 1/2 teaspoon salt
- 1 small clove garlic, crushed
- freshly ground pepper

1. Mix the dressing ingredients in a jar with a tight lid, and shake to blend. Boil the pasta in salted water with 2 tablespoons oil, and drain. Rinse the pasta with plenty of cold water. Remove to a clean bowl.

2. Rinse the artichokes well and leave to drain. Cut in half or in quarters and mix in with the pasta. Remove the tough stalks and fibers from the asparagus and boil for 5 minutes in salted water. Drain, chop in pieces and add to the pasta. Drizzle the contents of the bowl with half the dressing and mix thoroughly. Cover the salad and stand in the refrigerator for about 1 hour.

3. Serve on plates accompanied by the remainder of the dressing and plenty of freshly ground black pepper.

Puff Pastry Cornets with Wild Mushroom Filling

Yields 4 cornets
Preparation time 15 minutes
Baking time 30 minutes
Degree of difficulty ♥

- 2 long thin strips cut from a puff pastry sheet, cut in half
- 1/3 cup dry white wine
- 1oz (35g) dried wild mushrooms (chanterelles, shiitake, porcini)
- 3 tablespoons olive oil
- 1 very small clove garlic, crushed
- 6oz (200g) canned sliced mushrooms, drained
- 1/4 cup finely chopped parsley
- 1 teaspoon corn-starch, dissolved in 1 tablespoon water
- salt and freshly ground black pepper

1. Lay out the puff pastry sheet and cut 2 1/3-inch (1cm) thick strips from the shorter side. Cut each strip in half, so that you have 4 1/3-inch (1cm) thick short strips. Starting from the narrow end, roll each one about a small metal funnel, which you have previously coated with a little oil. The strip should cover about half the funnel, so that when cooked, the cornet will be smaller than the metal funnel.

2. Place the wrapped funnels on an unbuttered baking sheet and bake at 400°F (220°C) for 15 minutes. Lower the temperature to 300°F (150°C) and keep baking for another 15 minutes. Remove from the oven, unstick from the pan and leave to cool. At this stage you can store the pastry cornets in an airtight container, in the freezer.

3. Soak the dried mushrooms in the wine for 15 minutes. Drain and reserve the wine. Chop up all the mushrooms. Heat the oil in a large skillet and sauté the garlic and all the mushrooms.

4. Add the parsley and mix over high heat for a few minutes. Douse with the wine and let it evaporate for a few minutes over strong heat. Add the corn-starch and mix until the sauce sets. Season to taste and serve the filling in the puff pastry cornets.

Cauliflower and Mushroom Risotto

Yields 4 portions
Preparation time 20 minutes
Cooking time 20 minutes
Degree of Difficulty ♥

- half a small cauliflower divided into florets (2 cups cauliflower florets)
- 1/2 cup butter
- 1 small clove garlic
- 1 small onion, grated
- 14oz (400g) canned sliced mushrooms, drained
- 1 cup carnaroli or Carolina rice
- 1/2 cup dry white wine
- 4 cups chicken stock
- 1/2 cup grated hard cheese (Kefalotiri)
- salt and white pepper
- grated black truffle for sprinkling (optional)

1. Wash and clean the cauliflower. Boil in salted water for about 15 minutes, until it is almost soft and can be cut into florets.

2. Melt half the butter in a large deep skillet and sauté the garlic, onion and mushrooms. Stir in the rice. Add the wine and mix over strong heat, until evaporated.

3. Add the stock little by little, stirring constantly and waiting for the stock to be absorbed before adding more. Once you have added half the stock, add the cauliflower pieces. Add the remaining stock little by little, and keep stirring. Add as much stock as necessary for the rice to soften externally, but remain hard on the inside. You may not have to use all the stock. The whole process takes about 15 minutes.

4. Take the risotto off the heat, and add the remaining butter and the cheese. Taste and add more salt and white pepper if necessary. Serve the risotto on hot plates. If you like, sprinkle with shavings of black truffle.

5. Halve the ingredients to prepare exactly 2 portions of risotto. The risotto will keep in the refrigerator for 2 days. In my opinion, it is better to use the larger dosage, so you can enjoy the dish on the next day, too.

Royal Scallops with Prawns and Velvet Sauce

Yields 2 portions
Preparation time 20 minutes
Cooking time 20 minutes
Degree of Difficulty ♥♥

For the Scallops
- 6 royal scallops, shelled
- 1 cup dry white wine
- 1 teaspoon fresh rosemary
- 1 teaspoon dried thyme, crumbled
- 1 bay leaf
- 10 black peppercorns

For the Prawns
- 12 large prawns
- 1 cup water
- 1/4 cup olive oil
- 1 teaspoon seafood seasoning

For the Sauce
- 2 tablespoons butter
- 1 small clove garlic, crushed
- 1 cup cold stock from the seafood
- 1 tablespoon corn-starch
- 1 teaspoon Dijon mustard
- salt and freshly ground pepper
- 8oz (250g) fresh baby carrots, to serve

1. Rinse the scallops well and arrange them in an oven-proof dish. Pour over the wine, sprinkle with the herbs and cover with aluminum foil. Bake in a 350°F (180°C) oven for 20 minutes. Remove from the oven, cover, and keep warm. Drain, and keep 1/2 cup of the stock for the sauce.

2. Shell the prawns and remove the black intestine. Boil the water, oil and herbs in a large pan for 5 minutes. Add the prawns with their heads and simmer for 7 minutes. Remove from the heat, tear off the heads, add the prawns to the dish containing the scallops and strain their juices. Keep 1/2 cup of the stock for the sauce.

3. Melt the butter in a small pan and sauté the garlic. Mix the scallop stock with the prawn stock and dissolve the corn-starch and the mustard in the mixture. Add this to the pan. Add salt and pepper and stir the sauce until it sets. Drizzle the seafood with the sauce and serve garnished with baby carrots, boiled and sautéed in 2 tablespoons butter.

Yields 2 portions
Preparation time 30 minutes
Cooking time 25 minutes
Degree of Difficulty ♥♥

For the ginger-scented pink mashed potato
- 2 pounds (1kg) potatoes
- 1 teaspoon salt
- 1/2 cup evaporated milk
- 3 tablespoons butter
- 4 green onions, finely chopped
- white pepper and 1/8 teaspoon Chinese 5-spices
- 1 teaspoon various peppercorns, crushed
- 2-3 tablespoons ginger preserve juice
  (or 1 tablespoon grenadine and 1/2 teaspoon ginger powder)

For the Salmon
- 1 salmon fillet, 1¼ pounds (600g), skinned
- 2 tablespoons butter
- 2 tablespoons finely chopped fresh cilantro
- 1 teaspoon Chinese 5-spices
  (or 1 teaspoon of the following powdered spice mix: allspice, cinnamon, cloves, ginger and pepper)
- 1 cup dry white wine
- fresh cilantro leaves for garnishing
- 1 dose ginger preserves (recipe follows) or
  2 tablespoons ready-made ginger preserves

1. Prepare the mashed potato. Peel the potatoes and cut into pieces. Place in a pan, pour over water to cover them, add the salt and boil until very soft, about 35 minutes. Mash with a special tool or with a presse-purée into a clean bowl. Add and mix in the milk. Sauté the onions in the butter and add to the mashed potato while hot. Add a little white pepper, the powdered spices, the peppercorns and the red juice. Stir until the mashed potato is uniformly colored and scented.

2. Remove the skin from the salmon fillet with a sharp knife or ask your fishmonger to do it for you. It will be easier to remove the skin is you store the fresh salmon in the freezer for 30 minutes. Cut the fillet into four long thin strips, two for each plate. Place the salmon pieces in a baking dish, coat with butter, sprinkle over the herbs and spices and pour over the wine. Cover with aluminum foil and bake in a 350°F (180°C) oven for 25 minutes or until the salmon is cooked through and falls apart when pricked with a fork.

3. Transfer the salmon pieces onto the plates, cover and keep warm. Strain the juices from the fish and measure out 1 cup. Melt 2 tablespoons butter in a small pan. Stir in 1/2 tablespoon flour, until golden. Add all the juices at once and stir the sauce until it sets. Blend in 3 tablespoons double cream, salt and white pepper. Serve the salmon with the ginger preserves. Pour the sauce over the fish and accompany with scoops of pink mashed potato, served with an ice cream scoop. Garnish with fresh cilantro leaves.

Ginger Preserves

Yields 2 portions
Preparation time 25 minutes
Cooking time 1 hour
Degree of Difficulty ♥

- 1 large gingerroot
- 1 cup white vinegar
- 1 tablespoon grenadine
- 1 teaspoon sugar
- 1/2 teaspoon salt

1. Select the smoothest gingerroot you can find. A fresh root will be pale colored and its surface will not have any protrusions. Also fresh roots are hard. Wash well and peel with a potato peeler.

2. Cut very thin, almost transparent, slices off the root with the peeler. Cut as many slices as you can, up to where the root starts to become fibrous. Throw away the hard bit left at the heart of the root. You cannot eat fibrous ginger, as it is very hard.

3. Place the ginger slices in a small pan with the vinegar, grenadine, sugar and salt. Boil the mixture over high heat, cover, and leave to simmer for 1 hour, or until there is a small amount of thick red juice left in the pan. Store the ginger preserves in a sterilized jar in the refrigerator for up to 2 months.

4. The preserves are usually served between courses to cool the palate and prepare it to receive new flavors, especially when the previous course has a stronger taste than the one following. They are particularly spicy.

Duck with pomegranate sauce and red wine pasta

Yields 2 portions
Marinating time 24 hours
Preparation time 25 minutes
Cooking time 30 minutes
Degree of Difficulty ♥

- 2 duck breasts, skinned
  (8oz – 250g – each)
- 1 tablespoon butter
- 1 small clove garlic, crushed
- 1 small onion, grated
- 1/4 cup sweet red wine
- 1/4 cup pomegranate sauce
  (recipe follows)
- salt and freshly ground pepper

For the Marinade
- 2 tablespoons pomegranate sauce
  (recipe follows)
- 1/2 cup dry red wine
- salt and freshly ground pepper

For Garnishing
- 8oz (250g) fresh red wine pasta
- 2 tablespoons olive oil

1. Wash and clean the duck fillets well. Remove the skin with a sharp knife. Coat with the pomegranate sauce for the marinade, place in a deep bowl and pour over the wine. Stand in the refrigerator for 24 hours.
2. Melt the butter in a large deep skillet or a wok, and sauté the garlic and onion. Drain the fillets, place in the skillet, and sauté for a few minutes on either side, until they change color. Add the wine and simmer for a few minutes until it evaporates.
3. Add the pomegranate sauce. Cover and let the fillets simmer for 20 minutes. Drain off the sauce and cut the fillets into very thin long slices.
4. Boil the pasta in salted water with 2 tablespoons oil. If you are using fresh pasta, you will need to boil it for a shorter time, until it is al dente. Drain the pasta and serve with the duck fillets. Pour over the duck sauce and serve immediately. Sprinkle with plenty of freshly ground black pepper.
5. Alternatively, prepare the recipe with fillet of beef or porterhouse steak.

Pomegranate Sauce

Yields 2 cups
Preparation time 1 hour
Cooking time 1 hour and 20 minutes
Refrigeration time 1 to 2 days
Degree of Difficulty ♥♥

- 10 pounds (5kg) juicy ripe
  pomegranates
- 1/2 cup freshly squeezed lemon juice
- 1 cup sugar

1. Squeeze the pomegranates with your hands until soft, to free their juices. Cut in half. Wrap each piece in a square of cheesecloth and squeeze over a clean bowl, pressing with your palms to extract all the juice. You may use a juice extractor. At the end you should have about 4 pints (2 liters) of juice. The process is necessary for the juice not to go bitter.
2. Stand the juice in the refrigerator for 1 or 2 days, until it is clear and all the sediment is collected at the bottom. Pour the clear juice carefully into a jug or jar.
3. Place the pomegranate juice in a clean pan with the lemon juice and sugar, and heat the mixture over low heat, stirring constantly until the sugar dissolves. Simmer without the lid for about 1 hour and 20 minutes, until you are left with half the original mixture. Remove from the heat, and once cold, transfer the dark tangy syrup to a sterilized jar. The sauce can be stored in the refrigerator for several months.
4. Use this thick and tasty sauce to coat a fillet of beef before cooking, to add taste to your salad dressings or to prepare delicious sweet and sour sauces.

Gianduja Chocolate Pie

Yields 8-10 portions
Preparation time 30 minutes
Baking time 1 hour
Degree of Difficulty ♥

For the cake
- 1 pound (500g) unsalted butter
- 3 sachets (3 tablespoons) instant cappuccino
- 1 cup sugar
- 14oz (400g) fine quality dark cooking chocolate, cut in pieces
- 1 cup finely ground hazelnuts
- 1/2 cup self-raising flour
- 5 large eggs

For the chocolate icing
- 8oz (250g) fine quality cooking chocolate
- 1/2 cup unsalted butter
- 1/4 cup icing sugar
- 3 tablespoons milk
- 2 teaspoons glucose

1. Place the butter, coffee and sugar in a large pan, and boil until the sugar has dissolved completely. Add the pieces of chocolate and stir until they melt. Remove the mixture from the heat and pour into a large bowl. Leave to cool slightly. Add and mix in the hazelnuts and flour.

2. Beat the eggs lightly until just frothy. Transfer to the bowl with the chocolate mixture, and blend well until you obtain a uniform batter.

3. Line the bottom of an 8-inch (24-cm) hexagonal baking tin with non-stick paper, and butter the bottom and sides thoroughly. Pour the cake batter into the lined tin. Place the baking tin in a larger deep pan half-full of water and bake in a 350°F (180°C) oven for 1 hour.

4. Remove the cake from the oven and leave to cool in the tin. Place the cake, with the tin, in the refrigerator and stand for 3-4 hours.

5. Mix all the icing ingredients together in a small pan and heat until the chocolate has melted. Whisk the mixture well, until smooth. Turn the cake over onto a serving platter and carefully remove the paper. Can be stored in the freezer, without the icing, for 2 months. Pour the icing over the cake and refrigerate for 1 hour. Before serving, place a stencil with hearts on the surface, and sprinkle with pink sugar. Remove the stencil carefully, to leave the heart shapes on the icing.

Love Cake à la crème

Yields 12 portions
Preparation time 1 hour
Baking time 35 minutes (x2)
Degree of Difficulty ♥♥

- 1 recipe vanilla sponge cake (see "Vanilla Lemingtons" recipe)
- 2 pints (1 liter) whipping cream
- 1 cup icing sugar
- 2 sachets (60g each) instant vanilla-flavored pudding
- a few drops red food coloring
- 2 teaspoons strawberry essence (optional)
- 1/2 cup fresh or frozen raspberries, mashed (optional)
- white icing or whipped cream for decorating

1. Butter 2 round deep (10cm high x 20cm across) baking pans. Line the bottoms with non-stick oven paper. Prepare the sponge cake mixture and divide it between the two pans. Bake the sponge cakes separately in the oven for 35 minutes, at 350°F (175°C).
2. Remove from the oven, turn out onto non-stick oven paper sprinkled with icing sugar, and leave to cool. Once cool, separate each sponge into 3 layers using a sharp knife or a cake-separator. Sprinkle all the layers with half the icing sugar.
3. Prepare the filling. Beat the cream in the mixture with the remaining icing sugar, the instant custard powder, the food coloring and the essence, until you obtain a silky smooth mixture. At this stage you may add 1/2 cup of mashed raspberries to the mixture and stir well.
4. Spread one of the baking pans with plastic wrap and place one of the cake layers on the bottom. Cover with cream and top with another layer of cake. Repeat the process until you have used all the cake layers. Store the remaining cream in the refrigerator.
5. Now, you can place the cake in the freezer for 30 minutes, or the refrigerator for 1 hour, until the filling sets. Remove from the refrigerator and overturn the dessert onto a serving dish. Carefully remove the plastic wrap and coat the cake surface with the remainder of the cream. Press a metal heart shape all about the cake and in the center, and fill in the outline with white icing or whipped cream, using a piping bag with a thin straight nozzle (No.2) .

Amaretti Cappuccino Trifle

Yields 2 portions
Preparation time 15 minutes
Degree of Difficulty ♥

- 1 cup whipping cream
- 3 tablespoons icing sugar
- 1/2 sachet (30g) instant vanilla-flavored pudding
- 1 layer ready-made sponge cake
- 2 tablespoons instant Amaretto coffee dissolved in 1/3 cup boiling water
- 3 tablespoons Amaretto liqueur
- 5-6 Amaretti biscuits, crumbled
- 1oz (50g) chocolate flakes or grated good quality cooking chocolate
- 2 tablespoons unsweetened cocoa
- pink or chocolate sprinkles for decorating

1. Beat the cream with the sugar and custard powder in the mixer, until soft peaks form.
2. Cut 2 small and 2 larger discs, 1½ and 2½ inches (5 and 8 cm) in diameter respectively, from the sponge cake using round pastry cutters. Mix the coffee, water and liqueur in a small bowl. In a different bowl mix the crumbled Amaretti with the chocolate flakes and the chocolate powder. Use ready-made Amaretti, or make your own pink Amaretti, following the recipe on page 120.
3. Place the small cake discs on the bottom of two cappuccino mugs. Drizzle with a little of the coffee-liqueur mixture, sprinkle over some of the Amaretti and chocolate powder and cover with 2 spoonfuls of cream.
4. Cover with a second cake disc. Repeat the process, finishing with the cream. Decorate with some pink or chocolate sprinkles. Place the dessert in the refrigerator to cool. Serve cold.

Alternatively make tiramisu trifles: Prepare half the cream and blend it with 1/2 cup Italian mascarpone cheese. Replace the Amaretto liqueur with Kahlua and sprinkle with chocolate flakes and cinnamon.

DIAMONDS FOR BREAKFAST III.

A marriage proposal is always accompanied by diamonds. A romantic breakfast will show him your love in the sweetest possible way.

From movie stars to our best friends, from our grandmothers to the girls yet to be born, there is no woman who can resist diamond jewelry. The classic diamond ring is unsurpassable for a beautiful and romantic marriage proposal, and is a classic gift "for life".

Advice for him: A proposal can be made at night, under the candlelight, and the ring can be the surprise at breakfast in bed for two. By hiding the ring in a sweet made to look like a jewelry box, or inside a fortune cookie, you can create a unique moment of surprise and tenderness. Prepare a full surprise breakfast for your beloved, as there is no male more charming than one bringing a breakfast tray to the bed. So move and touch her – these moments before the wedding are the most memorable ones. If you keep up the habit after you are married, you will definitely make your companion very happy.

Advice for her: To return the trust and love that he has shown you, prepare him a breakfast fit for a king. Pamper your beloved, giving promises of a happy life together, just like the first breakfast you enjoy together.

If you propose to him, and go against tradition, make a fortune cookie and write a message that reads "I offer you my heart and my hand" or more directly "Will you marry me?" If you want to take it a step further, buy him a set of silver worry-beads or golden cuff-links, and offer them wrapped in a small velvet box.

The secret for a successful "surprise" breakfast is good organization. No matter how much you want it to look casual, it is extremely difficult to bake English muffins, while poaching eggs and preparing sweet croissants, and all of this just before your beloved wakes up. So make sure that your croissants, Danish pastries, muffins and pancakes have been prepared beforehand and stored in the freezer. Take them out as soon as you wake up and heat them in the oven for 20 minutes, or defrost them the night before. In the morning, just brew the coffee and cook the eggs. Poached, soft-boiled with caviar, or in the oven with snowy whites, you are sure to enjoy anything you make when you have it in bed with your beloved.

Don't forget to put some tulips on the tray. Hide your gift among their petals, to complete the magic of the moment.

Muffins with raspberries or blackberries

Yields 18 mini muffins
Preparation time 20 minutes
Baking time 20 minutes
<u>Suitable for freezing</u>
Degree of Difficulty ♥

- 2½ cups cake flour (not self-raising)
- 1/4 teaspoon bicarbonate of soda
- 2 teaspoons baking powder
- 1/3 cup sugar
- 1/2 cup dark brown sugar
- 2 eggs, slightly beaten
- 1/2 cup milk
- 1 cup yogurt
- 1/4 cup melted unsalted butter
- 1 teaspoon vanilla essence
- 1 cup blackberries or raspberries

1. Sift the flour, soda and baking powder into a bowl. Stir in the white and brown sugar. Mix the eggs with the milk, yogurt, butter and the vanilla and pour the mixture into the bowl with the dry ingredients. Add the fruit and stir the mixture slightly, just to wet the flour. The mixture should be smooth and homogeneous.
2. Grease three 6-hole muffin trays with corn-oil. Half-fill the muffin holes with the batter and bake the muffins at 400°F (200°C) for 18 to 20 minutes. Remove from the oven and leave the muffins in the tray for 5 minutes. Turn the muffins out onto a rack and allow to cool. At this stage you can store the muffins in plastic food bags in the freezer. Defrost for 1 hour before serving. Serve with coffee.

Jam pastries

Yields 6 pastries
Preparation time 20 minutes
Baking time 15 to 20 minutes
Degree of Difficulty ♥

- 1 packet ready-made croissant pastry
- 1 egg, slightly beaten
- 1/3 cup apricot, orange, strawberry of berry jam
- 1/2 recipe easy vanilla icing
- turquoise-colored granulated sugar

1. Open the packet of pastry and lay the oblong piece over a slightly floured surface. Press with a rolling pin to join any cuts in the pastry. Cut the sheet of pastry into 6 even square pieces.

2. Brush the pieces of pastry with the beaten egg and place a teaspoon of jam in the center of each square. Lift the edges of the square, right and left, and fold over the filling pressing so that the edges stick together. You may use a little water to make the dough stick. Put the little bundles on a buttered baking tray and bake in a fan oven, at 350°F (180°C) for 15 to 20 minutes. Remove the pastries from the oven and when cool pour over some icing and sprinkle with colored sugar.

Easy vanilla icing

1 recipe icing (covers an 8-inch - 24cm cake)

- 4 cups icing sugar
- 1/3 cup water or milk
- 2 tablespoons glucose (corn syrup)
- 1 teaspoon vanilla or almond essence
- food coloring, to tint the icing

1. Sift the sugar into a small saucepan. Add the water and glucose and stir over low heat until the icing is smooth and shiny. Do not allow the temperature to exceed 80°F (40°C).

2. Remove the icing from heat, add the essence and food coloring, if used, and stir. If you wish, you can divide the icing into 2 or 3 bowls and mix it with different food colors. Use the icing immediately as it dries quickly. If the icing dries, warm it up until soft.

Eggs Benedict with English muffins

2 portions
Preparation time 30 minutes
Degree of Difficulty ♥

- 4 warm English muffins (recipe follows)
- 4 eggs
- 4 oyster mushrooms, trimmed
- 2 green onions, finely chopped
- 2 tablespoons butter
- 1½oz (50g) alfalfa sprouts

1. Grease the egg poachers with olive-oil and place in a shallow frying pan with boiling water. Break the eggs into the poachers, season with salt and poach for 10 minutes or until the yolk has set.

2. Wash and clean the mushrooms, cut them in strips and sauté slightly in butter together with the green onions. Wash the sprouts and strain.

3. Serve each egg on a muffin together with the sautéed mushrooms. Pour over a spoonful of sauce and garnish with the alfalfa sprouts. Serve the eggs and muffins warm.

English muffins

Yields 14 muffins
Preparation time 1 hour
Baking time 15 minutes
Suitable for freezing
Degree of Difficulty ♥♥

- 2 sachets (2 tablespoons) active dry yeast
- 1/2 cup warm water
- 3 tablespoons sugar
- 1 cup warm buttermilk
- 2 eggs
- 1/2 cup melted unsalted butter
- 2 cups all-purpose flour
- 1/2 teaspoon salt

1. Put the yeast, water and sugar in a bowl. Allow to stand until frothy. Add the milk, eggs and butter and stir.

2. Add the flour and salt and beat the mixture to a smooth batter. Pour the batter into the buttered holes of a muffin tin, half filling them. Set aside for 45 minutes and then bake the muffins at 400°F (200°C) for 10 to 15 minutes, until risen and golden brown. When cool, store in pairs in food bags in the freezer for up to 1 month. In the morning, defrost as many muffins as you need.

Hollandaise sauce

- 3 egg yolks
- 1 tablespoon water
- 2-3 tablespoons freshly squeezed lemon juice
- salt and white pepper
- 8oz (250g) melted unsalted butter

1. Beat the egg yolks, water, lemon juice, salt and white pepper in a food processor at medium speed. Continuing to beat, add the warm melted butter gradually, at a thin constant flow, through the food processor opening, until the sauce is smooth and homogeneous. Keep the sauce warm until serving time or warm it up in a double boiler.

Snow White Eggs

Preparation time 8 minutes
Baking time 15 minutes
Degree of Difficulty ♥

- 2 large eggs
- 1/8 teaspoon cream of tartar
- salt and white pepper
- 1/3 cup pesto sauce, toasted bread slices and cherry tomatoes for garnishing

1. Break the eggs carefully and save the unbroken yolks in half the egg-shell. Pour the egg whites into the mixer bowl. Beat the egg whites with a little salt and the cream of tartar until stiff.
2. Place spoonfuls of beaten egg white on a buttered baking tray to form two heaps and make a hole in the middle using a greased spoon. Place an egg yolk in each hole. Season with salt and pepper and bake in a fan oven at 350°F (180°C), for 15 to 18 minutes or until the meringue begins to go golden brown. Remove from the oven and serve hot on toast with pesto sauce and cherry tomatoes. It is best to bake the eggs in small ovenproof soufflé bowls.

Eggs with caviar

Preparation time 15 minutes
Degree of Difficulty ♥

- 2 large eggs
- salt and white pepper
- 1oz (30g) Beluga caviar

1. Boil two large eggs for 8 minutes. While hot, cut the top off with a sharp knife, season with salt and pepper and serve in eggcups topping each with 1/2oz (15g) Beluga caviar for each egg.
2. Alternatively: After cutting off the top of the eggs, remove the half-cooked yolk with a teaspoon and place in a bowl. Add 2 tablespoons mayonnaise, 1 teaspoon lemon juice, salt and white pepper and beat to a smooth mixture. Fill the eggs with the mixture and cover with 1/2 oz (15g) black caviar. Serve immediately.

Pancakes with mozzarella and prosciutto

Yields 2 sandwiches
Preparation time 15 minutes
Degree of Difficulty ♥♥

- 4 fresh and warm pancakes (recipe follows)
- 2-4 tablespoons pesto sauce
- 6oz (200g) mozzarella fior di latte, cut in slices
- 4 fine slices of prosciutto crudo
- 1/3 cup Parmigiano-Reggiano flakes

1. Stack two pancakes together, spreading them with a little pesto sauce and filling them with slices of mozzarella and prosciutto, and topping with parmesan flakes. This is a tasty and filling snack.

Pancakes

Yields 8-10 pancakes
Preparation time 15 minutes
Frying time 15 minutes
Degree of Difficulty ♥

- 1 teaspoon baking powder
- 1/2 teaspoon bicarbonate of soda
- 1/2 teaspoon salt

For the pancakes
- 1 egg
- 1½ cups buttermilk
- 2 tablespoons melted butter
- 1 cup all-purpose flour
- 1 tablespoon sugar

For the aromatic butter
- 1 cup unsalted butter, softened
- 1 tablespoon lemon or orange peel or 2 tablespoons peach preserves

1. Beat the egg in a large bowl. Add the rest of the ingredients and beat to a smooth batter. Butter the bottom of a small frying pan and place over high heat. Pour in as much batter as necessary to cover the bottom of the pan. When the pancake rises and before the bubbles that form on the surface have burst, turn the pancake over and cook until golden brown.

2. Serve the pancakes warm straight from the pan for breakfast, with butter and honey. If you wish, you can serve them with the aromatic butter. **To prepare the butter:** let it soften at room temperature and mix with your preferred ingredient. Place in a plastic case or divide among special miniature butter molds and refrigerate until set. **Alternatively:** spread the pancakes with sour cream and pour over maple syrup.

Honey, ricotta and dried fruit

Serves 2
Preparation time 15 minutes
Degree of Difficulty ♥

- 4oz (150g) ricotta or anthotyro or light cream cheese
- 1 tablespoon sugar
- 1 teaspoon lemon juice
- 2 tablespoons strained thick Greek yogurt
- 2/3 cup thyme-scented Greek honey
- 2 tablespoons brown sugar
- 2/3 cup sliced dried fruit such as bananas and figs
- 1/2 cup shelled walnuts

1. Beat the ricotta together with the sugar, lemon juice and yogurt in a food processor until fluffy and smooth.
2. Serve the honey in stemmed bowls with a scoop of cheese mixture. Sprinkle with fruit, brown sugar and walnuts. Serve immediately. **Alternatively:** serve with cashew nuts or pecans instead of walnuts.
3. If in season, serve with fresh figs, cut in quarters, sprinkled with brown sugar and grilled slightly.

Cappuccino freddo

Yields 2 glasses
Preparation time 15 minutes

1. Put 4 portions of espresso coffee in the coffee maker for espresso but double the quantity of water, i.e. as if you were making 2 cups of cappuccino. When the coffee has cooled down, pour it into two tall glasses and refrigerate. Meanwhile, beat 1/3 cup milk with an electric shaker until frothy and thick. Divide between two glasses and serve immediately.
2. Alternatively, beat 1/3 a cup whipping cream with a Nescafe mixer until thick and serve the cappuccino freddo with cream. Add as much sugar as you like before covering the coffee with frothy milk or whipped cream.

Strawberries with Cardamom and Cointreau

Yields 2 servings
Preparation time 15 minutes
Degree of Difficulty ♥

- 2 cups small strawberries
- 1/3 cup castor sugar
- 1 teaspoon vanilla essence or
  1/2 teaspoon ground cardamom
- 1/3 cup Cointreau

1. Wash the strawberries and lay them on kitchen paper to dry. Mix the sugar with a little powdered vanilla in a bowl. Coat the strawberries with the scented sugar or drizzle with vanilla essence and place them in two tall glasses. Pour over the Cointreau and serve. If you wish, omit the cardamom and Cointreau, place the strawberries in crystal bowls and serve with a glass of fine champagne. Another elegant idea to serve strawberries is to half dip them in melted chocolate, dark or white. After the chocolate has set, arrange them on a silver stemmed platter and accompany them with "clouds" of whipped cream served in a fine crystal bowl.

Greek coffee

Medium sweet coffee
For 2

- 2 small cups of water (2/3 of a cup)
- 2 teaspoons sugar
- 2 teaspoons Greek-type coffee

1. Put the water in a traditional Greek copper coffeepot and bring to the boil. Add the coffee and sugar and place over low heat until frothy. Do not allow to boil. Remove from heat and pour the froth carefully into two espresso-size coffee cups. Then place the coffeepot over high heat and bring to the boil again. Pour the coffee carefully into the cups so that the froth does not sink. Serve immediately.

Sugar roses

Preparation time 15 minutes
Drying time 2-3 hours
Degree of Difficulty ♥

- 2 cups castor sugar
- 1/8 teaspoon light green or turquoise food coloring paste
- 2-3 drops peppermint essence
- 1-2 teaspoons cold water

1. Place the sugar in a bowl. Add the coloring and mix first with a toothpick to distribute the coloring evenly and then knead the sugar with your hands to a uniform color. Add the essence diluted in water and knead with your hands to a sandy texture.
2. Fill the special rose shaped cases with the mixture. Leave the sugar in the cases for 5 minutes and then turn over the cases onto a plate lined with non-stick oven paper. Set the sugar roses aside at room temperature for 1 or 2 hours until firm. The longer they stand the harder they get. They can be kept for quite a long time in a sugar container.

Miniature ring box cakes

12 1½ x 1½ x 1½ inch (5x5x5cm) cakes
Preparation time 2 hours
Baking time 35 minutes
<u>Suitable for freezing</u>
Degree of Difficulty ♥♥♥♥

- 1 recipe vanilla sponge cake
  (see "Vanilla Lemingtons " on page 110)

For the garnish
- 8oz (250g) raspberry jam
- 1 recipe Royal icing (recipe on page 183)
- 1 packet Regalice (sugarpaste)
- 1-2 drops blue, red, yellow food coloring

1. Prepare one recipe of vanilla sponge cake and bake in a square 8-inch (25cm) pan. Remove from the oven and turn out onto a cloth to cool. Cut the sponge into 5 parallel strips and then into 5 vertical strips to form 25 square miniature cakes. Join pairs of squares with jam (one square in excess).

2. Divide the Regalice paste into 3 parts and color one part turquoise using 2 drops blue and 1 drop yellow food coloring. Color the second part blue or pink with 1 drop blue or red food coloring respectively. Knead until uniformly tinted. Gently warm the royal icing until of pouring consistency. Put the cakes on a rack and pour over the royal icing to coat evenly.

3. Cut pieces of the colored paste with which you want to cover each cake and, using a small rolling pin, roll out into 5-inch (15cm) square sheets onto a surface sprinkled with icing sugar. Transfer each sheet carefully onto each cake while the icing is still soft, and smooth with your hands to cover the cake. Cut the edges off with a pair of scissors and smooth the rim at the bottom part of each cake with a knife. Cover all the cakes in the same way. Roll out the white part of Regalice into a thin square sheet and cut it into long strips. Stick the strips on the cakes with a little water so that the cakes look like boxes tied with a bow. The miniature cakes can be kept for 2 months in the freezer or 2 to 3 days in the refrigerator.

Yields 24 small pastries
Preparation time 3 hours
Baking time 20 to 25 minutes
<u>Suitable for freezing</u>
Degree of Difficulty ♥♥♥♥

For the pastry
- 1½ tablespoons active dry yeast
- 1½ cups warm milk
- 5½ cups all-purpose flour
- 1/2 cup castor sugar
- 1 teaspoon salt
- 5 egg yolks
- 1½ cups soft unsalted butter
- 1⅓ cups glucose or honey
- 1⅓ cups dark brown sugar

For the cream filling
- 1/4 recipe crème pâtissière (recipe on page 240)

For the walnut filling
- 3 tablespoons whipping cream
- 1 cup crushed walnuts
- 1 teaspoon ground cinnamon
- 1/4 teaspoon ground cloves
- 3 tablespoons dark brown sugar

For the apple filling
- 2 tablespoons unsalted butter
- 2 tablespoons dark brown sugar
- 2 large Granny Smith apples peeled and cut in pieces
- 1 teaspoon apple pie spice

1. Mix the tepid milk and yeast in a small bowl, cover with plastic wrap and set aside for 10 minutes until frothy. Place the flour, sugar and salt in the food processor bowl and mix the ingredients gently with a dough hook. Add the yeast and eggs and beat for 10 minutes. Continuing to beat, add the butter, one spoonful at a time to form a soft, smooth and shiny dough.
2. Transfer the dough to a well-greased cookie sheet and spread it with your hands to cover most of its surface. Cover with plastic wrap and store the dough in

the refrigerator until the following day.

3. Butter two 12-hole muffin tins and pour a teaspoon of glucose or honey in each case and then sprinkle with 1 tablespoon of dark brown sugar. Prepare the crème pâtissière and cool covered. Prepare the apple filling by mixing all the ingredients together over low heat for 5 minutes until the apples have softened. Transfer to a clean bowl and cool. Mix all the ingredients, except for the cream, for the walnut filling in a third bowl.

4. Remove the dough from the refrigerator and let stand 1 hour at room temperature. Press the dough to deflate it and divide it into three oblong pieces. Divide each one vertically into two even pieces. Brush the two pieces with a little cream and sprinkle with the walnut filling. Roll up each strip from its long side. Divide each roll into 4 small 1/2-inch (2cm) thick pieces. Place the pieces with the cut side downwards in the muffin cases. Spread the two next strips of dough with crème pâtissèrie, roll them up, cut the rolls into slices and place them into another 8 cases.

5. Finally, spread the apple filling on the last two pieces of dough, roll them up and cut them in slices and place them in the remaining cases. At this stage, you can cover the tins with plastic wrap and deep freeze for up to 1 week. Defrost the rolls when you need them, let them rise for another 20 minutes, and follow the instructions in step 6.

6. Bake at 350°F (175°C) for 35 to 40 minutes until golden brown. Remove from the oven and turn over immediately onto a rack to cool. Serve immediately.

Cappuccino Raspberry shake

Yields 2 shakes
Preparation time 20 minutes
Degree of Difficulty ♥

- 1/2 cup ready-made espresso coffee, cold
- 1/2 cup yogurt
- 1/2 cup raspberries or strawberries
- 3 tablespoons chocolate syrup
- 1 teaspoon vanilla essence
- 1/4 - 1/3 cup castor sugar
- 1/2 cup whipping cream whipped with
  a little vanilla and
  1 tablespoon icing sugar (optional)
- chocolate flakes to serve

1. Pulse the first 6 ingredients in a blender to a smooth purée. Taste and add more sugar if needed. Divide the mixture between two glasses and top with spoonfuls of whipped cream or whipped milk. Sprinkle with chocolate flakes and serve immediately.
Alternatively: blend frozen strawberries or raspberries to make a delicious sorbet-like drink.

Sugar hearts with cinnamon and chocolate powder

Preparation time 15 minutes
Drying time 2-3 hours
Degree of Difficulty ♥

- 2 cups castor sugar
- 1 cup unsweetened cocoa powder
- 1 teaspoon ground cinnamon
- 1 – 1½ teaspoons cold water

1. Mix the sugar, chocolate powder and cinnamon. Add water and knead the mixture with your hands to a sandy texture.
2. Fill special heart, leaf or flower-shaped cases with the mixture. Leave the sugar in the cases for 5 minutes and then turn over the cases onto a plate lined with non-stick oven paper. Set the sugar roses aside at room temperature for 2-3 hours until firm. The longer they stand the harder they get.

Fortune Cookies

Yields 12 cookies
Preparation time 20 minutes
Baking time 25 minutes
Degree of Difficulty ♥♥

- 3 egg whites
- 6 tablespoons icing sugar
- 2½ tablespoons all-purpose flour
- 2½ tablespoons corn-starch
- 1 teaspoon vanilla essence
- 1½ teaspoons corn oil

1. Write a message to your beloved on a 2x1½-inch (7x5cm) piece of paper. Preheat the oven to 400°F (200°C). Draw 4 circles, 2½ inches (10cm) in diameter on non-stick paper and line the oven tray with the piece of paper. Grease the surface with a little corn oil.

2. Beat the egg whites in a food processor until frothy. Add the sugar and beat for another minute. Continuing to beat, add the flour and corn-starch. Finally, add the vanilla and corn oil and mix with a spatula. The mixture should be thick and smooth.

3. Place 2-3 teaspoons of the mixture in the centre of each circle and spread to cover the entire surface of the circle. Bake the cookies in the middle of a pre-heated oven at 350°F (175°C) for 7 to 8 minutes.

4. Remove from the oven and immediately place your message written on a piece of paper or the engagement ring wrapped in soft wrapping paper, if you wish, in the center of the cookies. Fold one side over the other to form a half-moon and press the two edges of the cookie together to seal them. Bend the cookies over the rim of a glass. Prepare all 4 cookies in the same way before they dry up. If they do dry up, place them in the oven for a short while to soften.

5. Spread the rest of the dough on the circles and repeat the process. Cool the cookies on a rack. The longer they stand the crispier. It is better to prepare the cookies several days in advance. Store them in a cookie tin, in a dry place and remember to mark with ribbon the cookie that contains the precious ring!

Pastelitas de Bodas

Yields 25-30 cookies
Preparation time 30 minutes
Baking time 15 minutes
Degree of Difficulty ♥

- 1 cup unsalted butter
- 1/4 cup icing sugar
- 2 teaspoons vanilla essence
- 2 cups all-purpose flour
- 1/4 teaspoon salt
- 1/2 cup pecans or macadamia or almonds or hazelnuts, roasted and coarsely ground
- 1 cup icing sugar to fold in the cookies

1. Beat the butter and sugar with the vanilla in a mixer until fluffy and white. Meanwhile, mix the flour with the salt. Stop beating and add the flour a handful at a time, gently kneading the mixture with your hands. Add the nuts and knead gently, to incorporate. Do not over-knead or the cookies will turn out stiff.

2. Roll out the dough in parts into 1/2-inch (1cm) thick sheets and cut out small flowers using an appropriate cutter. You may cut out small hearts with a cookie cutter or roll the dough up using your hands to form crescent-shaped cookies. Place the cookies on a non-buttered baking sheet and bake at 350°F (180°C) for about 15 minutes. Remove the cookies from the oven and while still hot dust generously with icing sugar. These fluffy cookies are served at weddings in Mexico.

2

ORGANIZING A WEDDING

Let me not to the marriage of true minds
Admit impediments. Love is not love
Which alters when it alteration finds,
Or bends with the remover to remove
O, no! it is an ever-fixed mark
That looks on tempests and is never shaken;
It is the star to every wandering bark,
Whose worth's unknown, although his height be taken.
Love's not Time's fool, though rosy lips and cheeks
Within his bending sickle's compass come.
Love alters not with his brief hours and weeks,
But bears it out even to the edge of doom.
If this be error and upon me proved,
I never writ, nor no man ever loved.

William Shakespeare, Sonnet 116

"Marriage is and will remain the most interesting voyage of discovery man will ever attempt to make".

Sören Kierkegaard

The groom goes to the bride's home for the official proposal. To avoid the anxiety and nervousness that go with the first meeting, invite both families to a rich meal at home, and break the ice by offering ouzo and Mediterranean piquant appetizers to start with.

Follow some simple and useful advice, so that the first meeting between the two families goes smoothly and without undesired friction. A wedding is a very moving event, which often brings together families with different experiences, social backgrounds or even financial positions. Also, due to their age, parents are set in their ways and opinions. Don't try to force the families to get along, give them the chance to feel free and relaxed, reminding them that the evening is centered around the couple, on the way to their life together. Their opinions are respected, but not necessarily accepted. Make sure that you have other guests, who can help keep the conversation flowing, such as siblings, grandparents or the best man and maid of honor, because they will express the middle way. Although it may seem the most fitting subject for conversation, the upcoming wedding can be rather controversial. Make sure you drop hints in advance to both your mother and your mother-in-law with regard to the tasks you intend to allot them regarding the wedding preparations. When the subject comes up, hopefully they will have already accepted their role in the organization of your wedding.

Inviting both families to a dinner prepared by you can be quite an experience. Face it as a challenge and involve your partner in as many tasks of the preparation as he is willing to take up. Preparing everything together can be a fun experience and a great rehearsal for your future life together.

The in-laws' comments will be minimized if they know that their precious son has prepared some of the dishes or at least has contributed somehow to their preparation. You don't have to be perfect, just thoughtful and relaxed. Make sure you know the eating habits of your parents and your future husband's parents in advance, so that you can surprise them pleasantly. Take into consideration the religious and cultural aspects of your in-laws' background, making sure you ask your fiancé about them.

Choose a variety of light Mediterranean dishes that will transform your evening into a culinary experience. Start the meal with Greek ouzo and appetizers adapted to modern Greek cooking. Serve slices of toasted pitta bread with traditional Greek salads, such as eggplant salad or tirokafteri or octopus marinated in vinegar and olives. The appetizers can be served in the living room, to make everyone feel more comfortable. Serve a light Greek dry white wine with the main meal. Complete the meal with liqueurs and honey sweets. If you wish, peel three oranges in long chunks and boil the pieces in aromatic syrup, prepared according to the recipe "Baclava Roses". Drain the orange preserves and dip each slice in melted chocolate to coat. Let the orange pieces set on non-stick paper and serve this delightful delicacy with liqueur. Relax and get organized. Both your parents might surprise you, and their love for you will make itself felt in the sweetest way.

Ricotta and pistachio flutes

Yields 30 flutes
Preparation time 40 minutes
Baking time 30 minutes
Degree of Difficulty ♥♥

- 1½ cups ricotta or anthotyro cheese
- 7oz (200g) mascarpone or cream cheese
- 3 tablespoons light brown sugar
- 2/3 cup coarsely ground pistachio nuts
- 1/2 teaspoon cardamom powder
- 1 teaspoon orange zest
- 16 thin phyllo pastry sheets for desserts
- 2/3 cup melted butter
- 1 recipe syrup (as in recipe "Baklava roses")
- 1 teaspoon saffron threads
- a piece of orange rind

1. Prepare the filling. Beat both the cheeses with the sugar in the mixer until creamy. Mix in the pistachios, cardamom and orange zest.

2. Layer 4 sheets of pastry, brushing the first three layers with melted butter. Place 1/4 of the filling along the short end of the pastry, slightly overturn the long side of the phyllo on the left and right of the filling, so that it doesn't escape while baking, and roll up. Prepare 4 rolls in the same way. Place the rolls on a buttered baking sheet, one next to the other. At this stage, you can store the rolls in the freezer. Brush the rolls with melted butter just before baking. Bake in the oven at 400°F (200°C), for about 20 minutes, until golden brown.

3. Prepare the syrup, as in recipe "Baklava roses", adding 1 teaspoon of saffron threads and a piece of orange rind. Pour the hot syrup over the rolls as they come out of the oven. Sprinkle with some ground pistachio nuts. Cut each roll into 4 equal sections, once cold, and serve on a tray.

Fillet of sole in vinegar

Appetizer ("meze") for ouzo
Preparation time 20 minutes
Refrigeration time 48 hours
Degree of Difficulty ♥

• 1 pound (500g) fresh fillet of sole, well cleaned
• salt
• 2-3 tablespoons small capers
• 2 cups vinegar
• 2-3 cloves garlic, thinly sliced
• olive oil
• crumbled dried oregano and thyme

1. Ask your fishmonger to prepare you some fillets of sole, without the skin and bones. Wash thoroughly and dry on absorbent paper. Cut into very thin slices or long thin strips. The fish is easier to cut if it has been in the freezer for 30 minutes. Arrange the pieces of fish in an oven-proof dish, sprinkle with some salt, the capers and slices of garlic.

2. Pour over the vinegar until the fish is submerged, and cover with cling-film. Stand in the refrigerator for 2 days. Remove from the refrigerator and drain away the vinegar. Place on a dish, drizzle with good quality olive oil, and sprinkle with some oregano and thyme. The fish can be preserved in olive oil in the refrigerator for up to 1 week.

Eggplant terrine (cold dish)

Yields 16 portions
Preparation time 1 hour + 1 hour
for salting
Refrigeration time 4 hours
Degree of Difficulty ♥♥

- 6 medium-sized long eggplants
- oil for frying
- 1/4 cup balsamic vinegar
- 1 bunch rocket or watercress
- 1 pound (450g) Parmigiano-Reggiano very thinely sliced or 2/3 cup Reggiano parmesan shavings
- 2 jars (14oz or 400g each) red pimientos
- 2 cups black olive paste
- a few sprigs of basil
- 14oz (400g) mozzarella fior di latte, cut in slices

For the dressing
- 1/4 cup balsamic vinegar
- 1/2 cup extra virgin olive oil
- 1 tablespoon Dijon mustard
- 2 tablespoons sugar
- salt and freshly ground black pepper

1. Most of the ingredients used in this recipe can be purchased at an Italian Deli. Cut the eggplants into long thin slices, cover with plenty of salt and stand for 1 hour in a colander. Wash with plenty of cold water and squeeze between your palms to remove all the water. Dry on absorbent paper and fry in hot oil until crispy at the edges. Drain and arrange on an oven-proof dish. Once cold, pour over the balsamic vinegar, cover and stand in the refrigerator for up to 2 days.

2. Wash and dry the rocket. You will need a large spring mold. Remove the bottom of the mold and place the ring on the platter you intend to use for serving.

3. Arrange a layer of eggplant slices, drained of the vinegar, to cover the bottom. Cover with half the parmesan shavings. Spread with half the olive paste, and cover with half the peppers, split lengthways and opened up. Cover with half the rocket and basil leaves, and finish with the thin slices of mozzarella. Repeat the layers in reverse, starting with the rocket and ending with the eggplants or red peppers.

4. Cover the dish and place it in the refrigerator. If you wish, prepare the salad in advance. It will keep in the refrigerator for up to 5 days. As the terrine may let out juices, cover the ring with kitchen paper. Remove the paper and the ring just before serving.

5. Serve the terrine cold, cut in thick slices and drizzled with the dressing. To prepare the dressing, place all the ingredients in a jar with an airtight lid and shake well.

Carrot Bread

Yields 2 loaves
Preparation time 30 minutes + 2 hours to rise
Baking time 30 minutes
<u>Suitable for freezing</u>
Degree of Difficulty ♥♥

- 1½ cups warm carrot purée (5 medium carrots, boiled and mashed)
- 2/3 cup warm broth from the carrots
- 1½ tablespoons active dry yeast, or 1oz (43g) fresh yeast
- 6 - 6½ cups all purpose flour
- 1/4 cup extra virgin olive oil
- 3 tablespoons honey
- 2 tablespoons finely chopped fresh mint

1. Dissolve the yeast in the warm carrot broth. Add and mix in 3-4 tablespoons flour, cover with cling-film and leave to rise for 10 minutes.

2. Set aside 1/2 cup flour. Place the remaining flour in the mixer bowl, add and mix in the salt. Open a hole in the center and pour in the oil, honey, carrot purée, yeast and mint. Beat with the dough hook for 10 to 15 minutes, adding as much flour as necessary, until the dough sticks to the hook and not to the bowl.

3. Place the dough in a bowl, coated with a little oil. Cover with cling-film and stand for 2 hours. Press down to let the air out and knead for 5 minutes, adding 1 to 2 tablespoons flour, until you have a smooth, non-sticky dough. The reason you will need more flour is that the carrot releases humidity as it stands. For the same reason, the bread remains fresh for several days after baking.

4. With your hands, form the dough into a large oblong piece to make one large loaf (for 40-inch or 1m ovens) or cut in two and form each into a smaller oblong piece. Roll up each piece. Place in ungreased baking pans, cover with cling-film, and stand for 30 minutes, until they rise. If you wish, brush with one egg yolk beaten with 1 teaspoon olive oil, and sprinkle with black sesame or poppy seeds. Bake in a 400°F (200°C) oven for 30-35 minutes, or until golden-brown. Freeze while fresh.

Seafood Bourekia

Yields 16 patties
Preparation time 30 minutes
Baking time 30 minutes
Degree of Difficulty ♥♥

- 1 pound (500g) white fish fillet (sole or cod)
- 2 pounds (1kg) medium prawns
- 7oz (200g) mussel flesh
- 1 cup dry white wine
- 1/4 cup lemon juice
- 1/4 cup finely chopped parsley
- 1/2 cup butter or margarine
- 1/2 cup finely chopped green onions
- 1/4 cup flour
- 2 cups milk
- 1 tablespoon mustard
- 1/2 cup grated soft white cheese ("kefalograviera")
- 1 pound (500g) thin phyllo pastry
- 1/3 cup olive oil, for coating

For the lemon sauce
(Yields 1½ cups sauce)

- 1/4 cup unsalted butter or margarine
- 1 clove garlic, crushed
- 2 tablespoons corn-starch
- 1/2 cup water
- 1 cup freshly squeezed lemon juice
- 2 teaspoons lemon zest
- 1 tablespoon mustard
- 1 teaspoon powdered saffron threads

1. Boil the fish fillets in salted water for around 10 minutes, until soft. Drain, place in a clean bowl and mash with a fork. Remove the shell, tail and intestine from the prawns and boil in salted water for 4 minutes. Drain, remove the heads, chop finely and mix with the fish.

2. Wash the mussels thoroughly, to remove all the sand. The best way is to submerge them in a bowl of water for 15 minutes. Drain and repeat the process until the water is clear when drained. Place in a small pan, pour over the wine and boil for 4 minutes, uncovered. Do not overboil. Drain and mix with the prawns and fish. Add salt and pepper, drizzle with the lemon juice and sprinkle with parsley.

3. Melt half the butter in a pan and sauté the onions. Add to the bowl containing the seafood and mix together. Melt the remaining butter in a clean pan and sauté the flour. Add all the milk at once and stir over high heat until it sets. Add and mix in the mustard and cheese until it melts. Remove from the heat, transfer to the bowl with the seafood and blend gently.

4. Lay three sheets of pastry out on your workbench, one on top of the other, brushing each sheet with olive oil. Fold the sheets in half from the short side, and cut the oblong piece into three long, narrow strips. Place a spoonful of the filling on the short side of each strip, Fold the sheet left and right over the filling, and roll it up. Make similar rolls until you have run out of filling.

5. Arrange the rolls on a well-buttered baking sheet, brush with a little olive oil and sprinkle with sesame and paprika, if you like. Bake in a 360°F (180°C) oven for about 30 minutes, until golden brown. Serve warm or cold, with the lemon sauce.

6. Melt the butter for the sauce in a small pan. Add the garlic and sauté slightly. Add the cornstarch, having first dissolved it in the water, lemon juice, lemon zest, mustard and saffron. Stir for a few minutes over medium heat, until the sauce sets. Remove from the heat and serve immediately.

Yields 12 portions
Preparation time 25 minutes
Cooking time 40 minutes
Degree of Difficulty ♥
<u>Light</u>

- 4 medium-sized celeriacs
- 1/2 cup freshly squeezed lemon juice
- 1/3 cup olive oil
- 1/3 cup grated onion
- 5 green onions, finely chopped
- 2 large ripe tomatoes, finely chopped
- 1 cup tomato juice
- 8 bottled sun-dried tomatoes, finely chopped
- 3 tablespoons small capers
- 1/4 cup finely chopped celery leaves
- 1/4 cup finely chopped parsley
- 1/8 teaspoon hot red pepper

1. Wash and peel the celeriacs. Cut each one into thick slices and place them in a large pan with the lemon juice and enough water to cover them. Boil for 10 minutes. Drain, and when cool, press the centers with your fingers to create a groove.

2. Heat the oil in a pan and sauté all the onions. Add the fresh tomato, sun-dried tomatoes, capers, celery leaves, parsley, salt and pepper and bring to the boil. Add the celeriac slices to the pan and simmer for about 30 minutes. Arrange the slices of celeriac in the center of a platter and fill with spoonfuls of the sauce mixture.

Brisket of Beef stuffed with Ground Meat, Pistachios and Cashew Nuts

Yields 10-12 portions
Preparation time 30 minutes
Baking time 5 to 6 hours
Degree of Difficulty ♥♥

- 4 pounds (2kg) brisket of beef
- 1/4 cup butter, softened
- 1 medium-sized red onion, finely chopped
- 5 green onions, finely chopped
- 2 cloves garlic, finely chopped
- 10oz (300g) ground pork
- 1/2 cup grated soft white cheese ("Kefalograviera")
- 2 tablespoons Ketchup
- 2 tablespoons mustard
- 1 egg
- 1/4 cup coarsely ground pistachios
- 1/4 cup coarsely ground cashew nuts
- salt, pepper
- 1/3 cup unsalted butter or margarine
- 1 cup Cognac
- 1/4 cup freshly squeezed lemon juice
- 1 sprig parsley, 1 sprig dill, 1 sprig celery and 2 bay leaves, tied in a bouquet garni

1. Ask your butcher to remove the bones and prepare the roast for filling. Melt the butter in a small pan, add and sauté the onions and garlic, until soft. Remove from the heat and mix with the ground meat. Add the cheese, Ketchup, mustard, egg, nuts, salt and pepper, and knead with your hands to incorporate into the ground meat mixture.

2. Shape a long roll out of the mixture, as long as the meat cut, place it in the center of the meat and roll it up. Tie up the roast with cotton thread, so that it doesn't open up while cooking. Sprinkle with salt and pepper to taste and place in a large oven-proof dish. Coat with the butter. Pour over the cognac, lemon juice and 1/2 cup water, and add the bouquet garni. Cover with aluminum foil and bake slowly in a 325°F (160°C) oven, for 5 to 6 hours, until the meat is tender. Open the oven every 1 hour and baste the meat with the juices.

3. When ready, remove from the oven and drain off the juices. If less than 2 cups, replenish with Worcestershire sauce, or soy sauce, or water. Melt 2 tablespoons butter in a pan, and sauté 2 tablespoons flour. Add the meat juices and stir over high heat, until set. Add and stir in 2 tablespoons fine mustard. Carve the meat and serve with the sauce.

Millefeuilles with marinated octopus and red pepper relish

Yields 6 portions
Preparation time 30 minutes
Refrigeration time 24 hours
Cooking time 1 hour
Degree of Difficulty ♥

- 3 2-pound (1kg) frozen octopuses, thawed and cleaned
- salt
- 1 cup vinegar
- 1/2 cup olive oil
- 1 bouquet garni (1 sprig celery, 2 cloves garlic, 1 small onion, 1 sprig parsley, 10 black peppercorns, 2 bay leaves)
- 8oz (250g) puff pastry (1 sheet)
- red pepper relish, fresh rocket and a little balsamic vinegar for serving

1. Wash the octopuses well, place in a large pan, add enough water to cover them, a little salt, and the vinegar and simmer for 1 hour or until sufficiently soft. Frozen octopus cooks faster.

2. Drain, rinse with cold water and remove the membrane carefully. Return the octopuses to a clean pan, fill with water to cover them, add the bouquet garni and simmer for another 30 minutes, until very tender. Drain, cut into pieces and pour over oil and vinegar, while still warm. Refrigerate the marinated octopus for at least 24 hours.

3. Prepare the puff pastry. Roll out the pastry sheet on an ungreased baking sheet, and cut into 12 oblong pieces. Make pretty shapes and parallel lines on the pastry surface, using a pizza cutter. If you wish, drizzle the dough with a little melted salted butter, for extra taste. Bake the pastry in the oven at 425°F (210°C) for 25 minutes or until golden brown. Turn off the oven, open the door, and let the pastry cool inside.

4. Remove the pastry pieces to plates with a metal spatula. Assemble the millefeuilles just before serving, by joining two pieces of pastry with 1 or 2 tablespoons relish, and a few pieces of octopus. Garnish with fresh rocket drizzled with balsamic vinegar and serve as a first course.

Red Pepper Relish

Preparation time 20 minutes
Cooking time 1 hour and 30 minutes
Refrigeration time 2 weeks
Degree of Difficulty ♥

- 1 teaspoon black peppercorns
- 1 bay leaf
- 5 allspice corns
- 2 teaspoons mustard seeds
- 2 pounds (1kg) sweet red bell peppers, cut in julienne pieces
- 2 vindallia onions, sliced
- 4 cloves garlic, finely chopped
- 1½ cups good quality wine vinegar
- 2 green apples, peeled and grated
- 1 teaspoon grated fresh gingerroot
- 1 cup dark brown sugar

1. Wrap the peppercorns, bay leaves, allspice and mustard seeds in a piece of muslin and place in a large saucepan with the peppers, onions, garlic, vinegar, apple and ginger. Simmer for 30 minutes, until the peppers are soft.

2. Add the sugar and stir until it melts. Simmer for 1 hour and 15 minutes, stirring occasionally, until the sauce sets. Remove the muslin with the spices and let the mixture cool.

3. Store the relish in sterilized jars, and stand for 2 weeks before using. Will keep for up to 1 year in a cool dry place. Once opened, keep refrigerated. Don't forget to label the jars of homemade relishes and preserves, mentioning the content and the production date.

Baklava Roses

Yields 24 small baklava
Preparation time 30 minutes
Baking time 10 minutes
Degree of Difficulty ♥

- 1/3 cup coarsely ground
  pistachio nuts
- 1/3 cup coarsely ground walnuts
- 2 tablespoons dark brown sugar
- 1 teaspoon ground cinnamon
- 1/4 teaspoon ground cloves

- 8oz (250g) thin phyllo pastry,
  for sweets
- 1/3 cup unsalted butter or
  melted margarine

For the syrup
- 1 cup castor sugar
- 2 tablespoons lemon juice
- 1 cup honey
- 1/2 cup water

1. Mix the walnuts with the pistachios, sugar, cinnamon and cloves. Layer three sheets of phyllo pastry brushing each sheet with melted butter. Sprinkle the pastry surface with the nut mixture. Cut out 4-inch (10-cm) circles with a pastry cutter. Press the center of each circle down to form a flower and place them in the holes of a well-buttered muffin tray.

2. Repeat the process with another 3 sheets of pastry, making a total of 24 roses. Brush with melted butter. Bake at 350°F (170°C) for 8 to 10 minutes. Boil the sugar with the juice, honey and water for 7 minutes, or until a light syrup forms. Drizzle the baklava roses with the hot syrup as soon as you take them out of the oven.

Saragli Lilies

Yields 20 pieces
Preparation time 30 minutes
Baking time 30 minutes
Degree of Difficulty ♥

- 3 cups coarsely ground walnuts
- 2 teaspoons ground cinnamon
- 1 teaspoon ground cloves
- 1 cup melted vegetable shortening
  or unsalted butter

- 8oz (250g) phyllo pastry

For the syrup
- 2 cups castor sugar
- 2/3 cups water
- 1/4 teaspoon cream of tartar or
  1 tablespoon lemon juice
- 1/4 cup glucose

1. Mix the walnuts with the cinnamon and cloves. Spread out a sheet of pastry on your workbench, brush well with melted butter and sprinkle over a little of the mixture. Placing a very thin rolling pin at one end of the pastry, roll it up loosely. Tuck it in on either side.

Remove the rolling pin and place the roll on a well-buttered baking sheet.

2. Prepare all the rolls in the same way. Cut into thick pieces and arrange them on the cookie sheet with the cut side facing up, so that they look like lilies. Sprinkle with a little melted butter, and bake in a 370°F (180°C) oven, for 30 minutes, or until golden brown.

3. Prepare the syrup while the lilies are baking. Boil all the syrup ingredients without stirring, in a small saucepan for 5 minutes. Pour the hot syrup over the saragli as soon as they come out of the oven. The saragli can be stored at room temperature for up to 2 weeks. If you wish, serve with scoops of mocha ice cream.

Miniature Kataifi nests with sweet lemon-scented anthotiro cream

Yields 24 miniature kataifi
Preparation time 15 minutes
Baking time 25 minutes
Degree of Difficulty ♥
Light

- 8oz (250g) anthotiro or ricotta cheese
- 1 tablespoon milk
- 1/3 cup icing sugar
- 2 egg yolks
- 2 tablespoons Grand Marnier
- 1 teaspoon lemon or orange zest
- 7oz (200g) kataifi pastry

1. Brush 2 or more mini muffin trays with a little corn oil. Tear off small bundles of kataifi pastry. Wrap them around your finger to form small rolls and place them in the grooves of each tray.

2. Cream the cheese, milk and sugar in the mixer. Add the egg yolks, liqueur and zest, and beat to incorporate.

3. Fill a piping bag with the cream and pipe rosettes into each kataifi nest. Bake the mini kataifi at 375°F (190°C) for 20 to 25 minutes, or until golden brown. Store at room temperature and consume on the same day. Store the remaining nests in the refrigerator. Once refrigerated, they will taste good but they will lose their crispiness. Serve with coffee, and cherry preserve, if you like.

THE ENGAGEMENT II.

Spring is an ideal time for an engagement in the garden, surrounded by blossoming flower-beds.

Traditionally, an engagement is the couple's official announcement to their families and friends of their intention to get married. Unofficial vows have already been exchanged at the time of the marriage proposal, but the event is made official and celebrated with an engagement party.

Today it is not obligatory for a priest to be present at the engagement, as it was in older times. The duration of an engagement is not fixed, but usually fluctuates between 2 and 13 months. The period elapsing before the wedding day is necessary, both for all the procedures related to the preparation of the wedding, and for the two families to get to know each other before the big day. The engagement is also a very good marriage rehearsal, as for the first time the couple is treated as one entity, and has to resolve all the issues related to its life together. A good time for an elegant engagement party in the garden is Easter day.

When Shakespeare wrote the greatest love story of all time, the custom was for a man and the woman of his dreams to elope. Centuries later, the bride's father was required to pay his future son-in-law a dowry for taking his daughter. The engagement gave the bride time to collect a magnificent trousseau to take with her to her new home.

Usually, engagements are held at the future bride's home, where traditionally the groom goes to ask her father for her hand in marriage. Although all the old traditions have eclipsed, certain events that are central to our lives, such as an engagement, are happy events and a beautiful memory for the couple.

The silver tray bearing the sugared almonds and rice is placed on a table covered with a snow-white tablecloth. When the groom crosses the threshold, he places the rings on the tray. When all the relatives are gathered together, the couple exchanges loving words and the rings. The rings can also be exchanged by the father of the bride or the best man.

The engagement ceremony, as well as most of the customs associated with marriage, is dedicated to the bride. At the engagement, the groom's relatives bring her gifts of jewelry. The bride's family gives the groom a watch, a custom referring to the fact that he must get to the church on time for the wedding.

The engagement can be a simple meeting between the two families, or a grand event with a large number of guests. An official engagement requires a lot of preparation, including printing invitations, arranging a banquet, music, flowers and decorations. Many couples offer their guests a small bonbonnière, as a souvenir from the big event. The engagement can be a good rehearsal for the wedding.

Roquefort and salmon rolls

Yields 30 rolls
Preparation time 30 minutes
Degree of Difficulty ♥

- 5 tortilla-type wrappers
- 8oz (250g) anthotyro or ricotta
- 8oz (250g) Roquefort or other high-quality blue cheese
- salt and white pepper
- 1 pound (500g) smoked salmon or trout, cut in thin slices
- 4oz (100g) red caviar

1. Fold out a tortilla wrapper on the workbench. If refrigerated, warm the tortilla wrappers in a microwave oven for a few seconds until pliable. Beat the anthotyro and roquefort in a food processor together with a little salt and white pepper to a smooth creamy mixture. Spread each tortilla with 2 to 3 tablespoons of the mixture and cover with a few slices of smoked salmon.
2. Spread a little more cheese mixture over the salmon and 1 to 2 teaspoons red caviar. Prepare the rest of the tortillas in the same way to form 5 rolls. Wrap the rolls in plastic wrap and store in the refrigerator for 30 minutes until the cheese filling has set.
3. Remove the rolls from the refrigerator and cut them into 1/2-inch (1cm) thick slices. Store in the refrigerator covered until serving time. You can prepare them on the previous day.

Engagement almond cookies

Preparation time 20 minutes
Baking time 10 to 12 minutes
Degree of Difficulty ♥♥

• 2 pounds (800g) almonds, blanched
• 3 cups icing sugar
• 1 teaspoon vanilla or almond essence
• 2 egg whites (large)

1. Place the almonds in a food processor together with the icing sugar and grind to a smooth powder. Continuing to beat, add the essence and egg whites. Beat the mixture to a soft and supple dough. Let the dough stand for a while, until hard enough to shape. The longer the dough stands uncovered, the harder it gets.

2. Form marriage wreaths or the initials of the bride and groom using your hands and decorate with small flowers also made of dough. Stick the dough flowers on the wreaths or monograms with a little water. Place on a baking sheet lined with non-stick oven paper and bake at 350°F (180°C) for 10 to 12 minutes avoiding browning.

Spring canapés

For a buffet
- 1 packet of sliced bread or
  1 packet of white Italian Spuntinella bread
- 1 packet of square or round slices of Pumpernickel
- mayonnaise for spreading
- fresh broad bean sauce
- trout mousse (recipe on page 88)
- dill, red and black caviar, pistachios, red pimientos, cashew nuts, parmesan cubes, black and green olive paste, taramosalata, various pickles and edible flowers, to garnish

For the cheese mixture
- 2oz (50g) cream cheese or 2oz (50g) ricotta cheese
- 2oz (50g) cream of French goat's cheese or 2oz (50g) manouri cheese
- 3 tablespoons finely chopped parsley or mint
- 1/3 cup ground nuts

1. Cut the white bread with a heart-shaped cutter. Spread the hearts with mayonnaise and top with a creamed trout rosette (follow the instructions in the recipe: artichokes with creamed trout, omitting the egg white). Garnish with a little dill.

2. Mix the cheeses with the parsley, nuts, salt and pepper. Beat in a blender and spread a fair amount of mixture over the pieces of pumpernickel. Garnish with a little red and black caviar.

3. Boil 2 cups of shelled fresh broad beans in salted water for 10 minutes and mash them in a food processor. In a saucepan, sauté the onion and garlic in 2 tablespoons olive oil. Place the bean purée in the saucepan and add 3 tablespoons finely chopped parsley, 3 tablespoons lemon juice, salt and white pepper and stir over low heat to thicken. Strain in a sifter lined with absorbed paper for 2 hours, until cool. Beat in the food processor adding 1/3 cup olive oil in a thin steady flow. Keep refrigerated. Spread the mixture over square canapés and garnish with pistachios or hearts cut out of red pimientos.

4. Alternatively, for tasty canapés, you can pipe rosettes of black or green olive paste and garnish them with whole cashew nuts or cubes of Parmigiano-Reggiano. You can also garnish the bread hearts with taramosalata rosettes and pickles.

5. Place the canapés on a platter, cover them with plastic wrap and store in the refrigerator. You can prepare the canapés on the previous day. Decorate with edible flowers such as calendula, hibiscus, jasmine or pansies.

Devilled eggs

With chicken livers
- 8 hard boiled eggs
- 7oz (200g) chicken livers
- 1/4 cup butter
- 3 tablespoons water
- salt and pepper
- 1/4 cup mayonnaise

1. Chop the livers finely. Melt the butter in a small saucepan without bringing it to the boil and add the liver, water, salt and pepper. Cover and simmer over very low heat for 1 hour until soft.
2. Shell the eggs carefully and using a sharp knife cut them in half lengthways. Place the yolks in the food processor bowl, add the liver and blend. Stir the mayonnaise gently into the mixture. Place the cream in a piping bag and fill the eggs.

With mayonnaise and mustard
- 8 hard boiled eggs
- 1 tablespoon mustard
- 1 teaspoon saffron threads
- 1/4 cup strained Greek yogurt
- 1/4 cup mayonnaise
- salt and white pepper

1. Shell the eggs gently and using a sharp knife cut them in half lengthways. Place the yolks in a bowl and mash together with the rest of the ingredients. Place the smooth paste into a piping bag and pipe rosettes into the empty eggs halves.

With porcini tartar cream
- 8 hard boiled eggs
- 1/2oz (15g) dried porcini
- 1/4 cup freshly squeezed lemon juice
- salt and white pepper
- 1 cup olive oil
- 1 teaspoon dried chives

1. Shell the eggs and cut them in half lengthways. Use the yolks for the filling and set aside the empty egg halves. Place the porcini in a bowl, pour over the lemon juice and set aside for 20 minutes or until soft and swollen. Strain the porcini and preserve the juice. Place the porcini together with the egg yolks, a little salt and pepper in the food processor bowl and blend to a smooth mixture.
2. Continuing to beat, add the oil to the bowl a little at a time at a steady flow. It will take 15 minutes to add all the oil to the bowl and form a smooth and thick mayonnaise-type sauce. Flavor the sauce with 1 or 2 tablespoons of the reserved lemon juice and finely chopped chives. Fill the egg halves with the porcini tartar cream.

Pretzels

Yields 24 soft pretzels
Preparation time 30 minutes + 2 hours to rise
Baking time 12 to 15 minutes
Degree of Difficulty ♥♥♥

- 1½ tablespoons active dry yeast
- 1 tablespoon sugar
- 3 cups tepid water
- 2 pounds (2kg) all-purpose flour
- 1½ teaspoons salt
- 6 tablespoons bicarbonate of soda, diluted in 2 liters of water

1. In a bowl, dilute the yeast and sugar in half the water and add a few tablespoons of flour to form a thick batter. Cover and set aside for 15 minutes until the yeast rises.

2. Place 2 cups of the flour, salt, the risen yeast and the rest of the water in the mixer bowl and beat for 2 minutes. Add the rest of the flour a little at a time kneading with the dough hook for 10 minutes and adding as much flour as needed until the dough no longer sticks to the dough hook and is smooth and pliable. Or knead with your hands for 20 minutes adding as much flour as needed. Place the dough in a well-buttered bowl, cover with plastic wrap and set aside for 2 hours until double in volume.

3. Press the dough to deflate and using your hands shape it into an oblong piece on a slightly floured surface. Using a floured sharp knife, cut the dough into narrow strips along the short side of the piece of dough. Shape each strip carefully with your hands into a cord on the floured surface and wrap the two ends of the cord left and right by placing one end over the other to form a pretzel. Stick the ends in place with a little water. Lay the pretzels on a baking sheet lined with non-stick paper. Let the pretzels rise, uncovered, for about 25 minutes.

4. Boil the water and soda in a large stainless steel saucepan (do not use an aluminum one as it will go black). Place the pretzels in the boiling water one at a time and let them rise for a few seconds, turning them once. Remove them from the water with a slotted spoon and place again on the baking sheet lined with non-stick paper. When all the pretzels are ready, bake them at 425°F (220°C) for 12 to 15 minutes or until golden brown. When cool, you can store them in the deep freeze in hermetically sealed containers. Serve them elegantly tied with a pink or lilac bow.

Artichoke hearts with trout mousse and shrimps

Yields 24 starters
Preparation time 35 minutes
Cooking time 30 to 35 minutes
Degree of Difficulty ♥

- 24 fresh artichokes
- 1 cup freshly squeezed lemon juice
- 1 tablespoon flour
- 24 medium-sized shrimps
- 1 teaspoon seafood seasoning

For the trout mousse
- 2 pounds (800g) smoked trout fillets
- 7oz (200g) cream cheese
- 1/3 cup finely chopped dill
- 1/3 cup freshly squeezed lemon juice
- 2-3 tablespoons crème fraîche
- salt and a little white pepper
- 1 egg white (small egg), beaten to a soft meringue
- parsley sprigs to garnish

1. Clean the artichokes and reserve the hearts only. You can also use frozen artichokes as long as they are tender and without fibers. Choose small and uniform artichokes, as far as size is concerned. After cleaning the artichokes, place them immediately in a saucepan with the lemon juice and flour and then cover with salted water. Boil them until very soft.

2. After removing any bones, cut the trout fillets into small pieces. Place them in the food processor together with the cream cheese and beat to a smooth cream. Add the dill, lemon juice, salt and white pepper and as much cream as needed to obtain a soft creamy mixture. Beat the egg white with a little salt and two drops of lemon juice to a stiff meringue and mix gently with the trout cream. Fill a large piping bag with the trout mousse and place in the refrigerator for 30 minutes to set slightly.

3. Shell the shrimps and remove the black intestine. Then boil them in salted water with 2 tablespoons olive oil and 1 teaspoon seafood seasoning. Drain and remove the heads.

4. Place the artichokes on a platter one next to the other and pipe a large rosette of trout mousse in the centre. Garnish with the boiled shrimps and parsley. If you wish, serve the artichoke hearts on finely chopped iceberg lettuce to avoid slipping.

Elegant spring beetroot soup

Serves 12
Preparation time 1 hour and 20 minutes
Cooking time 40 minutes
Degree of Difficulty ♥♥

- 12 medium-sized beetroots
- 1 large onion, grated
- 4 leeks, cut in pieces
- 2 carrots, cut in pieces
- 8 cups water
- 3 tablespoons olive oil
- 1/2 cup freshly squeezed lemon juice
- 3 tablespoons honey
- salt and white pepper
- 1 pound (450g) Greek strained yogurt or crème fraîche

1. Wash the beetroot well without peeling. Wrap in aluminum foil and bake in the oven at 350°F (180°C) for 50 minutes to one hour until soft. Remove from the oven, dip in cold water until cool enough to handle, peel and grate.
2. Wash and peel all the vegetables and place them in a large saucepan with water. Add the oil and grated beetroot and bring to the boil. Lower the heat and simmer for 40 minutes until soft.
3. Remove the vegetables from the saucepan using a slotted spoon and transfer to the food processor bowl. Reserve the liquid. Add the lemon juice and honey and pulse to mash adding the reserved liquid a little at a time. Transfer to a clean saucepan and season to taste. Store the soup in the refrigerator to chill. Before transferring the soup to a serving tureen, mix with the yogurt.

Perch timbale with baked vegetables and creamy fish sauce

Serves 12
Preparation time 1 hour
Baking time 30 minutes
Degree of Difficulty ♥♥

- 3 medium-sized eggplants, cut in thin slices
- 4 medium-sized zucchini, cut in thin slices
- 6 long red peppers, cleaned and cut in two
- 12 medium-sized oyster mushrooms, trimmed
- 1/4 cup olive oil
- 1 teaspoon Italian herbs or various dried and ground herbs
- 7 pounds (3kg) perch, barramundi or salmon fillet, cut in uniform pieces
- 1/2 cup black olive paste
- a few sprigs of basil or tarragon or sorrel
- 2 cups dry white wine
- a bouquet garni, consisting of 10 black peppercorns, 1 bay leaf, 10 sprigs of basil or tarragon wrapped in muslin
- 2½ pounds (1kg) baby carrots, to garnish

1. Sprinkle the slices of eggplant and zucchini with salt and stand in a colander for 1 hour. Rinse well with plenty of cold water and squeeze with your hands to remove excess water. Dry the vegetables on absorbent kitchen paper and place on a buttered baking sheet together with the peppers and mushrooms. Drizzle the vegetables with the olive oil and sprinkle with the herbs. Bake at 425°F (220°C) for 35 minutes. After removing the vegetables from the oven, peel off the blackened skin of the peppers.

2. Bone and skin the fish fillets. Wash well and place half the fillets in a slightly oiled oven-proof dish. Spread with the olive paste and place the baked vegetables over the fish. Top with the rest of the fillets and secure with toothpicks. Place the sprigs of basil, tarragon or sorrel on top.

3. Pour over the wine and place the bouquet garni in the Pyrex dish. Cover with aluminum foil and bake at 350°F (180°C) for 35 to 40 minutes or until the fish comes apart when pricked with a fork. Remove from the oven and serve on plates. Strain the juices to a clear liquid and reserve 1 cup for the sauce.

4. Serve the fish with baby carrots sautéed in a little butter.

Creamy fish sauce with tarragon or sorrel

Yields 1½ cups sauce

- 6 green onions, finely chopped
- 1 cup dry white wine
- 1 cup fish stock
- 2-3 sprigs parsley
- 3 leaves sage
- 1 cup cold butter, cut in pieces
- 1/4 cup crème fraîche
- 2 tablespoons small capers
- 2 tablespoons chives, finely chopped
- 4oz (100g) fresh tarragon or sorrel, finely chopped
- salt and white pepper

This sauce, like all buerre blanc-based sauces, cannot be reheated as the butter will melt and separate from the sauce. You should therefore prepare the sauce just before serving or a bit earlier and keep it at stable temperature in a double boiler.

1. Boil the onions together with the wine, stock, herbs, salt and pepper in a saucepan until the mixture reduces to 1/3. Remove from the heat and strain. Add the pieces of butter all at once to the clear stock and blend until you obtain a smooth, uniform and thick mixture. Add the cream, capers, chives and fresh tarragon or sorrel, salt and white pepper and stir gently in a double boiler.

Kid roll stuffed with manouri cheese, spinach and asparagus pesto

Serves 12
Preparation time 30 minutes
Baking time 3 hours and 30 minutes
Degree of Difficulty ♥♥♥

- 7 oz (200g) manouri cheese
- 4 oz (100g) anthotyro cheese
- 1 egg yolk
- salt and freshly ground pepper
- 1/4 cup finely chopped fresh mint
- 14 oz (400g) fresh spinach
- 1 tablespoon oil
- 1 clove garlic, crushed
- 8 pounds (4kg) boneless kid
- 1/2 cup freshly squeezed lemon juice

For the asparagus pesto
- 1 pound (500g) fresh green asparagus
- 1/4 cup fresh mint leaves
- 1 cup grated dry mizithra or parmesan
- 2/3 cup ground roasted pine nuts
- salt and a little white pepper
- 1 cup extra-virgin olive oil

1. Prepare the asparagus pesto. Trim the asparagus, cut in pieces and boil in salted water until soft. Strain and when cool transfer to the food processor bowl. Add the mint and mash. Add the grated cheese, ground pine nuts, salt and pepper and blend. Continuing to beat, add the oil gradually at a thin constant flow until incorporated in the sauce. This procedure lasts about 10 minutes but it is necessary to avoid the oil curdling.

2. You can purchase the manouri and antotyro cheeses from a Greek deli. You may substitute with ricotta, although manouri is a more aromatic cheese. Pulse the manouri in a food processor together with the anthotyro, egg yolk, salt, white pepper and finely chopped mint to a smooth and uniform cream. Wash the spinach well and blanch. Strain the spinach with your hands to remove excess water and sauté together with the garlic and oil.

3. Ask your butcher to remove the bones and most of the fat from the meat without tearing the skin. Wash the meat well, spray with lemon juice and sprinkle with salt and pepper. Line a work surface with non-stick oven paper and place half the pieces of meat on the paper one next to the other with the skin facing downwards. Using a kitchen hammer, flatten the meat to form a single oblong piece of meat. Spread the meat with some spoonfuls of asparagus pesto sauce. Place half the sautéed spinach over the meat and cover with a layer of the cheese mixture. Roll up into a regular thick roll. Wrap the roll carefully in non-stick paper and tie the ends, right and left.

4. Repeat the process with the other pieces of meat to form another roll. To make things easier, place the rolls in two meat loaf tins and bake slowly at 350°F (160°C) for about 3 hours. The slower you cook the meat, the more tender it will become. Serve the roll cut in thick slices with sweet potato or pumpkin purée, blanched asparagus sautéed in butter and the remaining asparagus pesto.

Sweet potato purée

Serves 12
Preparation time 30 minutes
Cooking time 30 to 35 minutes
Degree of Difficulty ♥

- 6 medium-sized sweet potatoes or yams, scrubbed (about 5 pounds or 2kg)
- 2 tablespoons olive oil
- 2 leeks, only the white part, finely chopped
- 1 small clove garlic, crushed
- 4 green onions, finely chopped
- 1 teaspoon dry chives
- 2 tablespoons finely chopped parsley
- 1/4 cup cold butter, in small pieces
- salt and freshly ground pepper

1. Boil the sweet potatoes in salted water for 30 to 35 minutes until thoroughly tender. Remove from the heat, drain, remove the skins and when slightly cool mash in the food processor adding as much liquid as necessary using the water in which the sweet potatoes were boiled. Transfer the purée to a colander and strain for 1 to 2 hours.

2. Heat the oil in a large saucepan over high heat and sauté the leeks, garlic and onions. Add a few spoonfuls of the liquid the potatoes were boiled in, and simmer until the leeks are tender. Remove from the heat and add the dried chives and finely chopped parsley. Mix in the purée and blend in the butter, a piece at a time. Season and serve the purée hot.

3. Alternatively, prepare pumpkin purée in the same way. To clean the pumpkin easily, place it in the oven at 400°F (200°C) for 15 minutes. Instead of chives, add 1 teaspoon dry or 1 tablespoon fresh rosemary.

Meringue boxes
with strawberries and Chantilly

Yields 6 meringue boxes
Preparation time 1 hour
Baking time 1 hour and 30 minutes + several hours for drying
Degree of Difficulty ♥♥♥

For the meringues
• 1 recipe meringue mixture
  (recipe on page 241)

For the filling
• 1 pound (500g) ready-made whipped cream (Chantilly)
• 1 pound (500g) fresh strawberries cleaned and sliced
• strawberry sauce for serving (recipe on page 129)

One recipe of meringue mixture fits in the bowl of a domestic mixer. Meringues made using this recipe fit exactly in a 24-inch (60cm) conventional oven. To make more meringues, repeat the process.

1. Cut out two pieces of non-stick paper the size of the oven grid. Draw 20 2x2 inch (5x5cm) squares on each piece of paper. Spread the paper over the oven grids.
2. Put the meringue mixture in a piping bag and using a small nozzle (number 7) pipe horizontal and vertical lines to cover the surface of the squares forming lace-type patterns. If you wish, use a larger nozzle and after forming the perimeter of the square draw a small heart in the center of the square. Fill the entire surface of 6 squares with meringue to use as the bases of the boxes.
3. Bake the meringues in a conveyor oven at 200°F (90°C) for 1 hour and 30 minutes. Switch off the oven and cool the meringues in the oven. Store the meringues in airtight boxes, in a dry place. In dry weather, they will keep for several weeks.

To assemble
Place the compact squares on serving plates and pipe a large rosette of whipped cream over them. Stick the four sides of the box on the cream and fill the boxes with more cream. Garnish with some strawberry slices and serve with spoonfuls of strawberry sauce.

Strawberry cheese cake with mascarpone

Serves 12
Preparation time 35 minutes
Refrigeration time 4 hours
Degree of Difficulty ♥♥

For the base
- 18 oz (600g) digestive biscuits
- 14 oz (400g) cream filled digestive biscuits
- 6 oz (150g) blanched almonds
- 2/3 cup vegetable shortening or butter

For the filling
- 1 pound (500g) mascarpone (or cream cheese)

- 1/2 cup white vegetable shortening or unsalted butter
- 1 cup icing sugar
- 1/3 cup milk
- 3 cups whipping cream
- 3 sachets (60g each) instant strawberry flavored pudding
- 7 oz (200g) fresh or frozen strawberries, cleaned

For the meringue
- 4 egg whites
- 1/2 cup castor sugar
- a little vanilla essence

1. Grind all the biscuits in a food processor together with the blanched almonds to a smooth powder. Add the butter that should be at room temperature and beat until blended with the biscuits to form a soft mixture. Place the ring of a 10-inch (25cm) spring-form pan on a serving plate. Make sure it is fastened. Oil the inside surface of the ring and the plate slightly. Pour in the biscuit mixture and press with your hands to evenly cover the bottom and the sides of the mold.

2. Place the mold in the refrigerator while preparing the filling. Beat the cheese, butter and sugar with the mixer at medium speed. The cheese and butter should be at room temperature. Dilute the instant pudding in the milk and add the mixture gradually to the mixer bowl. Continue to beat until blended with the previous mixture. Mash the strawberries and add to the mixer bowl. Beat at medium speed for a few seconds until the mixture is a uniform color. Whip the cream separately to form soft peaks. Blend the two mixtures gently in the mixer bowl until no lumps remain.

3. Pour the filling into the mold and store the cake in the refrigerator for at least 4 hours or until the following day. Remove the ring on the day of serving and tie a pink ribbon round the cake.

4. Beat the egg whites in the mixer until frothy, add the sugar and vanilla and beat to a stiff meringue. Spoon the meringue over the cake. If you wish, you can put the cake under the grill for 5 minutes until the meringue is slightly golden brown.

Rose engagement cake

Serves 24
Preparation time several hours
<u>Suitable for freezing</u>
Degree of Difficulty ♥♥♥♥

For the almond cake
- 3½ cups self-raising flour
- 2 cups sugar
- 5 eggs
- 1 cup soft unsalted butter
- 1 cup milk
- 1/2 teaspoon almond essence
- 1 cup ground blanched almonds
- 1 heart-shaped 12-inch (30cm) mold

For the cherry à la crème filling
- 2 cans (14 oz or 400g) cherry pie filling or 1 recipe sour cherry sauce (recipe on page 113)
- 1 recipe vanilla buttercream icing (recipe on page 132)

To garnish
- 1 garland of Regalice paste (see "Heart Cake with wedding rings" on page 131)
- 120 small marzipan roses (recipe on page 203)

1. Beat all the cake ingredients, except for the ground almonds, in the mixer for 4 minutes. Then add the almonds and mix for a few seconds to blend into the mixture. Pour the cake batter into a well-buttered heart-shaped mold and bake at 350°F (180°C) for about 1 hour and 10 minutes. Remove from the oven and turn out onto a grid.
2. When the cake is cool, divide it into three layers. Join the layers by spreading buttercream icing and cherries or cherry sauce in between. Cover the entire surface of the cake with the rest of the icing and stick a Regalice paste border about the base of the cake. Prepare the Regalice paste as described for the "Ring Pillow cake".
3. Stick the small roses on the top of the cake. To make the roses, follow the instructions given for "Marzipan Sugared Roses". Color the almond paste with a few drops of pink food coloring and cut out circles of marzipan using a small pastry cutter. You will need 3 to 4 circles for each rose. The garnished cake will keep in the deep freeze for up to 1 month.

Royal Almond Hearts

Yields 12 hearts
Preparation time 1 hour
Degree of Difficulty ♥

- 2 cups finely ground blanched almonds
- 1 cup sugar
- 1/2 cup water and 3 tablespoons flower water

1. In a saucepan, boil the water and sugar until diluted. Add the flower water and the ground almonds. The dough should have an oozing sticky texture. If it is too runny, add more almonds (always keep 2-3 spoonfuls). If it is too hard, add some water. Remove from heat, cover with plastic wrap to avoid drying and cool until it can be handled.

2. Shape large pieces of dough and cut out small hearts using a 1½-inch (4cm) pastry cutter. Coat the hearts with icing sugar. Place the hearts on a baking sheet dusted with icing sugar. Leave the hearts uncovered to dry for a few hours. The longer they stand the crispier they will be. Use cloves to stick small pink bows on the hearts.

WEDDING DRESS FITTING III.

"…they stared at her (Aggeliki), surprised by her beauty, as she was standing on the stool,
wearing her wedding dress made of Belgian lace – Mrs Thalia called it "chantilly"…
So fine-spun, with such delicate designs, minute flowers, and then bigger ones. It was "Renaissance" style…

"Wedding Dress Fitting", Dora Giannakopoulou

*At the final fitting, the bride 'sweetens' the seamstress with homemade sweets.
Don't forget the champagne…*

One of the nicest tasks in preparing a wedding is searching for the ideal wedding dress. There is no task more pleasant for a woman than trying on different dresses, and seeing her beauty shine through even more than the happiness reflected in her face. Before you decide on the wedding dress of your dreams, dedicate as much time as you possibly can to research. A strange fact is that, although with any other item of clothing a woman can change her mind many times, when it comes to a wedding dress, most women recognize what they are looking for and fall in love with it as soon as they try it on. Perhaps, of course, this 'love' is premeditated, as, more than any other evening dress, every woman has thought and dreamed about her wedding dress long before she starts looking for it.

Dressing the bride has always been more expensive and much more complicated than dressing the groom; but then that is in accordance with feminine nature. And that is also why a wedding is considered to be exclusively the bride's celebration. The search, the fittings, and the final selection of the wedding dress, jewelry, and all other necessary accessories are a woman's idea of heaven, even if her companion often hears her complaining about the trials and tribulations of the purchase. Enjoy your wedding dress fittings without anxiety, as they will be one of the most beautiful memories to accompany you in life.

Remember that the only dress that can have a train, countless layers of tulle, lace, a rich underskirt and veil, is your wedding dress. Enjoy it, design it, and don't be afraid of excess in the fittings. Try on as many dresses as you can, and spend as much time as possible at the fittings, in the company of your best friends. Wedding dress fittings are a party. Don't be afraid to try dresses that are totally unrelated to your usual style, as the result in the mirror might be a very pleasant surprise. Consult with the experts and trust their opinion, as making you beautiful is a live promotion for them. However, make sure that the wedding gown you choose reflects the mood and style of the wedding you have envisaged.

Extra attention must be paid to the back of the wedding dress, as it will be the focal point of attention during the ceremony. Choosing a majestic train for a formal ceremony in a Cathedral can be very appropriate, but you should simply avoid it for a less formal reception or garden party. Choose a detachable train in order to feel more at ease at the reception. A gown with a majestic train must be accompanied by an equally imposing veil, preferably one of similar proportions, while a more simple strapless wedding gown should be matched with a short, shoulder-length veil.

At the time of the final fitting, make sure your weight is stabilized, so that further alterations that might take more time than you actually have do not become necessary. Don't forget to bring the shoes you plan to wear for the wedding to the fittings, so that the hem is at the right length.

At the final fitting, the bride 'sweetens' the seamstress with home-made sweets. Don't forget the champagne…

Palmier Hearts

Yields 20 hearts
Preparation time 15 minutes
Cooking time 15 minutes
Degree of Difficulty ♥

- 8oz (250g) puff pastry (one sheet)
- 2/3 cup fine sugar
- red and white crystallized sugar
- 1/4 cup melted unsalted butter

1. Roll out the pastry on a slightly floured surface. Sprinkle the entire pastry surface with the crystallized sugar. Roll up on either side until the folds meet in the middle of the sheet, to form "binoculars".

2. Cut thin slices from the short side of the roll with a sharp knife and arrange on a non-buttered baking tray lined with non-stick oven paper. Press down each shape to form a pretty heart.

3. Brush the hearts with a little melted butter. Bake in a 425°F (210°C) oven for 15 minutes. When cooked, sprinkle again with red, white or pink crystallized sugar. Can be stored in a biscuit tin for up to 1 week.

4. Alternatively: prepare the palmiers with marzipan filling. Roll a 7oz (200g) piece of marzipan into a very thin sheet and spread over the pastry sheet. Fold and shape as before and cut little hearts from the roll. Bake as above.

Cappuccino truffles

Yields 24 truffles
Preparation time 40 minutes
Baking time 15 minutes
Degree of Difficulty ♥♥

- 1/2 recipe pâte brisée (recipe page 228)
- 1/2 cup double cream
- 2/3 cup chocolate chips
- 1/2 cup mini marshmallows
- 1 sachet (1 tablespoon) vanilla-scented instant cappuccino
- whipped cream and chocolate flakes for decorating
- 2 12-case mini muffin baking tins.

1. Prepare the pastry dough. Cut little pieces of the pastry and roll them out with a small rolling pin onto a floured surface. Cut out circles with a 3-inch (7-cm) pastry cutter. Place the circles you have cut out on the buttered baking tins. Prick holes in the pastry with a wooden skewer.

2. Bake the tartlets for 15 minutes at 350°F (180°C). Remove from the oven and leave to cool inside the tins. Transfer to a serving platter.

3. Prepare the filling. Heat the cream in a small pan. Add the chocolate chips, marshmallows and coffee, stir and warm up over low heat, until the chocolate melts and you have a smooth, shiny mixture. Divide the chocolate mixture among the tartlets and refrigerate for 30 minutes, until set. Garnish with whipped cream and chocolate flakes. The perfect accompaniment for a mug of cappuccino.

Yields 12 portions
Preparation time 30 minutes
Degree of Difficulty ♥

- 24 lace-shaped meringues, ready-made or homemade (1 recipe meringue)

For the mocha cream
- 8oz (250g) cream cheese
- 1/2 cup unsalted butter
- 1/3 cup icing sugar
- 3 tablespoons evaporated milk
- 2 sachets instant cappuccino
- 1 sachet (60g) instant custard, vanilla or chocolate flavored
- 1 cup whipping cream
- 1 cup milk

For the chocolate ganache icing
- 2 cups double cream
- 8oz (250g) fine-quality cooking chocolate, in pieces
- 1 teaspoon vanilla essence
- 1 teaspoon glycerin (optional)

1. You can order the meringues from a good patisserie, in any shape you like, or prepare home-made ones with 1 recipe meringue (recipe on page 241). Prepare the meringues when you have time and store them in a hermetically sealed box, in a cool, dry place. To make garter-shaped meringues pipe the meringue onto non-stick paper on the oven grid, with a large nozzle (127D) for large ones, or a smaller nozzle (403) for smaller ones.

2. Prepare the mocha cream. Beat the cream cheese with the butter, icing sugar, evaporated milk and instant cappuccino, to form a soft and light mixture. Beat the instant custard separately with the milk and cream, until set. Blend the two mixtures, stirring carefully. Fill a piping bag with the cream, using the same nozzle as the one you used for the meringues, and store in the refrigerator.

3. Prepare the ganache icing. Heat the cream in a saucepan, without boiling it. Remove from the heat, add the chocolate, vanilla essence and glycerin, and stir until the chocolate melts and you have a smooth and shiny mixture. Leave to cool before using. Stick the meringues together two by two using the cream and refrigerate without covering. Drizzle with the ganache icing or with warm chocolate fudge sauce just before serving.

Easy solution: Buy any shape of ready-made meringues from a patisserie, place them on a stemmed bowl, cover with the mocha cream and drizzle with the chocolate fudge sauce. An amazing dessert ready in just 20 minutes.

If you are having the wedding dress fitting at the atelier, and not at home, follow these instructions for transporting the dessert: Place the meringues in a pretty basket. Place the cream in a porcelain bowl and refrigerate until you are ready to transport it. Heat the chocolate sauce you prefer over low heat just before leaving home and transport it in an oven-proof sauce boat.

Chocolate Fudge Sauce

- 8oz (250g) fine-quality cooking chocolate
- 1/2 cup golden syrup
- 2 tablespoons unsalted butter

1. Melt the chocolate with the syrup and butter over very low heat. Once melted, beat briskly to form a thick and shiny sauce.

Vanilla Lemingtons

Yields 16 vanilla lemingtons
(2½ inches - 7cm)
Preparation time 1 hour
Baking time 35 minutes
Degree of Difficulty ♥♥

For the vanilla sponge cake
- 4 eggs
- 2/3 cup fine sugar
- 1 cup vanilla essence
- 1 cup self-raising flour
- 3 tablespoons warm water
- 3 tablespoons melted butter

For the filling and icing
- 8oz (250g) strawberry or raspberry jam
- 1 cup fluffy white icing (recipe on page 241)
- 1 cup unsweetened shredded coconut

1. Prepare the sponge cake. Beat the eggs and sugar in the mixer, at medium speed, until double in bulk, about 15 minutes. Add the essence without stirring. Sift the flour little by little into the egg mixture, beating constantly at very low speed, or stirring with a wooden spoon, until the mixture is smooth. Take care not to deflate the eggs.

2. Mix the water with the butter and add to the mixture little by little, stirring gently. Pour the mixture into a well-buttered square baking pan, 10x10 inches (25cm x 25cm), or a jelly roll pan, lined with buttered grease-proof paper. Bake the sponge cake at 350°F (180°C) for 30 to 35 minutes, or until a skewer comes out clean. Unmold on a grid, remove the paper and leave to cool.

3. Cut out hearts with a 2½-inch (7-cm) pastry cutter. Cut each heart shape in two lengthways and join the two halves with a little jam. Arrange on a grid and spread icing on the surface with a metal spatula. Sprinkle with the shredded coconut.

Cream éclairs

Yields 14 medium pastries
Preparation time 1 hour
Baking time 40 minutes
Degree of Difficulty ♥♥

- 1 recipe choux pastry (recipe on page 183)
- 8oz (250g) whipped cream
- some drops of bitter almond essence
- 1/2 cup finely chopped maraschino cherries (optional)
- 1/2 cup easy vanilla icing (recipe on page 51)
- some drops of red food coloring (for pink icing)

1. Prepare the choux pastry according to the recipe and place it in a piping bag fitted with a number 8B nozzle. Design 14 2-inch (5-cm) circles on non-stick paper and line the grid with it. Pipe pretty rings of pastry 2/3-inch thick over the perimeter of the circles.

2. Bake the choux for 15 minutes in a 425°F (210°C) oven, until they rise and become golden-brown. Lower the temperature to 300°F (150°C), and keep baking for another 25 to 30 minutes, until the inside of the choux is dry. Remove from the oven and leave to cool.

3. Cut each choux in half lengthways and join the two halves with whipped cream mixed with a little bitter almond essence and the chopped maraschino cherries. Arrange on a serving dish and drizzle with pink and white icing or chocolate ganache sauce (recipe on page 107).

Mini ricotta cheesecakes with morello cherries

Yields 48 mini cheesecakes
Preparation time 20 minutes
Baking time 1 hour
Refrigeration time 4 hours
Degree of Difficulty ♥♥

For the base
- 3 tablespoons unsalted soft butter
- 16 Oreo cookies, crumbled
- 1 teaspoon orange zest

For the filling
- 1 cup ricotta cheese (7poz - 200g)
- 1/3 cup icing sugar
- 1 teaspoon orange zest
- 2 tablespoons lemon juice
- 2 eggs
- 1 tablespoon all-purpose flour
- 1/3 cup double cream
- morello cherry sauce for garnishing
  (recipe follows)

1. Line the holes of 4 12-case mini muffin baking tins with paper cases. Mix the butter with the cookies and zest for the base, and divide the mixture among the cases, pressing down with your thumb to cover the bottom.

2. Cream the cheese in the mixer with the icing sugar, orange zest and lemon juice. Incorporate the eggs and flour into the mixture, beating constantly.

3. Add the cream and beat for 1 minute, at maximum speed. Divide the mixture among the cases, covering the biscuit base, without reaching the rims.

4. Bake the mini cheesecakes for 1 hour at 300°F (150°C). Leave to stand in the oven until cold, about 1 hour, with the oven door ajar. Place on a dish without removing the paper cases and refrigerate for 4 hours or until the next day.

5. Just before serving, tear the paper cases and remove them carefully, arrange the cheesecakes on a platter and garnish with morello cherry sauce.

Morello Cherry Sauce

- 1½ pounds (750g) fresh or
  1 pound 10oz (800g) canned
  morello cherries, stoned
- 1/4 cup corn-starch
- 1/2 cup sugar
- 3 tablespoons Calvados Brandy

1. If you are using fresh cherries, remove the stones with a special tool, without ruining the shape. Place the stones and juice in a pan, together with any cherries that have been spoilt. Add 1 cup water, boil for 10 minutes and drain the juice into another pan. There should be 1½ cups of juice, if not, add some water.

2. If you are using canned cherries, simply drain the juice from the can and make sure it is 1½ cups. Place the juice in a pan and add the sugar, corn-starch and a tiny pinch of salt. Simmer until you obtain a thick, transparent sauce.

3. Remove the sauce from the heat, leave to cool a little and add the Brandy. Pour the stoned cherries into the sauce and stir gently.

Vol-au-vent hearts with jam

Yields 12 hearts
Preparation time 20 minutes
Baking time 15 minutes
Degree of Difficulty ♥

- 1 packet of 20 square puff pastry pieces (18 needed)
- 4oz (100g) marzipan (optional)
- 1/2 cup strawberry or forest fruit jam
- icing sugar for sprinkling

1. Join the pastry pieces three-by-three, coating each with a little water. Roll out with a small rolling pin into a larger sheet of pastry, big enough to cut out 2 hearts with a small vol-au-vent heart-shaped cutter.

2. Cut out the hearts and arrange on an ungreased baking sheet. Refrigerate for 15 minutes.

3. If you like, roll the marzipan out into a thin sheet and cut out heart shapes with a 1-inch (3-cm) cutter. Place the mini hearts in the center of the pastry hearts.

4. Bake the pastry for 15 minutes at 425°F (210°C), until they rise and turn golden. Remove from the oven, and once cold, fill with jam. Sprinkle the borders of each heart with a little icing sugar.

In Athens, the bed was made by the bride's closest relatives, happily married men and women.
Under the cushions they would put 9 almonds, for 9 sons, an open pair of scissors, to cut off evil tongues,
and protect against curses, spells, the evil eye, and a piece of net belonging to a retired fisherman.
In the island of Lefkada, the bed is made by a male, whose mother and father are both alive.
In Goudi in Pafos, they make the bed and then spread a sheet on the part where the single girls are sitting, so that they may find a suitable husband.
When the bed is made, a pretty baby is rolled on it, so that the bride may soon have one of her own.

"Traditions and customs of our folk history", Kiveli Editions

On the last Thursday before the wedding, invite your single girlfriends to afternoon tea, and to participate in the traditional custom of making the wedding bed.

The tradition of making the bed has been preserved until today, and is one of the important celebrations preceding the big day. Single girls, married couples or young boys, depending on the particularities of each area of Greece, are invited to make and decorate the bridal bed on the last Thursday before the wedding. They shake and spread the white sheets and the hand-woven bridal bedcovers happily, while the groom unmakes one corner of the bed three times so that they have to start again. Traditionally, bridal bedcovers were sewn by young girls when preparing their trousseau; today, they are bought by the bride, together with her mother or mother-in-law. Making the bed is a good opportunity for modern couples to open up their new home for the first time, and receive wedding gifts from their close relatives and friends.

Once the bed is made, the guests shower it with gold sovereigns and money, rose petals for "a life strewn with flowers", sugared almonds for fertility, and rice for the marriage to take roots. According to tradition, a pretty baby is rolled on the bed three times, also to bring fertility and good luck. The bed must remain thus until the couple's wedding night, and that is why the bride and groom usually sleep separately for the nights remaining until the wedding. The hostess offers her guests home-made sweets, to thank them for honoring her with their presents and gifts.

A wedding should be celebrated with plenty of good food and traditional sweets, such as almond cakes and honey sweets, according to the customs of each area. The future bride is required to exercise self-control before the plethora of food on offer each time friends and relatives are celebrating in her honor, as the wedding is only a few days away, and the dress fittings are getting "tighter". For making the bed, the last of the pre-wedding celebrations, just before the wedding of your dreams, make sure the recipes you choose are light, without extra calories that could spoil your diet.

In different countries the equivalent event of "making the bed" is the bridal shower, where the bride invites her closest girlfriends to show them her engagement ring, her wedding gown, as well as her new house. At the same time, her friends have the chance to offer their gifts in person and express their best wishes of happiness for the wedding. The maid of honor is the honored guest of the bridal shower. The event nowadays often includes the groom and the couple's best friends.

Avoid the stress caused by a formal evening invitation, and organize an afternoon gathering for tea or coffee, where you can serve light but mouth-watering sweets. Accompany with a good quality peach-flavored French champagne. For a more classic touch, champagne and strawberries will add finesse to your evening.

Pink Amaretti

Yields 35 mini cookies
Preparation time 20 minutes
Baking time 15 minutes
Degree of Difficulty ♥

- 1 cup blanched almonds
- 1 cup icing sugar
- 1 egg white
- 2-3 tablespoons Amaretto liqueur
- 1/2 teaspoon bitter almond essence
- some drops of red food coloring

1. Grind the almonds with the icing sugar in the blender to obtain a smooth powder.
2. Add the egg white, liqueur, essence and food coloring and keep beating for another 2 minutes, to form a smooth, sticky, relatively thick pink dough.
3. Spoon the dough into a piping bag with a round 1/2 inch (1½ cm) nozzle and pipe small cherry-sized balls onto a cookie sheet lined with non-stick oven paper. If you like, use a star-shaped nozzle to form pretty rosettes.
4. Bake the amaretti in the oven at 350°F (180°C) for 12 to 15 minutes. Remove from the oven and leave to cool on the sheet. Store in a cookie tin. The longer they stand, the crunchier they will become. Will keep for 1 month in a biscuit tin.

Bitter almond bavaroise

Yields 12 portions
Preparation time 1 hour
Refrigeration time 4 hours
Degree of Difficulty ♥♥
<u>Light</u>

- 1 tablespoon gelatine, dissolved in 1/4 cup water
- 3 large eggs, separated, and 3 egg yolks
- 1/2 cup sugar
- 1/8 teaspoon salt
- 3½ cups low-fat milk
- 1 teaspoon bitter almond essence
- 2 tablespoons Amaretto liqueur
- 1 sachet (60g) vanilla-flavored instant pudding
- 1/2 teaspoon vanilla essence

1. Stir the gelatine in the water and let it swell. Then, heat the mixture over low heat, until the gelatine dissolves.

2. Whisk the egg yolks, sugar and salt until they thicken to a lemony pale mixture. Bring the milk to the boil in a large pan. Add 3-4 tablespoons hot milk to the egg yolk mixture and then transfer the mixture to the pan with the rest of the milk, stirring briskly. Stir the milk with the beaten egg yolks over medium heat until the mixture thickens enough to cover the back of a spoon. Add and mix in the gelatine. Remove the cream from the heat and add the essence and liqueur. Let the cream cool and refrigerate for about 2 hours, until it starts to set.

3. Beat the egg whites with clean beaters to a soft meringue. Remove the semi-set cream from the refrigerator, add the instant custard and whisk briskly. Fold in the beaten egg whites gently.

4. Transfer the mixture to a pudding mold and refrigerate for at least 4 hours, or until the next day. Unmold the bavaroise onto a serving platter. If you wish, serve with morello cherry sauce (recipe on page 113).

Dobos Torta

Yields 12 portions
Preparation time 1 hour
Baking time 45 minutes
Degree of Difficulty ♥♥

- 1 recipe butter sponge cake (recipe on page 156)
  baked in three deep baking tins, 7 inches (20cm) in diameter,
  buttered and lined with non-stick oven paper

For the easy buttercream chocolate filling
- 1 tablespoon instant coffee
- 1 tablespoon cocoa powder
- 3 tablespoons boiling water
- 8oz (250g) good quality cooking chocolate, in pieces
- 1½ cups unsalted butter
- 1 cup icing sugar

An ideal opportunity to try out your wedding cake is to prepare a miniature version and serve it at the bridal shower. It is also a good idea to ask the store preparing your wedding cake to send you a trial version to serve at your bridal shower.

1. Prepare the sponge cakes, following the directions of the recipe. Once cold, divide each sponge cake into 2 layers, so that you have a total of 6 layers.
2. In a small pan or double-boiler, mix the coffee and cocoa with the water. Add the chocolate pieces and stir over low heat until melted. Remove from the heat and let the chocolate mixture cool.
3. Cream the butter with the sugar. Add the melted chocolate and mix to obtain a smooth silky icing. The filling will keep in the refrigerator for 1 week, covered.
4. Join the layers together with the chocolate filling. Coat the cake with the same icing. Garnish with fresh roses or chocolate marzipan flowers, prepared according to the instructions on page 203.

Strawberry Caramel Flan

Yields 16 portions
Preparation time 1 hour
Baking time 1 hour
Degree of Difficulty ♥♥♥
<u>Light</u>

For the strawberry-flavored caramel
- 1½ cups castor sugar
- 1/4 cup water
- 1/4 teaspoon cream of tartar or a few drops lemon juice
- a few drops red food coloring
- 1 teaspoon strawberry essence

For the meringue mixture
- 12 egg whites
- 1 cup castor sugar
- 1 teaspoon cream of tartar or 1/2 teaspoon lemon juice
- a little vanilla essence
- a few drops red food coloring (optional)
- 8oz (250g) fresh strawberries to garnish

1. Place all the caramel ingredients in a small pan and boil until the mixture reaches 245°F (120°C), until it reaches the soft ball stage. To ascertain whether the caramel is ready, dip a small spoon in the pan and drop it into a glass of cold water. If the caramel forms a soft ball in the water, remove from the heat immediately. If not, repeat the experiment with a clean spoon after 1 minute. Empty the caramel in a deep 10-inch (25-cm) cake ring mold and turn, so that the sides of the pan are coated with caramel.
2. Beat the egg whites with the cream of tartar at the mixer's top speed until set, and while beating, add first the vanilla essence and then the sugar in two parts. Keep beating until stiff peaks form.
3. Spoon the meringue into the mold and spread with a spatula, so that there are no air pockets. The mold should be full to the rim. Half-fill a large deep baking pan with water, place the mold with the meringue inside the pan and then put the pan in the oven. If the baking pan is made of aluminum, put 2 or 3 slices of lemon in the water so that the pan doesn't turn black. Bake the soufflé at 350°F (175°C) for 55 to 60 minutes. The flan will rise about 4 inches (10cm) above the mold. Open the oven and let the flan cool inside it. It will deflate to just above the rim of the mold.
4. Wait until it is cold and unmold onto a dish. Garnish with fresh strawberry slices. Pour 2 or 3 tablespoons water in the mold, heat until the caramel has melted and pour over the flan and strawberries. Keep refrigerated.

Bride's Angel Cake

Yields 12 portions
Preparation time 30 minutes
Cooking time 40 minutes
Degree of Difficulty ♥
<u>Light</u>

- 1 cup self-raising flour
- 2/3 cup icing sugar
- 12 egg whites from large eggs
- 1/4 teaspoon salt
- 1½ teaspoons cream of tartar or 1/2 teaspoon lemon juice
- 2/3 cup castor sugar
- 1 teaspoon bitter almond essence
- 3 tablespoons cocoa powder
- 1 tablespoon instant coffee
- 2 tablespoons sugar
- mocha ice cream for serving (optional)

1. Sift the flour with the icing sugar. Beat the egg whites with the salt in the mixer until frothy. Add the cream of tartar and beat until soft peaks form. While beating, add the castor sugar in 2 parts, until you have a stiff meringue. Stop beating, add the bitter almond essence and mix gently with a spatula. Add the sifted flour little by little to the meringue, stirring lightly with a wooden spoon or beating at the mixer's lowest speed. Beware not to deflate the egg whites.

2. Place 1/3 of the mixture in an ungreased angel cake pan, 10 inches (25cm) in diameter. Mix the cocoa with the coffee and sugar and sprinkle half of it over the mixture. Add another 1/3 of the mixture and sprinkle with the remaining cocoa. Top with the remaining mixture. Stick a metal spatula vertically into the mixture and pull out all about to make shapes.

3. Bake the cake in the lower part of the oven, at 375°F (190°C) for 35 to 40 minutes. Remove from the oven and leave to cool, overturning with the tin. The tin will stand on its special feet. The cake will take about 2 hours to cool.

4. To remove the cake easily from the tin, pass a knife around the tin, between the cake and the walls, overturn the tin, and hit lightly with your palms. Serve with mocha ice cream and strawberries if you like.

Vanilla Lace Cheesecake

Yields 12 portions
Preparation time 20 minutes
Baking time 1 hour
Refrigeration time 4 hours
Degree of Difficulty ♥♥
Light

For the base
- 3 tablespoons margarine
- 1 tablespoon unsweetened cocoa powder
- 1½ cups corn flakes

For the filling
- 1½ pounds (800g) ricotta or light cream cheese
- 2 tablespoons corn-starch, diluted in 2 tablespoons cold water

- 2 teaspoons vanilla essence
- 1 teaspoon lemon zest
- 2 tablespoons lemon juice
- 2/3 cup fat-free yogurt
- 1/2 cup sugar
- 1 egg, separated, and 2 egg whites
- 1/2 cup icing sugar, mixed with a split vanilla pod, for sprinkling

1. Oil a heart-shaped spring baking tin, 10 inches (24cm) in diameter, using corn oil. Line the bottom with non-stick oven paper. Brush it with a little oil. Grind the corn flakes in the blender and mix with the margarine and cocoa. Spread the mixture in the tin, to cover the bottom.

2. Place the ricotta or cream cheese, corn-starch, vanilla, lemon zest and juice, yogurt, half the sugar and the egg yolk in the mixer bowl and beat to a light and uniform mixture.

3. Beat the egg whites and the remaining sugar separately until soft peaks form. Add the beaten egg whites to the cheese mixture and fold in gently so as not to deflate them. Transfer the batter to the lined pan. Bake inside a pan with water up to the middle at 325°F (160°C) for 1 hour and 30 minutes.

4. Let the cheesecake cool inside the oven, with the door half-open. Remove from the oven and, once cold, cover with plastic wrap and store in the refrigerator until the next day. Unbuckle the baking tin, remove the ring, and transfer the cake to a platter. To serve, sprinkle icing sugar scented with vanilla over a lacy stencil placed on the cake's surface. Remove the stencil and the designs will stay on your cheesecake.

Meringue muffins with strawberries and cream

Yields 18 meringue muffins
Preparation time several hours
Degree of Difficulty ♥♥

- 1 recipe meringue (recipe on page 241)
- 1 cup strawberry sauce
- 8oz (250g) strawberries, sliced
- 1 cup whipping cream, whipped with
  1/4 teaspoon vanilla powder and a few drops lemon juice

1. Prepare the meringue. Using a spoon, fill 18 paper muffin cases placed in the grooves of 3 muffin trays. Bake at 200°F (100°C) for 1 hour and 30 minutes. Switch off the oven and let the muffins cool inside it until the next day. Can be stored for 2 weeks in a box.
2. Before serving, remove the paper cases from the meringues. Serve with the whipped cream, slices of fresh strawberries and strawberry sauce.

Strawberry sauce

- 4 cups strawberries
- 1½ cups sugar
- 4 tablespoons corn-starch
- 4 tablespoons lemon juice
- 4 tablespoons Cognac

1. Mix the strawberries, sugar, corn-starch and lemon juice in a large saucepan. Simmer slowly and stir periodically, until the mixture sets and a glossy transparent sauce forms. Remove from the heat. Add and stir in the Cognac.
2. If you want to make strawberry coulis, that is a transparent sauce, boil the strawberries with 2 cups water for 10 minutes. Drain and keep the juice. Measure to see that you have two cups; if not, add some water. Mix the corn-starch and sugar in a small saucepan. Add the strawberry juice and lemon juice. Boil while stirring constantly, until the sauce is set and transparent. Remove from the heat, add and stir in the Cognac. Store the sauce in a plastic bag in the freezer for long-term storage or in a jar in the refrigerator if it is to be used within a few days. Yields about 4 cups of sauce.

Ring pillow cake

Yields 20 servings
Preparation time 2 hours
Suitable for freezing
Degree of difficulty ♥♥♥

• 1 heart-shaped baking pan 11 inches width x 2 inches height (28x5cm)

For the chocolate sponge cake
• 4 eggs
• 1 cup sugar
• 1 teaspoon vanilla essence
• 2/3 cup self-raising flour
• 1/3 cup unsweetened cocoa powder
• 2 tablespoons melted unsalted butter

For the velvet chocolate mousse filling
• 1/2 tablespoon gelatine powder
• 1/2 cup milk
• 1/4 cup unsalted butter
• 1/4 cup unsweetened cocoa powder
• 5oz (125g) cooking chocolate, cut in pieces
• 2 tablespoons Kahlua liqueur
• 1 egg white
• 1/4 cup icing sugar
• 1/2 cup whipping cream
• 1 teaspoon vanilla essence

For the decoration
• 1 jar (15oz – 450g) Royal icing
• 1 pound (500g) ready-to-roll fondant icing (Regalice)

1. Prepare the sponge cake. Beat the eggs with the sugar and vanilla at the mixer's highest speed for 15 minutes until set and double in volume. Mix the flour with the cocoa and sift gradually into the egg mixture. Keep beating very slowly or mixing with a spatula, until the mixture is uniform. Do not deflate the eggs. Add the melted butter and fold gently into the batter, so as not to deflate it.

2. Pour the batter into a well-buttered and floured heart-shaped baking pan. Bake the sponge cake in the oven at 370°F (180°C) for 35 minutes, or until a skewer inserted in the middle comes out dry. Remove the cake from the oven. Overturn onto a rack spread with non-stick oven paper sprinkled with icing sugar, and leave to cool.

3. Prepare the filling. Dissolve the gelatine in the milk and let the mixture swell. Melt the butter in a large pan and stir in the cocoa. Add the milk and gelatine and stir until the mixture is well heated and the gelatine dissolves. Add the chocolate pieces and stir over low heat, until you obtain a thick and uniform chocolate mixture.

4. Remove from the heat and add the liqueur. Stir gently and allow the mixture to cool. Whip the whipping cream with the vanilla essence until stiff and fold gently into the chocolate mixture. Whisk the egg white with the sugar to form a soft meringue and gently fold into the chocolate mixture.

5. Divide the heart-shaped sponge cake into 2 layers and join together with the chocolate filling. Heat 2/3 of the Royal icing until soft and pour over the cake to cover the entire surface of the heart. Using a rolling pin, roll out half of the fondant icing on a marble surface sprinkled with icing sugar, to form a thin sheet slightly larger than the heart. Fold the icing sheet over a thin wooden rolling pin and spread over the cake, like a tablecloth. Press lightly with your hands to smooth it evenly, so that it covers the entire cake, the surface and its sides. Cut off the bits of icing remaining around the border.

6. Roll out the remaining fondant, and cut out strips about 4" (10cm) wide with a jagged pastry cutter. Stick them around the cake with a little water to form the border. Place the remaining Royal icing in a piping bag with a very thin nozzle (No1) and draw delicate frills on the border. Place the cake in the refrigerator uncovered, until serving time, or store in the freezer in a cake box for up to 1 month.

Vanilla Chiffon Cake with buttercream icing

Yields 16 portions
Preparation time 20 minutes
Baking time 50 minutes
Degree of Difficulty ♥

For the cake
- 8 large egg whites
- 1 teaspoon cream of tartar or
  a few drops lemon juice
- 1/2 teaspoon salt
- 1 cup sugar
- 6 large egg yolks
- 1 cup self-raising flour
- 3 tablespoons Amaretto liqueur
- 3 tablespoons water
- 1 teaspoon vanilla essence

For the filling and the icing
- 1 recipe buttercream icing
  (recipe follows)

1. Beat the egg whites with the cream of tartar and salt at the mixer's top speed until frothy. Add half the sugar and keep beating until soft peaks form.
2. In a clean bowl, beat the egg yolks with the remaining sugar in the mixer until set. Add the flour, liqueur, water and vanilla essence and beat until thick but runny. If you don't like the Amaretto taste of bitter almond, substitute with water.
3. Fold the meringue mixture gently into the egg yolk mixture, taking care not to deflate the egg whites. Pour the batter into an ungreased angel cake pan. Bake at 325°C (160°C) for 50-55 minutes.
4. Remove from the oven, invert the pan with the cake and let it stand on its metal "feet". Let cool upside-down for at least 1½ hours. Once cool, pass the blade of a knife carefully between the cake and the pan, and unmold onto a serving dish.
5. Prepare the buttercream icing. Using a serrated knife or a cake separator, divide the cake into 3 layers. Spread half the buttercream icing on the two layers and stack all three together. Use the remaining icing to cover the cake. Decorate with the prettiest white roses from your garden.

Buttercream Icing

Yields 1 recipe icing
Preparation time 30 minutes
Degree of Difficulty ♥♥

- 2 cups sugar
- 1/2 cup water
- 6 egg whites
- a pinch of salt
- 1/2 teaspoon cream of tartar
- 2 cups unsalted butter, softened
- 3-4 tablespoons Amaretto liqueur or
  1 teaspoon vanilla essence

1. Prepare the icing after you have baked the sponge cake. It must be used immediately because if it sets or is refrigerated it cannot be heated or softened because the butter will separate. The recipe cannot be multiplied. Repeat the process for larger quantities of icing. Melt the sugar in the water in a small pan and bring to the boil. Keep boiling for 5 minutes over high heat, until caramelized up to the soft ball stage (see recipe "Strawberry Caramel Flan") or until the caramel thermometer shows 245°F (120°C).
2. In the meantime, beat the egg whites in the mixer with the salt and cream of tartar, until stiff peaks form. Continuing to beat, add the syrup to the egg whites, pouring with a slow constant flow. The pouring process will take about 12 minutes, so that the syrup is slowly incorporated into the egg white mixture, cooling down in the meantime. For better results, wrap a towel with ice cubes around the mixing bowl.
3. After adding the syrup and while still beating, add the softened butter to the mixture spoonful by spoonful. Note that the butter should be at room temperature and very soft, but not melted. Beat until you obtain a very light and fluffy white mixture. Stop beating and stir in the liqueur or vanilla essence.
4. Alternatively, prepare mocha flavored buttercream icing by adding 1 tablespoon instant coffee, mixed with 2 tablespoons Kahlua. For chocolate icing add 4oz (125g) melted chocolate to the butter. For fruity icing, add 1 teaspoon strawberry essence or 1 teaspoon lemon or orange zest. The icing can also be scented with 1 teaspoon coconut or peppermint essence. It can be colored pink or pale blue or turquoise with a few drops of red, blue or green food coloring respectively.

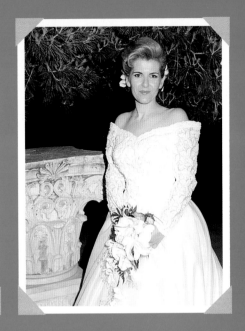

3

WEDDING RECEPTIONS

Love one another, but make not a bond of love
Let it rather be a moving sea between the
Shores of your minds
Fill each other's cup but drink not from one cup
Give one another of your bread but eat not
From the same loaf
Sing and dance together and be joyous but
Let each one of you be alone
Even as the strings of a lute are alone they
Quiver with the same music

On marriage, The Prophet, Khalil Gibran

THE MINIMAL RECEPTION I.

When he saw the warm, bright smile on her face and the snowflakes circling her hair and her cape,
he froze, as if he had been attacked by a spirit, through the haze of his dreams [...]
And as she (Shotoko) stooped to enter the rickshaw, one cheek came very close to Kiyoaki's face for a moment,
but she hurriedly pulled back her head, and nervously straightened her body; a movement that revealed her slender,
strong neck to Kiyoaki, and brought to his mind the white smooth neck of a swan.

Yukiyo Mishima, Spring Snow

If you are having a few special guests, plan a wedding reception at home, in minimalist style, with food inspired by the tastes, shapes and scents of the Far East.

A wedding at home requires much preparation and organizing. Choose to organize a reception for a limited number of guests, in a buffet style, where all your guests can sit about a few beautifully made and decorated tables. At a wedding reception, where each detail and your every choice is discussed exhaustively by all your guests, not only at the time but for long after, make sure that everything is perfect by adhering to your chosen style, without excessive deviations from the tone of the whole event. For a bride choosing a simple style, the ceremony and reception should be characterized by elegance and minimalism, from the invitations, the wedding dress, the bouquet and the church decorations, to the reception hall, the menu and the music.

For a minimalist menu, it is preferable to serve a few choice dishes. In the presentation of a modern minimalist menu, an important role is played by the size of the portions, which should be small and delicate, and the arrangement of the food on the dishes, which must be geometrically harmonized. Serve a tall pyramid cake for the guests, and personal pyramid-shaped desserts for the Bridal table.

Greet your guests at the atrium or the entrance with two large bonsai trees made of white winter truffles with chestnuts, and a glass of champagne. The truffles are ideally preserved in the cold winter air. If you wish keep the bonsai wrapped in tulle until the guests arrive. Inside, make sure there is a reception area where your guests can meet each other while drinking champagne or cocktails, before they take their places at the table. Cocktails can last from half an hour to an hour, until the bride arrives home from the church.

Make sure there are place-cards for the guests on the tables, so that everyone knows where to sit. If there are more than four tables, there should be one person responsible for directing each guest to the right table number. Correct arrangement of the guests requires for married couples to be separated and to mingle with the other guests, and for men and women to sit alternately at the tables, while engaged or newly married people should sit next to their companions.

The food can be served on a buffet or on dishes passed about by waiters and offered to the guests, depending on how much staff you are having at the reception. For a wedding reception at home, where the guests are in relatively small surroundings, the newlyweds may propose a toast to all the guests at once, without having to circulate and greet everyone personally.

White can be the predominant color. Decorate the area of the reception with beautiful arrangements of white tulips, orchids, chrysanthemums or Casablanca lilies. For centerpieces you may choose small bonsais made of white winter roses. Light tiny candles on each plate for an elegant yet simple touch.

Elegance, taste and discretion are the characteristics of the modern couple choosing the minimalist approach for their wedding. Choose it only if it expresses your general lifestyle.

Truffle Bonbonnières

Yields 50 bonbonnières

- 3 recipes white chestnut truffles
- 50 miniature silver-plated or silver cups
- white sugar-coated almonds
- 50 cinnamon sticks
- 50 miniature styrofoam balls, 2 inches (5cm) in diameter
- 50 white satin ribbons

1. Prepare the truffles well in advance and store in the freezer. Fill the silver cups with white sugar-coated almonds and secure a cinnamon stick in the center.

2. Fix the styrofoam balls onto the cinnamon sticks and attach the truffles to these with toothpicks.

3. When offering the bonbonnières, wrap the truffles in muslin tied onto the cinnamon stick with a white ribbon. You may want to print ribbons with the couple's names and the wedding date. Otherwise, wrap the entire bonsai in muslin, to make it steadier. Keep the bonbonnières in the refrigerator or somewhere cool, so that the chocolate does not melt. The truffles are very sensitive to the heat. Offer them to your guests at the end of the reception.

Fried ravioli with ricotta and nut filling

Yields 24 ravioli
Preparation time 30 minutes
Frying time 30 minutes
Degree of difficulty ♥

- 2 tablespoons vegetable oil
- 1 small clove garlic, minced
- 1 small shallot, grated
- 2oz (50g) hazelnuts, roasted
- 2oz (50g) almonds with their skin, roasted
- 2oz (50g) cashew nuts or pistachios or walnuts
- 8oz (250g) ricotta or anthotyro cheese
- 1 tablespoon dairy cream
- 1 teaspoon horseradish paste
- 1 teaspoon mustard
- freshly ground white pepper
- 8oz (250g) ready-made wonton wrappers or 1 recipe homemade wonton dough (recipe on page 161)
- 1 egg white for brushing
- blanched soybean sprouts and walnut oil for serving

1. Heat the oil in a small saucepan and sauté the garlic and onion. Coarsely grind the nuts in a blender. Cream the cheese in a bowl and incorporate the cream and sauces. Blend to a smooth and soft mixture. Add the nuts, sautéed ingredients and plenty of freshly ground white pepper.

2. Put a teaspoonful of filling in the center of each wonton wrapper and brush the edges with a little egg white. Cover with another wrapper and press to seal.

3. Place the ravioli one next to the other on a baking sheet lined with oven paper, cover with cling film and freeze. When frozen, transfer to a food bag and store in the freezer for up to 1 month. Keep well wrapped in cling film for future use. Beware, wonton dough should not dry as it will dissolve when fried.

4. Fry the frozen ravioli straight from the freezer by dipping them in boiling hot oil, in a wok or deep fryer for 5 minutes, until golden brown. For a buffet, serve immediately. If served individually on plates, garnish with steaming bean sprouts drizzled with a little walnut oil. You may accompany with sweet and sour sauce.

Fillet medallions
with béarnaise sauce and wasabi purée

Serves 50
Preparation time 1 hour
Cooking time 1 hour
Degree of Difficulty ♥♥♥

For the wasabi purée
• 8 pounds (4kg) potatoes
• 1/2 cup butter, softened
• 2 cups milk
• 8 eggs
• 1 cup grated parmesan
• 2 teaspoons wasabi paste or
  horseradish sauce
• salt and white pepper

For the fillet medallions
• 50 bite-sized beef fillet medallions

• 1 cup unsalted butter
• 50 thin slices of white radish,
  cut into butterfly shapes, for decoration

For the béarnaise sauce with horseradish
• 1 cup finely chopped green onions
• 1/3 cup finely chopped fresh tarragon
• 1 teaspoon dried thyme, crumbled
• 2 bay leaves
• 2/3 cup dry white wine
• 1/2 cup white vinegar
• 8 egg yolks
• 3 tablespoons water
• 1 pound (500g) butter,
  cut in small pieces
• 2 tablespoons horseradish sauce

1. Peel the potatoes and chop them up. Place in a pan with enough salted water to cover them, and simmer until the water has been absorbed and the potatoes are soft, about 30 minutes. In a large clean bowl, mash the potatoes, gradually adding the butter and milk. Make a well in the center of the purée, break in the eggs, add the grated cheese, paste, salt and pepper, and blend well to incorporate. Let the mixture cool. Fill a large piping bag with the purée and pipe rosettes in the form of small nests onto a well-buttered lined baking pan. Bake the purée nests at 400°F (200°C) for 25-30 minutes.

2. Place the chopped onions, half the tarragon, the thyme, bay leaves, wine and vinegar in a large pan, and simmer the mixture until it is reduced by 1/3. Remove and discard the bay leaves. Beat the egg yolks and water in a bowl. Add the concentrated mixture to the bowl little by little, whisking briskly, until it blends with the egg yolks. Transfer the mixture to a bain-marie and stir until it thickens. Little by little incorporate the butter to the mixture. Stir in the horseradish sauce. Prepare the sauce just before serving and keep it warm in the bain-marie pan.

3. Melt 2 tablespoons butter in a large deep skillet. Season the medallions and sauté a few at a time in the butter for 3-4 minutes, turning them over so that all sides are cooked. Remove from the skillet and keep warm. Add more butter until all the fillets have been sautéed. Place the purée nests in an oven-proof dish, on square baked puff pastry sheets which you can prepare according to the recipe "Millefeuilles with marinated octopus" on page 77. Place a fillet medallion on each nest and pour over 1 tablespoon sauce. Decorate with butterflies cut out of thin slices of white radish.

Sole, fresh salmon and scallop timbale

Yields 8 timbale
Preparation time 1 hour and 30 minutes
Baking time 30 to 35 minutes
Degree of Difficulty ♥♥♥

For the mousline
- 18oz (600g) cleaned, frozen scallops
- 2 medium eggs
- 1/2 teaspoon salt
- 1/4 teaspoon white pepper
- 1¼ cups double cream

For the timbale
- 8 slices of fresh salmon fillet
- 9 large fillets of Dover sole, cleaned, skinned and boned
  (each fillet is half a fish)

- salt and freshly ground white pepper
- 8 tablespoons black caviar

For garnishing
- 1 recipe creamy fish and sorrel sauce
  (recipe on page 91)
- 8 tablespoons black caviar
- assorted green salad
- a little red caviar

1. Prepare the mousline. Place the scallops and eggs, salt and white pepper in the mixer bowl and beat to a creamy mixture. While beating, add the cream slowly and steadily, until the mixture becomes uniform. Do not beat the mixture too hard, or the cream will curdle. Transfer the mousline mixture to a clean bowl, cover and refrigerate until you have prepared the timbale.

2. Butter 8 metal crème caramel molds. Line the bottom of the molds with non-stick oven paper. Season all the fillets. Cut the salmon fillet slices to fit the dimensions of the bottom of each mold and place them inside. Chop the remaining pieces and use them with the chopped ninth fillet of sole to form the middle layers of fish in the molds.

3. Cut and remove a large circle from the flat side of each fillet of sole. Roll up the remaining piece and spread it round the inside of each mold. Cut the ninth fillet into 8 pieces and mix it with the remaining salmon pieces

4. Place a few spoonfuls of mousline in each mold, and cover with the sole and salmon pieces. Add some more mousline until you have almost reached the rim of the mold and cover with the round piece of fish cut out of each fillet.

5. Cover the molds with aluminum foil and place them side by side in a large deep round baking pan. Fill the pan with water to the middle and place in a pre-heated 350°F (180°C) oven. Bake for 30 to 35 minutes. Remove from the oven, stand for 15 minutes and serve on beds of green salad, garnished with spoonfuls of red and black caviar and drizzled with creamy fish and sorrel sauce (recipe on page 91).

Stuffed vine leaves "dolmadakia" with salmon

Yields 30-35 dolmadakia
Preparation time 1 hour
Cooking time 30 minutes
Degree of Difficulty ♥♥

- 1 pound (500g) vine leaves
- 1/4 cup margarine
- 1/2 cup olive oil
- 28 green onions, chopped
- 1 cup grated shallot
- 1/3 cup pine nuts
- 1/2 cup finely chopped sultanas
- 1/2 cup Basmati or Carolina rice
- 1/2 cup finely chopped fresh parsley
- 1/2 cup finely chopped fresh dill or mint
- 1 teaspoon lemon zest
- 2 pounds (1kg) fresh salmon fillet, chopped
- 1/3 cup freshly squeezed lemon juice

1. Wash the vine leaves and remove the stalks. Blanch them by dipping a few at a time in boiling water for 5 minutes, and then drain.

2. Melt the margarine with 3 tablespoons of the oil in a large saucepan and lightly sauté the green onions and the shallot. Add the pine nuts and sultanas and stir over high heat for a few minutes. Add the rice, parsley, dill, lemon zest, salt, pepper and 2 cups boiling water to the pan, cover and simmer until all the water is absorbed and the rice is soft. Remove from the heat and let the mixture cool. Add and mix the pieces of raw fish in with the rice.

3. Press the rice into a 7½x7½ inch (22x22cm) square baking pan, which you have previously brushed with a little oil. Turn the molded rice out onto the work bench and cut into 1x1 inch (2x2cm) square pieces with a pastry cutter. Wrap each rice square in a vine leaf, to form small parcels.

4. Spread a few vine leaves on the bottom of a large heavy-bottomed saucepan and arrange the dolmadakia side by side, in layers. Put the pan over heat and add the remaining oil, lemon juice and 2 cups boiling water. Season, cover the pan and simmer until the dolmadakia are soft and only a tiny bit of juice is left, about 20 minutes. Serve the dolmadakia cold, sticking a pearl-tipped cocktail stick into each one. Can be prepared in advance.

Avocado and caviar sorbet

Serves 12
Preparation time 15 minutes
Freezing time 4 hours
Degree of Difficulty ♥

- 6 avocados, peeled and stoned
- 1/4 cup finely chopped fresh cilantro or parsley
- juice of 1 lemon
- zest from 1 lime
- 2oz (100g) Sevruga caviar
- salt and white pepper
- 2 egg whites
- pomegranate seeds, to garnish

1. Place the avocado pieces, cilantro, lemon juice, lime zest and caviar in the mixer bowl and beat to a pulp.

2. Beat the egg whites separately until stiff peaks form. Fold the meringue gently into the avocado mixture, taking care not to deflate the egg whites.

3. Freeze the mixture for 3-4 hours. Serve the sorbet in scoops in Martini glasses and garnish with pomegranate seeds. A delicious dish to guide you from the first to the second course.

Sweet and sour risotto

Yields 50 spoonfuls
Preparation time 1 hour
Degree of Difficulty ♥

- 3 tablespoons corn oil
- 1/2 cup butter
- 1/4 cup grated red onion
- 1 tablespoon grated fresh gingerroot
- 2 cups carnaroli or Carolina rice
- 1/2 cup dry red wine
- 1¼ liters vegetable stock
- 1/2 cup grenadine syrup
- 1/4 cup tinned pineapple juice
- 2 tablespoons pomegranate syrup (optional)
- 1/2 cup grated parmesan or hard gruyère
- salt and freshly ground pepper

1. Place the oil and half the butter in a large saucepan over high heat and when heated sauté the onion and ginger slightly. Add the rice and stir over high heat for 1 or 2 minutes. Pour in all the wine and stir for a few minutes until it evaporates.

2. Add the stock in portions, alternating with the grenadine syrup, stirring constantly and waiting for the stock to be absorbed before you add some more. Use as much stock as necessary for the rice to soften externally but remain "al dente" on the inside. Add the pineapple juice together with the last portion of stock. If you wish, season with 2 tablespoons pomegranate syrup for extra flavor (recipe on page 43).

3. Remove from the heat, blend in the rest of the butter and the parmesan. Season to taste. Serve the risotto warm in spoonfuls on a "réchaud" dish.

Miniature "kataifi" nests with salmon rolls filled with salad and horseradish vinaigrette

Yields 24 bite-sized salads
Preparation time 1 hour
Baking time 10 minutes
Degree of Difficulty ♥

For the vinaigrette
- 1 tablespoon horseradish sauce
- 2 tablespoons lemon or lime juice
- 2 tablespoons grated onion
- 1 egg yolk
- 1/4 cup rice wine or medium-dry sherry
- 1/4 cup balsamic vinegar
- 1 cup olive oil
- salt and freshly ground pepper

For the salad
- 24 mini kataifi nests (4oz -200g- kataifi or angel hair pastry)
- 1/4 cup melted salted butter
- 24 thin slices smoked salmon
- 4oz (200g) rocket
- 1oz (50g) fresh enoki mushrooms
- 1oz (50g) soy bean or mung bean sprouts, blanched and drained
- 1oz (50g) chives

For the horseradish vinaigrette:
1. Blend the horseradish sauce, lime juice and onion in the blender. Add the egg yolk, sherry, balsamic vinegar and beat until you obtain a uniform mixture. While beating, add the olive oil in a thin and steady flow, until it is blended with the rest of the ingredients. Season to taste.

For the salad:
1. Fluff up the kataifi pastry with your fingers. Take a few threads at a time and wrap them around your thumb to form tiny nests. Make a total of 24 nests, 2 inches (5cm) in diameter, and spread them on a buttered baking pan. Sprinkle with a little melted salted butter and bake at 400°F (200°C) for 10 minutes, until golden brown.
2. Fold a few rocket leaves, enoki mushrooms and sprouts in slices of smoked salmon to make pretty rolls. Place the rolls in the kataifi nests and serve on a platter. Serve the vinaigrette separately.

Yields 24 wontons
Preparation time 30 minutes
Cooking time 20 minutes
Degree of Difficulty ♥

- 1oz (35g) dried porcini or shiitake mushrooms
- 1 cup water
- 2 tablespoons olive oil
- 5 green onions, finely chopped
- 1 teaspoon grated fresh gingerroot
- salt and freshly ground pepper
- 8oz (250g) creamy goat's cheese or cream cheese
- 8oz (250g) wonton wrappers, thawed if frozen, or
  1 recipe home-made wonton dough (recipe on page 160)
- 1 egg white for brushing

1. Place the mushrooms and water in a small bowl and stand for 20 minutes until they swell. Drain and chop finely.

2. Heat the oil in a wok or small cast-iron skillet and sauté the onions and ginger. Add the mushrooms and stir over high heat, until all the water evaporates. Season the mixture and remove from the heat. Leave to cool. Add the cheese to the sautéed ingredients and mix thoroughly.

3. Place a spoonful of the mixture in the center of each square wonton wrapper. Brush the edges with a little egg white and pinch together to form a parcel. Attention, the wonton skins must not dry out or they will fall apart when fried. If you do not intend to use them immediately, keep them wrapped in cling film.

4. Once all the parcels are ready, cover tightly and store in the freezer. They will keep for up to 3 weeks. Fry straight from the freezer in hot oil, in a wok or fryer, for 5 minutes or until golden brown. Serve immediately.

Sushi with risotto al pesto and smoked trout

Yields 25 sushi pieces
Preparation time 40 minutes
Cooking time 15 minutes
Degree of Difficulty ♥♥

- 1/3 cup butter
- 1 cup carnaroli or Carolina rice
- 1/2 cup dry white wine
- 2½ cups vegetable stock
- 1/2 cup high quality ready-made pesto sauce
- 1/2 cup grated pamesan
- salt and white pepper
- 1 pound (500g) smoked trout
- 1 tube high quality fish roe paste

1. Melt half the butter in a medium pan and sauté the rice. Add all the wine at once and stir briskly over high heat, until the wine evaporates.
2. Gradually add the stock, stirring constantly and waiting until it is absorbed before you add more. Add as much stock as is necessary for the rice to soften externally but remain al dente on the inside. Add and stir in the pesto sauce together with the last addition of stock.
3. Remove from the heat, and blend in the remaining butter and parmesan. Place the mixture in a well-buttered 8-inch (20-cm) square baking pan and press down to cover the entire surface.
4. Cover and refrigerate the risotto for up to 1 day. Remove from the refrigerator, unmold onto non-stick paper and cut into 2-inch (5cm) square pieces with a pastry cutter.
5. Place the risotto squares on a serving dish and decorate with pieces of smoked trout and fish roe paste rosettes. Refrigerate until you want to serve the dish. You may purchase excellent fish roe paste from a Greek Deli.

Mediterranean salmon fillet rolls served in Portobello mushrooms

Yields 15 servings
Preparation time 1 hour
Baking time 20 minutes
Degree of difficulty ♥

For the garnish
- 4oz (100g) dried wild mushrooms (shiitake, chanterelles, porcini)
- 1 cup dry white wine
- 2 pounds (1kg) fresh spinach leaves
- 1/4 cup butter
- 8 green onions, finely chopped
- 1 medium-sized red onion, grated
- 1/3 cup finely chopped fresh tarragon
- salt and freshly ground pepper
- 15 Portobello mushrooms, trimmed
- a little lemon juice
- a little olive oil
- a little minced garlic
- 2 recipes tarragon sauce (recipe on page 91)

For the salmon rolls
- 6 pounds (3kg) fresh salmon fillets
- salt and white pepper
- 1/2 cup olive oil
- 1 cup dry white wine (plus the wine in which the mushrooms were soaked)
- 2 teaspoons crushed dried thyme

For the garnish

1. Soak the mushrooms in the wine for 15 to 20 minutes, until they swell. Strain and reserve the wine, to use in cooking the fish. Finely chop the mushrooms and set aside.

2. Wash the spinach and blanch in salted water, strain well and chop finely. Melt the butter in a large deep frying pan and sauté the green onions and onion until soft. Add the chopped mushrooms and sauté, stirring over high heat until all liquid evaporates. Stir in the spinach and tarragon. Turn off the heat, cover and keep the garnish warm.

3. Clean, dry and trim the Portobello mushrooms, trying not to damage their skin, and arrange them in an ovenproof dish. Chop up the removed stalks and add to the spinach garnish. Rub the trimmed mushrooms well with the lemon juice. Season and brush with a little olive oil and then grill for 15 minutes.

4. Prepare the sauce as directed, a short while before serving, and keep warm in a double boiler or use immediately.

5. Place a fish roll into each mushroom, toothpicks removed. Serve warm over the spinach and wild mushroom garnish, and top with tarragon sauce.

<u>For the salmon rolls</u>

1. Cut the fish fillets into strips, season and roll them up. Secure the rolls with toothpicks. Place the rolls in two slightly greased ovenproof dishes.

2. Put the oil, wine, thyme and a little white pepper in a large jar, screw the lid on and shake until well blended. Pour the mixture over the rolls and cook in the oven at 400°F (200°C) for 10 to 15 minutes. Keep warm until serving time. Strain the fish juices and reserve for the tarragon sauce, which you can prepare according to the recipe on page 91.

Sushi with puttanesca risotto and anchovies

Yields 25 sushi pieces
Preparation time 40 minutes
Cooking time 15 minutes
Degree of Difficulty ♥♥

- 1/4 cup margarine
- 2 tablespoons olive oil
- 1 small clove garlic, crushed
- 1 cup carnaroli or Carolina rice
- 3 cups vegetable stock
- 1/4 cup finely chopped sun-dried tomatoes
- 1/4 cup finely chopped black olives
- 2 tablespoons small capers
- salt and white pepper
- 1 jar anchovy fillets
- a few thin strips bottled red pimientos, and extra capers for decorating

1. Heat the margarine and oil in a medium pan and sauté the garlic and rice. Pour in the stock gradually, stirring constantly, and waiting for it to be absorbed before you add more. Add as much stock as necessary for the rice to soften externally, but remain al dente on the inside.

Add and stir in the sun-dried tomatoes, capers and olives together with the last addition of stock.

2. Remove from the heat and transfer to a well-buttered lined 8-inch (20-cm) square baking pan and press down to cover the entire surface.

3. Cover and refrigerate the risotto for up to 1 day. Remove from the refrigerator, unmold onto non-stick paper and cut into 2-inch (5-cm) square pieces with a pastry cutter.

4. Place the risotto squares on a serving dish and decorate with pieces of red Florina pepper, anchovy fillets and a few capers. Refrigerate until serving time. Serve cold

Individual Pyramid Cakes with Tangerine cream

Yields 6 individual cakes
Preparation time 1 hour
Refrigeration time 4 hours
<u>Suitable for freezing</u>
Degree of Difficulty ♥♥

- 14oz (400g) marzipan
- 14oz (400g) Regalice
- 1 cup royal icing (recipe on page 183)

- 1 recipe tangerine-flavored fruit cream (recipe on page 240)
- 6 small pyramid molds
- 6 10-inch (25-cm) ready-made sponge cake layers
- 1 cup raspberry jam

1. Prepare the tangerine cream. Mix with 2 cups whipped cream and refrigerate covered until you are ready to fill the pyramids. Buy ready-made sponge cake or bake the layers preparing 3 recipes sponge cake mixture, following the instructions in the "Vanilla Lemingtons" recipe and dividing them into 6 lined and buttered 10-inch (25-cm) round baking pans. You can prepare the sponge cake well in advance and store in the freezer covered with plastic wrap.

2. Secure the pyramid molds with the peak down in six cups. Cover the insides with plastic wrap. Cut four 4-inch (9-cm) isosceles triangles from each sponge cake layer, so that their bases form a 4-inch (9-cm) square in the center of the circle (see design on page 236). From the leftovers, make a smaller, 3-inch (7-cm) square piece for each pyramid. Attach the triangles on the internal walls of each pyramid.

3. Place 2 spoonfuls cream inside each pyramid. Cover with 2 tablespoons jam and then with the small square piece of cake. Add 3 tablespoons cream and more jam. Cover with the large square to close the pyramid. Freeze for 30 minutes for the cream to set.

4. Unmold the pyramids on a tray or dessert plates and spread all sides with jam, which you have previously heated and sifted, so that it is transparent. Sprinkle a surface with icing sugar and roll out thin round 8-inch (20-cm) sheets of marzipan with a small rolling pin, and use these to cover the pyramids all about.

5. Cut pieces out of the Regalice and roll each one out onto a surface sprinkled with icing sugar, using a small rolling pin to make thin sheets slightly larger than the marzipan ones. Sprinkle the pyramids with a little water and stick the Regalice sheets over the marzipan. Pipe small balls of royal icing on the corners of each pyramid. Refrigerate the cakes until the next day or freeze, covered, for up to 1 month.

White Chestnut Truffles

Yields 100 truffles
Preparation time 1 hour
Refrigeration time 12 to 14 hours
Suitable for freezing
Degree of difficulty ♥♥

- 2 pounds (1kg) fine white chocolate with a high content of cocoa solids
- 1/4 cup glucose
- 6 large egg yolks
- 14oz (400g) unsalted butter
- 1 cup whipping cream, whipped
- 1/2 cup Cognac or sherry or Armagnac
- 2 pounds (1kg) marrons glacés, puréed
- 2 pounds (1kg) fine white chocolate for coating

1. Melt the chocolate in a bain-marie together with the glucose. Mix well with a wooden spatula to a smooth mixture. Remove from the heat and leave to cool for 2 or 3 minutes. Blend in the egg yolks one by one, and the butter in small pieces, mixing constantly until you obtain a silky shiny mixture.

2. Add the whipped cream, the Cognac and the chestnut purée. Mix everything together well, spread the mixture on a lined jelly roll pan, and refrigerate for 12 hours. Shape the mixture into walnut-sized balls or use a miniature ice cream scoop to form balls, and arrange these in trays spread with non-stick oven paper. Refrigerate the trays containing the truffles for 2 hours until firm.

3. Melt the remaining chocolate in a bain-marie, with 1 tablespoon corn oil. Remove the truffles from the refrigerator, one tray at a time, and dip each truffle in the melted chocolate, using a fork or special tool for candy coating, until they are coated all over. Place carefully on trays lined with clean grease-proof paper. At this stage you can freeze the truffles. Once frozen, you can transfer the truffles to a large box, and arrange them in layers separated by non-stick paper. Avoid touching the coated truffles with your hands or the coating will become damp. You may handle them using confectioners' gloves.

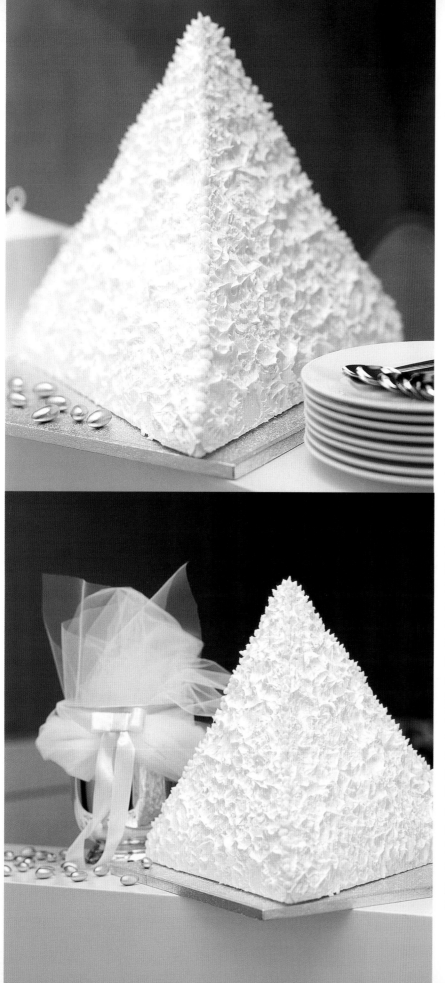

Pyramid Cake

Yields 100 portions
Preparation time several hours
Baking time several hours
<u>Suitable for freezing</u>
Degree of Difficulty ♥♥♥♥

For the butter sponge cake
- 8oz (250g) unsalted butter, melted
- 8 large eggs
- 2 cups fine sugar
- 2²/₃ cups all-purpose flour
- 1/2 teaspoon vanilla powder

- zest of 2 oranges (optional)

For the filling
- 6 recipes chocolate cream
  (recipe on page 239)

For the icing
- 3 recipes buttercream icing
  (recipe on page 132)

In order to make the pyramid cake, you will have to use four recipes of the above ingredients for butter sponge cake.

1. Melt the butter, remove from the heat and leave to cool slightly. Beat the eggs with the sugar at the mixer's top speed for 15 minutes, until thick and twice the original volume. Sift the flour with the vanilla powder into the egg mixture and fold it in gently so as not to deflate the beaten eggs. Add the melted butter a little at a time and the orange zest, stirring softly again, so as not to deflate the mixture.

2. For baking the four quantities of sponge cake, you will need in total: 3 square baking pans, dimensions 13, 11 and 9 inches (33, 28 and 23 centimeters). Butter the pans. Line with non-stick oven paper, and share one recipe of cake mixture between them. Bake separately at 350°F (180°C) for 20 to 25 minutes, until the cake is golden brown. Remove the pans from the oven and unmold onto a cloth sprinkled with icing sugar.

3. Repeat the process with the remaining cake mixture recipes, until you have 4 cakes of each size.

4. Join the square cakes using the chocolate cream. Cut the two smallest cakes in half to form the peak. Spread their surface with a light coating of cream, making sure the layer is not too thick and the cake too heavy. Secure the cakes with four 8-inch (20cm) long wooden skewers, sticking them vertically into the base of the pyramid from the four edges of the peak. Using a sharp knife, smooth off the sides of the pyramid.

5. Keep the pieces you have cut off the pyramid in the freezer, for future use in trifles. Prepare the buttercream icing and spread it over the pyramid, making patterns with a small spoon. At this stage the cake may be frozen for up to 1 month.

THE COUNTRY-STYLE WEDDING II.

Our bride is beautiful, and so is her trousseau,
And her friends, joining in her happiness.
I'm going to sing you a song with a chickpea,
Joy to the groom's eyes, who chose the bride-to-be.
I'm going to sing you a song with a guitar,
Long live the bride and groom, the best man and maid of honor.
I'm going to sing you a song with lemons,
Long live the bride and groom, and long live their parents.
I'm going to sing you a song with a cherry,
May this new couple made today, live to grow old and always be merry.

Greek Folk Song

A special wedding in a country house, in the shadow of green trees, with blossoming lemon trees in the background, can be particularly elegant in its simplicity.

The warm spring months are an ideal time to get married. A special wedding can be organized, away from the city, in the pleasant environment and peace offered by the countryside. There is nothing more beautiful than getting married in the white-washed church of a pretty village in the Greek or Italian countryside, with the bells pealing happily on a bright Sunday morning, and having a wedding party during the warm midday hours. In a countryside wedding, it is a must for the bride to go to church in a carriage, or even on a horse. At a midday wedding, you will also be able to enjoy the presence of small children.

Arrange the buffet under the trees and decorate it with tall cones adorned with lemons, lemon blossoms and leaves. The lemon tree's snow-white blossoms, with their strong scent and fragile beauty are a suitable adornment for the wedding scenery, as well as for the bride herself. In olden times, brides used to decorate their hair with lemon blossoms, for their unique scent. Braid lemon blossoms and small leaves into your wedding wreaths. The groom and best man's boutonnières can also be made up of lemon blossoms.

The buffet must also be simple, in the spirit of the season, with dishes inspired by Italian cooking, for the modern vegetarian couple. Prepare a large selection of cheeses and appetizers to serve to your guests, and accompany it with tasty white wine. An original idea, which gives the wine a special aroma, is to fill pitchers with cool wine and thin slices of peach.

Prepare a buffet with home-made fresh pasta, where each guest can choose the pasta and sauce they prefer. Choose to serve light sauces prepared with vegetables and olive oil. Serve a single meat dish, rabbit ragout (ragu al coniglio), from traditional Italian cuisine. The buffet can be decorated with fresh country produce, such as citrus fruits and vegetables. Place pretty artichokes in a brass vessel filled with water. Put small bunches of asparagus in vases of cold water. Little pots of basil and mint will give your buffet table scent and color. Serve rocket and carrot cut into sticks in glasses for your guests. Don't forget large mills for freshly ground pepper, and bottles of extra-virgin olive oil and balsamic vinegar, the quality of which might even be appreciated more than that of the wine you serve. A basil pot, a shallow plate with olive oil, a wreath of lemon blossoms and leaves, a pepper mill and a glass jar with fine vinegar can be placed as the centerpiece of the guests' tables.

The traditional Greek wedding sweet is bezedes (meringues). Prepare the wedding basket full of white meringues flavored with lemon, and decorate it with lemon leaves and blossoms. In certain parts of Greece and Italy, it is traditional to offer homemade sweets with the bonbonnières, such as honey cakes or crunchy almond sweets wrapped in transparent paper. An original idea for a countryside wedding is to set up a coffee machine, a coffee mill and an old-fashioned coffee pot for Greek coffee, so that your guests can choose between fresh hot espresso, cappuccino, or Greek coffee.

At the end of the meal serve shots of cold Grappa or frozen limoncello or Nocciolo liqueur, accompanied by Amaretti biscuits.

Yields 100 almond macaroons
Preparation time 30 minutes
Baking time 15 minutes
Degree of Difficulty ♥♥

- 1 pound (500g) or 3 cups blanched almonds
- 3 cups sugar
- 2/3 cup semolina
- 1 teaspoon vanilla essence
- 2 tablespoons bergamot or orange zest
- 1/3 cup Cognac
- 4 egg whites
- 1/4 teaspoon cream of tartar

1. When you prepare the lemon curd recipe on page 179, set aside all the egg-whites and use them to make elegant and tasty macaroons to offer to your guests with the bonbonnières. Place these, or some snow-white meringues (bezedes) in a large basket decorated with tulle and lemon leaves and flowers. The macaroons and lemon curd are a perfect combination.

2. Powder the almonds in a food-processor. Add the sugar, semolina, vanilla essence and orange or bergamot zest and beat to incorporate. Add the Cognac and beat this into the mixture as well. Empty the mixture into a large clean bowl.

3. Beat the egg whites until frothy. Add the cream of tartar and beat to a stiff meringue.

4. Fold the other ingredients into the meringue, taking care not to deflate the eggs. Place two baking sheets one on top of the other, and line the upper one with non-stick oven paper. (The double layer of pans prevents the macaroons from burning as they bake). Place the mixture into a piping bag with a star-shaped nozzle and pipe out rosettes at a short distance one from the other. Bake the macaroons at 350°F (18°C) for 15 to 20 minutes or until just golden. Leave to cool slightly and arrange on a rack to cool completely. The longer they stand, the crispier they will be. Will keep for 1 month in a cookie jar.

Bride's Diples-Cannoli

Yields 40 diples or 72 wonton wrappers
Preparation time several hours
Degree of Difficulty ♥♥

- 2²/₃ - 3 cups all-purpose flour
- 1/4 teaspoon salt
- 3 large eggs, beaten with 3 tablespoons water
- a little corn-starch
- 6 metal tubes for cannoli
- 2 cups honey and 1 cup water for the syrup
- coarsely ground walnuts and ground cinnamon for sprinkling, or whipped cream and chocolate flakes for cannoli

The same dough is used to prepare wonton wrappers.

1. Sift the flour and salt into a bowl and add the egg and water mixture little by little. Mix together and knead for 10 minutes, adding as much flour as necessary to form a stiff dough. Divide the dough into six pieces and form a ball with each piece. Cover with plastic wrap and stand for 5 hours. Roll out each ball into a very thin, almost transparent, sheet using a rolling pin. Sprinkle the surface often with corn starch, so that the dough does not stick. If you have a pasta machine, pass the dough through it a little at a time.

2. To make the "diples", cut the sheets into 4-6 inch (10x15cm) strips. Fill a large pan with oil and heat it up. Fold the strips around metal tubes coated with oil. Brush the sealing at the edges with a little egg white, to stick. Dip in the hot oil and fry until golden. Drain on absorbent paper and remove the metal tubes. Boil 2 cups honey and 1 cup water in a pan. Skim and drop in a few "diples" at a time and boil for a few minutes. Transfer them to a serving platter with a slotted spoon and sprinkle with chopped walnuts and cinnamon. Will keep 15 to 20 days without being refrigerated.

3. To make Italian cannoli, omit the syrup coating and fill the fried rolls with whipped cream using a pastry bag. Dip the ends in chocolate flakes. Store in the refrigerator.

4. Make wonton wrappers out of the same dough. Use one third of the ingredients to prepare 24 wonton wrappers. Roll out the dough on a surface sprinkled with corn-starch, to form a transparent sheet. Cut smaller pieces from the dough, with a round or square pastry cutter (3-4 inches - 7-10cm). Place the small sheets one on top of the other, sprinkling with a little corn-starch so that they don't stick. Will keep for 6 months in the freezer tightly covered.

Gazpacho shots with tequila

Yields 16-18 glasses
Preparation time 15 minutes
Refrigeration time 2 hours
Degree of Difficulty ♥

- 4 ripe tomatoes, skinned, cored and chopped
- 4 small gherkins
- 1 small clove garlic, crushed
- 1 large red bell pepper
- 2 tablespoons sugar
- 2 tablespoons Worcestershire sauce
- 1/4 cup freshly squeezed lemon juice
- 10 cups tomato juice
- 1/2 cup tequila
- salt and a little ground pepper
- 20-30 drops Tabasco sauce
- 1/4 cup finely chopped celery, to garnish

1. Pulse the first 7 ingredients in the blender. Add the tomato juice, tequila, salt, pepper and Tabasco and blend together. Refrigerate the gazpacho for 2 hours. Serve cold in short glasses. Add plenty of freshly ground pepper and garnish with finely chopped celery

Stromboli bread with smoked mozzarella

Yields 2 loaves
Preparation time 2 hours
Baking time 25 to 30 minutes
Degree of Difficulty ♥♥

- 3½ cups all-purpose flour
- 1/2 tablespoon active dry yeast
- 1½ teaspoons salt
- 3 tablespoons olive oil
- 1½ cups warm water (80°F - 40°C)
- 1/3 cup bottled sun-dried tomato
- 1 tablespoon tiny capers
- 1 small clove garlic, crushed
- 14oz (400g) smoked mozzarella, thinly sliced
- 1 teaspoon dried chives

1. In the mixer bowl, mix the flour with the yeast and salt. Make a hole in the center and pour in the oil. Add the water and beat the mixture with the dough hook for 10 minutes, until you have a soft, pliable dough that doesn't stick to the bowl. Cover the dough and stand for 2 hours, until double in bulk. Divide the dough in two and roll out into two rectangular sheets, 10x10 inches (25x25cm), with a rolling pin.
2. Brush the sheets with a little olive oil and sprinkle with the sun-dried tomato, capers, garlic and cheese. Roll up the two loaves and place them on a lightly oiled baking pan. Cover with a cloth and stand for 1 hour, or until double in size.
3. Brush with a little egg yolk and sprinkle over some dried chives. Bake the loaves at 400°F (200°C) for 25 to 30 minutes, until golden-brown. Serve the bread on the same day or wrap tightly in plastic wrap and store in the freezer.

Olive and rosemary focaccia

Preparation time 2 hours
Cooking time 45 minutes
Suitable for freezing
Degree of Difficulty ♥♥

- 6-6½ cups all-purpose flour
- 1 teaspoon active dry yeast
- 2⅓ cups warm water (80°F - 40°C)
- 1 tablespoon sugar
- 1 teaspoon Italian herbs
- 1/4 cup olive oil
- 2 teaspoons salt

For garnishing
- 1/4 cup olive oil
- 3 cloves garlic, finely chopped
- 2 tablespoons finely chopped fresh rosemary
- 2 cups sliced black olives
- salt and freshly ground pepper

1. Mix 6 cups flour with the yeast in the mixer bowl and make a hole in the center. Add all the other ingredients and mix with the dough hook for about 10 minutes, adding more flour if necessary until you obtain a soft and elastic non-sticky dough. Cover and stand until double in size.

2. Press the dough down to let the air out and knead for 5 minutes. Spread out on an oiled baking pan. Cover and leave to rise. Brush the surface with a little oil and press down using two fingers to make deep grooves all over the surface. Brush with the oil and top with the garlic, rosemary and olives. Sprinkle with a little salt and pepper.

3. Divide the surface of the dough into square pieces using a sharp knife. Bake the bread at 400°F (200°C) for about 45 minutes. Remove from the oven and cut into square pieces. Serve slightly warm. Prepare 2 or more recipes for the wedding buffet.

Portobello mushrooms with feta cheese and mint

- 30 medium Portobello mushrooms
- 1/3 cup freshly squeezed lemon juice
- olive oil, oregano and a little crushed garlic
- 1/4 cup olive oil
- 2 hot green peppers
- 10oz (300g) soft feta cheese
- 1/3 cup finely chopped mint
- 1 tablespoon vinegar
- salt and freshly ground pepper

1. Clean and trim the mushrooms. Remove the stems and arrange the mushrooms in a baking pan. Pour over the lemon juice, a little olive oil and sprinkle with a little oregano. Grill for 10 minutes.

2. In the meantime, fry the peppers in the oil. Drain and keep the aromatic oil. Remove the blackened skins and mash the flesh of the peppers with a fork, together with the cheese, mint, vinegar, a pinch of salt and freshly ground pepper. Add as much of the oil from frying the peppers as necessary to make the mixture soft and tasty.

3. Using a small spoon, fill the mushrooms with the cheese mixture and serve warm or cold; they are delicious either way.

Cheese board

- 1/4 head of Reggiano parmesan (around 16-20 pounds, 8-10kg)
- 4 pounds (2kg) each of gorgonzola, provolone and smoked mozzarella, in pretty pieces
- 1 small head kervella (white goat's cheese)
- 4 pounds (2kg) mozzarella – fior di latte
- several bunches of cherry tomatoes
- small pots of fresh basil and mint, for decorating

1. Prepare the cheese board; place small pots of basil and fresh mint all about the dish, for the scent. Make sure that there is a waiter/waitress at the buffet to carve pieces of the parmesan every now and then, so that there are always fresh pieces on the platter for your guests.

2. Serve the mozzarella in a large transparent jar, with sprigs of fresh basil and mint between the pieces of cheese, and fill with water. Guests can remove the cheese from the jar using a slotted spoon. Serve with bunches of cherry tomatoes.

Meat platter

- 40 thin slices each of prosciutto crudo, speck di prosciutto, bresaola, salami di Milano, coppa
- 2 jars anchovy fillets
- 1 jar mini gherkins
- a few figs and avocados
- 3-4 small melons
- slices of smoked salmon
- curly lettuce, to serve

1. Arrange the slices of meat, the anchovies and gherkins on a large platter. Quarter the figs with a knife and place them on a bed of curly lettuce. If you like, place a shallow bowl filled with extra-virgin olive oil in the center of the platter. Once removed from their packaging, the slices of meat should not stand in the open air for long. Sprinkle the bresaola with lemon juice and black pepper. Cut a few avocados into eighths, brush with lemon juice and wrap in thin slices of smoked salmon or prosciutto. Serve thin slices of melon also wrapped in prosciutto.

Marinated "married" baby artichokes

- 3 cans (3 x 14oz-400g) baby artichokes
- 1/3 cup balsamic vinegar
- 1/2 cup extra-virgin olive oil
- 8 cloves garlic, crushed
- 1/2 cup finely chopped parsley
- 2-3 teaspoons powdered dried red chilis
- 3 tablespoons small capers
- 10 bottled sun-dried tomatoes, chopped

1. Drain and rinse the artichokes. Cut in two. Mix the oil and vinegar in a large jar. Add the garlic, parsley, chili pepper, capers, sun-dried tomatoes, salt and pepper. Add the baby artichokes and marinate for several hours. You can also marinate cubes of feta cheese in the same way, or shelled and boiled scampi.

2. Remove all the ingredients from the marinade and stick them together with slices of lemon onto a tall ready-made Styrofoam cone (1m-2ft. tall). You will need 4 pounds (2kg) hard feta and 8 pounds (4kg) scampi. Remove the scampi heads but leave the tails intact. Boil in plenty of salted water flavored with seafood seasoning and olive oil. Cover the large Styrofoam cone first with fresh curly lettuce or endives and then stick on the rest of the ingredients, using pearl toothpicks.

Pasta di oliva nera

- 6 cups chopped black olives, stoned
- 2 cups ground cashew nuts
- 2-3 small cloves garlic, crushed
- 6-8 tablespoons olive oil
- 4-5 tablespoons balsamic vinegar

1. Blend all the ingredients together in the mixer, until you have a smooth mixture. Yields about 8 cups olive paste.

Pasta di oliva verde

- 6 cups chopped green olives, stoned
- 2 cups ground walnuts
- 6 bottled red pimientos, chopped
- 1/2 cup grated Reggiano parmesan
- 2 small cloves garlic
- 6-8 tablespoons olive oil and balsamic vinegar

1. Blend all the ingredients together in the mixer, until you have a smooth mixture. Yields about 8 cups olive paste.

Red Pesto

- 6 cups chopped bottled sun-dried tomato
- 3 cups grated Parmigiano-Reggiano
- 1 cup basil leaves
- 1/4 cup tiny capers
- 1 teaspoon grated red chilis
- 1 teaspoon sugar
- 2 cups pine nuts
- 3 cups olive oil

1. In a food processor, blend all the ingredients together, except the oil, until you have a smooth paste. Continuing to beat, add the oil, pouring slowly and steadily in a very thin flow until the sauce is uniform.

Pickled baby eggplants

Yields 12 pickled eggplants
Preparation time 1 week
Degree of Difficulty ♥♥

- 12 very small eggplants
- 12 cloves garlic, crushed
- 1 large green and 1 large red pepper, finely chopped
- 2 carrots, grated
- 2/3 cup finely chopped celery
- 6 long bottled red pimientos, cut in two lengthways
- celery sprigs, steamed
- 3 cups vinegar
- 4 cups water
- 1 tablespoon sugar

1. Remove the stems from the eggplants, make 3 incisions in each lengthways and season with plenty of salt. Stand in a colander for 1 hour. Rinse well with plenty of cold water and squeeze each one between your palms, to remove excess water. Blanch in hot water.

2. In a bowl, mix the garlic, peppers, carrots and chopped celery, and sprinkle with a little salt and plenty of pepper. Fill the eggplants with the mixture. Then wrap each one with a piece of bottled red pepper and a steamed sprig of celery.

3. Place the vinegar, water, sugar and one tablespoon salt in a pan and boil for 5 minutes, until the sugar dissolves. Remove from the heat, and once the liquid is cold pour it into two sterilized jars. Add the eggplants, making sure the liquid covers them. Screw on the lids and stand the jars in the refrigerator for 1 week.

Homemade pasta

Yealds 4 - 5 portions
Preparation time 1 - 2 hours
Drying time several hours
Degree of difficulty ♥♥

- 3 cups flour
- 1/8 teaspoon salt
- 4-5 large eggs beaten with 2 teaspoons oil

1. Mix the flour and salt in a large bowl. Make a hole in the center and pour in the beaten eggs with the oil. Taking a little flour from the sides, knead until you have a soft, elastic dough that doesn't stick to your hands. If the dough is too dry, add another egg. Alternatively, place all the ingredients in the mixer bowl and knead with the dough hook, to form a ball around it. Remove to the work surface and knead until smooth.

2. If you plan to mix the pasta with other liquid ingredients, omit the extra egg. Cover the dough with plastic wrap and leave to rise for 1 hour. Roll out with a pasta machine to the desired thickness and cut into various shapes. Hang the fresh pasta on a special pasta rail, and let it dry for several hours.

With spinach: grind 3oz (150g) fresh spinach leaves, blanched and well drained, in the mixer. Calculate the extra amount for each egg contained in the dough. Mix and knead in the spinach paste together with the eggs when preparing the dough.

With pesto: add 1 tablespoon of ready-made pesto sauce, draining off the oil, for each egg contained in the dough. With tomato: add 1 tablespoon tomato sauce for each egg contained in the dough, depending on how much you choose to make. You can also add 1 clove garlic, crushed, or 1/2 teaspoon dry red chili pepper to the tomato paste, for taste.

With red wine: prepare as above, only mix the tomato paste with 1 tablespoon sweet red wine.

With smoked salmon: grind 2oz (100g) smoked salmon in the mixer and add to the pasta dough.

All the sauces are enough for 8 portions of pasta at a family meal. At a buffet, guests will take smaller portions, so the following recipes will serve 12.

Siciliana sauce

- 4 pounds (2kg) eggplants
- 1/3 cup olive oil
- 3 cloves garlic, slivered
- 26oz (800g) ripe tomatoes, chopped
- 1 teaspoon sugar
- 3 tablespoons balsamic vinegar
- 1/2 cup finely chopped fresh basil and mint

1. Dice the eggplants. Sprinkle with plenty of salt and stand in a colander for 1 hour. Rinse and squeeze between your palms to remove excess water.

2. Deep-fry until crispy. Heat the oil in a pan and sauté the garlic. Add the tomatoes, sugar and vinegar. Simmer for about 15 minutes, until the sauce is almost set. Then add the herbs and eggplant and simmer for another 5 minutes. Season to taste.

Vegetable Napolitain sauce

- 1/4 cup olive oil
- 1 large onion, grated
- 1 leek, sliced
- 4 celery sticks, chopped
- 4 carrots, sliced
- 26oz (800g) small tomatoes, drained and chopped
- 7oz (200g) sliced white mushrooms
- 3 tablespoons Ketchup
- 1/4 cup finely chopped fresh basil
- 1/4 teaspoon Cayenne pepper

1. Sauté the onion lightly in the oil. Add the leek, celery and carrots, and stir for about 10 minutes over the heat. Add the tomatoes, mushrooms, ketchup, basil, a little salt and the Cayenne pepper. Mix together over high heat, cover, and simmer for 30 minutes.

Zucchini al pesto sauce

- 4 pounds (2kg) green zucchini, cut in julienne pieces
- 1/4 cup olive oil
- 1 large onion, thinly sliced
- 4 cloves garlic, crushed
- 2 cups pesto sauce
- salt and freshly ground pepper

1. Sprinkle the zucchini with salt and leave to stand in a colander for 30 minutes. Rinse well and squeeze between your palms to remove excess water. Dry on absorbent paper. Heat the oil in a large deep skillet and sauté the onion and garlic. Add the zucchini, a little at a time, stirring for 1 - 2 minutes, until the zucchini is soft but "al dente". Finally, blend in the pesto sauce, salt and pepper.

Tomato and basil sauce (Portobello à la greca)

- 4 tablespoons butter
- 1 medium onion, grated
- 2 cloves garlic, crushed
- 26oz (800g) canned tomatoes
- 1/2 cup chopped fresh basil leaves
- 1 teaspoon sugar
- 3 tablespoons balsamic vinegar
- 1-1½ teaspoons powdered red chili pepper (optional) and freshly ground pepper
- 20 medium Portobello mushrooms (optional)

1. Melt the butter with the oil in a small pan and sauté the onion. Add the remaining ingredients except the mushrooms, and simmer the sauce for 25 minutes.

2. Portobello mushrooms baked with tomato sauce are a delicious addition to your buffet. Arrange 20 medium mushrooms in a baking pan, pour over the sauce, add plenty of black pepper and cover with slices of ripe tomato. Sprinkle with 1/4 cup extra-virgin olive oil and bake at 375°F (190°C) for 1 hour and 30 minutes.

Baked conchiglioni with ricotta

Yields 12 portions
Preparation time 30 minutes
Baking time 40 minutes
Degree of Difficulty ♥♥

- 1 recipe tomato and basil sauce (recipe on page 171)
- 1 pound (500g) large shell-shaped pasta
- salt
- 1/4 cup olive oil
- 7oz (200g) grated mozzarella

For the filling
- 10oz (300g) frozen or 1½ pounds (600g) fresh spinach
- 1/4 cup butter
- 1/4 teaspoon nutmeg
- 1/4 cup pine nuts
- salt and freshly ground pepper
- 1/4 cup single cream
- 1 pound (500g) ricotta or anthotyro cheese
- 1/3 cup grated parmesan
- 1 egg (optional)

1. Prepare the tomato sauce according to the recipe. Blanch the spinach for the filling, drain and squeeze out the excess water. Melt the butter in a small pan and sauté the spinach. Add the nutmeg, pine nuts, salt and freshly ground pepper and stir slightly over the heat. Remove from the heat and once cool, blend in the cream, ricotta and parmesan. Finally, add and mix in the egg, if used.

2. Boil the pasta in a pan of salted water with the oil. Do not overboil. Drain the pasta and rinse under running tap-water until you can handle the shells. Fill each shell with the spinach and cheese mixture. Spread a few spoonfuls of the sauce in a deep baking pan and arrange the stuffed shells on top. Pour over the remaining sauce and sprinkle with the grated mozzarella. Bake at 375°F (190°C) for 35 to 40 minutes.

3. Alternatively: Omit the spinach, nutmeg and pine nuts, and prepare the dish with ready-made pesto sauce. Mix 1 cup pesto sauce with the cheeses, do not add cream or egg, and fill the shells with the mixture.

Ragu di coniglio

Yields 12 portions
Preparation time 30 minutes
Cooking time 1 hour 30 minutes
Degree of Difficulty ♥♥

- 2 large cleaned rabbits
- 4 bay leaves
- 20 peppercorns
- 20 allspice-corns
- 4 cloves garlic, cut lengthways
- salt and freshly ground pepper
- 2 bottles good quality red wine
- 1/4 cup butter
- 1/4 cup olive oil
- 1 large onion, grated
- 14oz (400g) canned tomatoes, finely chopped
- 1 teaspoon sugar
- 3 tablespoons balsamic vinegar
- 3 tablespoons tomato paste
- 1 teaspoon rosemary

1. Cut the rabbits into neat pieces, and remove all the bones. If you like, simmer the bones in salted water with some cleaned vegetables (onion, celery, carrot, peppers) for 2 hours to make a tasty meat stock, which you can strain and freeze for future use. Place the rabbit pieces in a large oven-proof dish, together with half the bay leaves, half the pepper and allspice-corns and half the garlic. Season and pour over half the wine. Marinate the meat for 2 hours or overnight.

2. In a large saucepan, melt the butter with the oil and sauté the onion, the remaining garlic and the meat, which you have drained from the marinade. Turn the meat using a fork so that it is cooked on all sides. Douse with the remaining wine.

3. Add the tomato, sugar, vinegar, tomato paste and rosemary, the remaining spices, salt and freshly ground black pepper, cover the pan, and simmer the food for 1 hour and 30 minutes, or until the meat is tender and the sauce thickens. Serve the ragu over large boiled fusilloni.

Mascarpone and morello cherry trifle

Yields one 20-pint (10-liter) bowlful
Preparation time 40 minutes
Degree of Difficulty ♥

- 6 cups (1½ liters) whipping cream
- 1 cup icing sugar
- 1 tablespoon gelatine, mixed with 2 tablespoons water and heated
- 3 pounds (1½ kg) mascarpone cheese
- 2 packets ladyfingers (1 pound 4oz – 600g)
- 2 cups ready-made espresso coffee
- 1 cup Kahlua liqueur
- 4 teaspoons vanilla essence
- 7oz (200g) chocolate flakes or grated chocolate
- 1 pound (500g) morello cherries or regular cherries stoned, and
  2 cans cherry pie filling or
  2 recipes morello cherry sauce

1. Whip the cream with the sugar and gelatine. Transfer the whipped cream to a clean bowl and place in the refrigerator. In the meantime, beat the cheese, which must be at room temperature, in the mixer until soft and creamy. Add the whipped cream to the cheese a little at a time and mix at medium speed, until the cheese and cream are blended.

2. Mix the coffee with the liqueur and vanilla essence in a large bowl, and dip the ladyfingers in the mixture one at a time. Arrange 10 to 15 ladyfingers to cover the bottom of the bowl, and add 1/3 of the cream. Mix the cherries with the pie filling or prepare the cherry sauce according to the recipe on page 113.

3. Pour 1/3 of the sauce carefully over the cream and sprinkle with 1/3 of the chocolate flakes. Repeat the process, ending with layers of cream, sauce and chocolate flakes. Keep refrigerated.

Lemon curd with Cookies

Yields 120 portions
(1 glass measuring 120cm – capacity
20 pints - 10 liters)
Preparation time several hours
Degree of Difficulty ♥♥

For the lemon curd (1 recipe)
• 1 cup lemon juice
• 1 cup sugar
• 1/3 cup corn-starch
• 3 egg yolks (from large eggs)
• 2/3 cup warm water
• 2 teaspoons lemon zest

For the biscuit base
• 1 pound (500g) digestive biscuits
• 1/2 cup unsalted butter
• 1/2 cup sugar

The ingredients for the lemon curd
will yield 1 home recipe (=3 cups).
Multiply the recipe by 4 and you will
have a 'party' dosage, whose
ingredients will fit in a large
saucepan. For the 120-portion
wedding dessert, you will need 5
times the party amount. Here is the
recipe for the large dosage (20 times
the home recipe).

For the wedding dessert
• 25 cups lemon juice
  (around 100 lemons)
• 20 cups sugar
  (around 10 pounds – 5kg)
• 6¹/₃ cups corn-starch
  (around 3 x 200g sachets)
• 60 egg yolks
• 10 cups warm water (2.5 liters)
• zest of 6 lemons
• 4 pounds (2kg) digestive biscuits
• 1 pound (500g) unsalted butter
  and 2 cups sugar (for the cookie
  mixture)

1. Place the corn-starch, sugar and egg yolks in a large saucepan and beat until the mixture is pale yellow. Add the lemon juice, a little at a time to start with, so that the mixture becomes gradually thinner without curdling. Heat over low heat and add the hot water to the pan. Keep stirring and let the mixture boil until you obtain a thick shiny custard covering the back of a spoon. Remove from the heat, add and mix in the lemon zest. Pulse the biscuits with the sugar and butter in the food processor. Spread 1/3 of the biscuit mixture to cover the base of a serving bowl, cover with 1/3 of the custard. Repeat the layers and finish with the lemon custard. Refrigerate until serving time. Will keep up to 1 week.

Lemon Curd – Wedding favors

Prepare as many recipes of lemon curd as you like, to fill small jars taking 1/2 or 1 cup lemon curd. Boil the jars to sterilize them. Fill the jars, screw on the lids and decorate with muslin and pretty ribbon. If you like, attach small paper labels to the ribbons, with the date of the wedding and the couple's initials. The jars of lemon curd will be a pleasant memento for your guests, who can enjoy it for breakfast on the next day, spread on slices of bread.

Si l' amour ne demande que des baisers
à quoi bon la gloire de cuisinier?

Rene Black, Chef, Waldorf-Astoria, New York 1948

Christmas is an ideal time for a luxurious wedding and a grand reception, with every pomp and ceremony, and a menu inspired by classic French cuisine.

If you belong to the class of people who cannot resist the glamour of extreme luxury and the grandeur of ceremony in every aspect of your life, then Christmas is the time of year to unleash your inspiration and plan the grandest wedding, without holding back.

From the tone of the reception, which can be rather classic and more imposing in relation to the soft colors of spring and summer weddings, to an incomparably luxurious, princess-style, wedding dress, with a lace veil and a long train fit to glide majestically over marble floors and Persian rugs, nothing is over the top for a wedding characterized by ultimate luxury.

Extreme attention must be paid to every single detail, from the bride's hairstyle, which should be an elaborate knot, the silver tiara, the jewelry, the satin gloves, the dress's expensive accessories, to the fourteen courses of the meal, which will be served at every single table at the precise same moment, covered with silver-plated bells, and ceremoniously uncovered for the guests by excellent waiting staff.

The invitation must absolutely indicate the atmosphere of the wedding and the reception, both in the style, the paper, the calligraphy, and in the content, which should have the indication: Evening Dress or Black Tie. The bridesmaids can wear organza dresses and velvet tops to match the rest of the decorations, and velvet bows in their hair.

No concessions in quality are allowed, both in decorating the church, the choice of car and reception hall, and in the quantity of the food, the champagne and the wine that are served, or in the correct attire of the large staff. Attention must be paid to detail, from the parking spaces, to the staff greeting the guests, the maître d' who will show them to their tables, and the waiters and waitresses who will obey their every order. Instead of greeting your guests at the church, you can do so at the reception hall, standing in the following order: first the wedding hosts, usually the mother and father of the bride, then the groom's parents, the couple, and finally the best man and maid of honor.

For a "French-style" reception at home, you should have enough room for all the guests, and all the necessary spaces, such as parking areas, a cloakroom, enough room in the kitchen for the catering staff, as well as sufficient storage space for preparing and decorating the dishes. Offer red and green sweets from two tall cones at the entrance to the reception hall, together with the champagne. Place a bonbonnière in front of each guest, and make sure there are as many glasses as the varieties of wine to be served with the meal. Tie snow-white meringue hearts with ribbon, to decorate the guests' chairs and the Christmas tree. Floral compositions of pink roses and orchids can decorate each corner, together with fir-tree branches. In order to complete the glamour of the occasion, choose a live orchestra, to fill the magic night with soft notes, and an expensive souvenir-gift for each of your guests.

Monogrammed bonbonnières

Yields 100 monograms
Preparation time several hours
Drying time a few days
Degree of Difficulty ♥♥♥

- 1 recipe meringue (recipe on page 241)
- 1/2 recipe egg icing
- cardboard monogram stencils

1. Cut out 1½-inch (4-cm) monogram stencils for the bride and groom from cardboard. Prepare 1 recipe meringue and pipe out the monograms with a No.4 nozzle, on ungreased non-stick paper, in baking pans. Bake at 200°F (90°C) for 1 hour and 20 minutes, switch off the oven and leave to dry for 24 hours.
2. Prepare the egg icing and coat one side of the cardboard monograms. Stick a meringue monogram on each piece of cardboard and stand in a cool dry place until the egg icing dries out, 1-2 days, and the meringue is fixed to the cardboard. Stick the monograms onto the ribbons of each bonbonnière.

Egg icing

- 2 egg whites
- 4 cups icing sugar

1. Beat the egg whites and sugar to a stiff meringue. Use the icing immediately, as it dries out very fast.

Mignardises

Yields 24 mini éclairs
Preparation time 30 minutes
Cooking time 30 minutes
Degree of Difficulty ♥♥

For the choux dough
- 1 1/3 cups water or milk
- 1/2 cup unsalted butter
- 1/4 teaspoon salt
- 1 cup all-purpose flour
- 4 large eggs

For the Royal Icing
- 2 egg whites from large eggs
- 1/4 teaspoon cream of tartar
- 4 cups icing sugar
- 1 tablespoon glucose (optional)
- 1/4 teaspoon glycerine
- 1/2 teaspoon vanilla essence
- red and green food coloring
- 1 cup whipped cream for the filling

1. Prepare the mini éclairs. Place the water or milk with the butter and salt in a large saucepan over high heat and stir until the mixture starts boiling. Remove from the heat, pour in all of the flour and stir briskly with a wooden spoon for about 1 minute, until the dough collects about the spoon and doesn't stick to the pan.

2. Place the dough in the mixer bowl and leave to cool for 2 or 3 minutes. While beating with the dough hook, add the eggs one by one, waiting until one is absorbed before adding the next one. Put the dough in a piping bag with a No.1A nozzle and pipe 1½-inch (4-cm) cords on buttered paper in a baking pan. Bake at 425°F (220°C) for 15 minutes and then lower the heat to 300°F (150°C) and let the éclairs dry out for another 15 to 20 minutes. Remove from the oven and leave to cool. Once cold, fill with a little whipped cream.

3. Prepare the icing, add coloring, and dip the éclairs lightly in the icing, to cover the surface. Serve on a platter with pearl-topped cocktail sticks. A good coffee accompaniment for the end of the meal.

4. **To make the icing:** beat the egg whites with the cream of tartar until you have a very light, not firm, meringue. Add the sugar, glucose, glycerine, and vanilla essence and beat for another minute. If the icing is too runny, add more icing sugar, and if it is too stiff, add another egg white. Divide the icing into 3 parts and color two parts green and pink with a few drops of green and red food coloring, respectively.

Blini

Yields 40 miniature blini (6 cm)
Preparation time 1 hour
Suitable for freezing
Degree of Difficulty ♥♥

- 2oz (40g) fresh yeast or
  1 tablespoon active dry yeast
- 2 cups wholemeal flour
- 1 cup warm water (100°F or 40°C)
- 1 cup warm milk (100°F or 40°C)
- 3 egg yolks
- 3 tablespoons melted butter
- 1 teaspoon salt
- 2 tablespoons sugar
- 3 egg whites, beaten

1. Stir the yeast into the water to dissolve and set aside for 10 minutes until frothy. Add a few tablespoons of the flour and stir the mixture to form a thick batter. Cover with a damp cloth and set aside for 30 minutes in a warm place until the batter rises.

2. Meanwhile, place the milk, egg yolks, butter and salt in the mixer bowl. Add the risen yeast and the rest of the flour and beat until blended. Whisk the egg whites and sugar separately, to a stiff meringue and fold into the previous mixture lightly, taking care not to deflate the meringue. Cover with cling film and set aside for 1 hour, until the mixture rises.

3. Heat a non-stick skillet and place 2-3 round 2½-inch (6-cm) ring molds inside. For mini blinis use smaller ring molds or just pour 1-2 teaspoons of the batter in the pan for each blini. Cook until bubbles form on the surface. Then remove the mold carefully and turn the blini over with a metal spatula. Cook for 1 minute and remove to a plate. Prepare all the blini in the same way. Cover and store in the freezer until needed.

Elegant blini canapés

Yields 40 hors d'oeuvres
Preparation time 20 minutes
Degree of Difficulty ♥

- 40 miniature blini, ready-made or homemade
- 7oz (200g) smoked trout
- 14oz (400g) smoked salmon, in thin slices
- 14oz (400g) foie gras
- 2 black truffles, shaved
- 1 jar black caviar (2-3oz or 60-80g)
- 1 jar red caviar (2-3oz or 60-80g)
- 7oz (200g) goat's cheese roll

For the cheese mixture
- 5oz (150g) cream cheese
- 5oz (150g) goat's cheese
- 2 tablespoons crème fraîche
- 1/2 teaspoon horseradish sauce (optional)
- 2 tablespoons finely chopped dill (optional)
- 2 teaspoons lemon juice
- salt and white pepper

1. Before garnishing the blini, arrange on a platter and drizzle with a little melted butter. Heat in the oven until the butter is absorbed, about 5 minutes.

2. Cream the two cheeses in the mixer. For a milder taste, prepare the mixture using only cream cheese. Add the cream, horseradish, dill and lemon juice and beat until you obtain a soft, uniform mixture.

3. Place a little of the cheese mixture on the blini, and top with a few pieces of trout or a salmon rosette with a little red or black caviar. Garnish with dill. Garnish the remaining blini with slices of goat's cheese roll and caviar, or spread with foie gras and top with shaved black truffles.

Salmon, caviar and crème fraîche trilogy

Yields 20 portions
(1-2oz or 40-50g of each salmon variety and 1/2oz or 15g caviar per portion)
Preparation time 15 minutes
Degree of Difficulty ♥

- 26oz (800g) smoked Norway salmon fillet
- 2 pounds (1kg) gravlax salmon or

- 2 pounds (1kg) wild Blanic salmon
- 1 pound 10oz (800g) fresh white marinated salmon
- 10oz (300g) Sevruga caviar
- 10oz (300g) red caviar
- 1 cup cream, French crème fraîche or sour cream
- slices of lemon for serving and slices of pumpernickel

1. You can either buy the different varieties of salmon or prepare the gravlax and marinated salmon at home.
2. Serve the salmon varieties on platters, cut into 1oz (40g) portions, or on plates accompanied by spoonfuls of Sevruga and red caviar and crème fraîche. Garnish with slices of lemon and pumpernickel. Choose good quality caviar, such as Beluga, Sevruga or Oscietre, to match the quality of the salmon you are serving.

Fresh marinated salmon

Yields 24 slices
Preparation time 15 minutes
Marinating time 24 hours

- 8 slices white salmon, skinned and boned
- white vinegar
- 1 tablespoon fresh rosemary

- 1 teaspoon dried thyme, crumbled
- 1 large red pepper, grilled and finely chopped
- olive oil
- salt, pepper

1. Wash the fish well, cut in long, thin slices and arrange in a baking pan. Attention, do not use an aluminum baking pan. Sprinkle the fish slices with the herbs and a little salt. Pour over plenty of vinegar to cover the slices and cover with cling film. Stand in the refrigerator for 24 hours.
2. Remove from the refrigerator and drain off the vinegar. Cover in olive oil and store in the refrigerator until serving time.

Gravlax salted salmon

Yields 25 portions
Preparation time 15 minutes
Salting time 3 to 4 days

- 2 pounds (1kg) fresh salmon fillet, chopped
- 1 cup coarse salt
- 1/4 cup sugar
- 1 cup finely chopped dill
- 1 teaspoon white pepper

1. Mix the salt with the sugar, dill and pepper. Spread 1/4 of the mixture in a round stainless steel, non-reactive, baking pan, big enough for all the salmon pieces. Arrange the salmon, skin down, on the salt, and cover with the remaining mixture, and stand in the refrigerator for 3 to 4 days. Remove the salmon from the salt when you are going to serve it. Wipe it with absorbent paper, remove the skin and cut into very thin slices.

Yields 18 brioches (1 recipe)
Preparation time 20 minutes + 2 hours to rise
Cooking time 20 minutes
Suitable for freezing
Degree of Difficulty ♥♥

- 2 tablespoons active dry yeast or 2oz (60g) fresh yeast
- 1⅓ cups warm milk (100°F or 40°C)
- 6 cups all purpose flour
- 1½ teaspoons salt
- 3 tablespoons sugar
- 1/4 cup melted butter
- 2 eggs and 4 egg yolks
- 2/3 cup cold butter, in pieces
- sesame or poppy seeds, to sprinkle

1. Dissolve the yeast in the milk and let stand until risen and frothy, about 10 minutes. Place the flour in the mixer bowl, make a hole in the middle and pour in the risen yeast and all the other ingredients, except the butter and seeds.

2. Beat the ingredients in the mixer using a dough hook for 10 minutes, until you have a smooth and elastic dough, that is not too sticky. Make a few holes in the dough with your fingers, and place the pieces of cold butter inside. Then beat again until the butter is mixed into the dough.

3. Transfer the dough to a buttered bowl, coat the surface with a little melted butter and cover with cling film. Stand for 2 hours, until double in size. Cut small balls, the size of a tangerine, off the dough, and place each one in the heart-shaped molds of a well-buttered muffin tray.

4. Cover the brioches in the pan and leave to rise for 20 minutes. Coat with egg yolk mixed with 1 teaspoon water and sprinkle with sesame or poppy seeds. Bake at 350°F (180°C) for 15 to 20 minutes, until golden brown. Once cold, store in the freezer, in plastic food bags.

Crayfish with Zabaglione sauce

Yields 12 portions
Preparation time 30 minutes
Cooking time 25 minutes
Degree of Difficulty ♥♥

- 24 large crayfish
- 24 prawns, shelled and deveined
- 3 tablespoons salted butter
- salt and white pepper
- 4 egg yolks
- 2 cups Champagne
- 1/2 cup double cream
- 1 jar red caviar and a few sprigs tarragon for garnishing

1. Boil the crayfish in salted water for 15 minutes. Strain and remove the flesh from the pincers and tails by splitting their underbellies, taking care not to damage the shells. Remove the black intestine. Keep the shell with the pincers for decorating.
2. Melt the butter in a large skillet and sauté the prawns for 4 minutes. Add the crayfish flesh and sauté for 2 more minutes. Season with salt and white pepper. Remove the seafood to a plate using a slotted spoon.
3. Pour the champagne into the skillet and simmer over medium heat, until half of it evaporates. Add the cream and stir briskly over the heat until warm but not boiling. Transfer the mixture to a double boiler.
4. Beat the egg yolks lightly in a bowl and pour in a few spoonfuls of the warm mixture. Then pour into the pan with the remaining mixture and stir briskly until thick. Whisk for 5 to 10 minutes. The mixture should be thick and airy. Prepare this sauce just before serving.
5. Serve the seafood on plates and pour over the warm sauce. Decorate the plates with the crayfish shells, a few sprigs of tarragon and a little red caviar.

Consommé with black truffle and foie gras ravioli

Yields 10 portions
Preparation time 1 hour
Cooking time 30 minutes
Degree of Difficulty ♥♥

For the consommé
• 2 liters (8 cups) meat stock
• 2 egg whites
• salt and white pepper
• 5 black truffles

For the ravioli
• 20 wonton wrappers, thawed if frozen, or
  1 recipe pasta dough (recipe on page 170)
• 1 egg white for brushing
• 7oz (200g) foie gras

1. Bring the stock to the boil. Whisk the egg whites lightly and add to the stock. Bring the mixture to the boil over medium heat, stirring constantly. When it starts to boil, stop stirring. Simmer until all the egg froth solidifies and rises to the surface.
2. Remove from the heat and stand for 10 minutes, until cool. Strain the stock through two sheets absorbent kitchen paper, until the stock is transparent. Repeat the process with clean paper if necessary. Season the consommé and serve immediately or refrigerate until the next day.
3. If you like, prepare the ravioli with home-made pasta dough. If you use wonton wrappers, arrange half the wrappers on the work surface and brush their edges with a little egg white. Place 1 tablespoon foie gras in the center and cover with the remaining wrappers. Press down so the wrappers stick to each other with the egg white.
4. Pour the consommé into a clean pan and bring to the boil. Add the ravioli. Boil for 5 minutes. Remove from the heat, season, and serve in soup plates with pieces of black truffle.

Iles flottantes d'amour with raspberry sauce

Yields 6 portions
Preparation time 30 minutes
Cooking time 30 minutes
Refrigeration time 12 hours
Degree of Difficulty ♥♥

For the crème anglaise
• 9 egg yolks
• 1 cup castor sugar
• 2 teaspoons vanilla essence
• 2 cups milk, boiled
• 1 cup double cream

For the meringue
• 6 egg whites
• 1/2 teaspoon cream of tartar
• 1/2 teaspoon vanilla powder or essence
• 1 cup castor sugar
• 1/8 teaspoon salt

For serving
• 10oz (300g) fresh raspberries
• 1/4 cup icing sugar

1. Prepare the crème anglaise custard. Beat the egg yolks with the sugar and vanilla until thick and frothy, add the warm milk and double cream and stir the mixture over a double boiler or very low heat, until thick enough to cover the spoon. The mixture must not boil. Remove the saucepan with the custard from the heat, and sink it in a pan of cold water, to cool down and avoid curdling. Cover the surface with cling film and stand in the refrigerator for 12 hours.

2. A few hours before serving the dessert, beat the egg whites with the cream of tartar until frothy. Add half the sugar and beat to a thick, stiff meringue. Add the remaining sugar and vanilla and stir the mixture for a few seconds, to fold in the sugar.

3. Fill a large deep skillet half-way with water, about 2 inches (5cm) deep. Heat the water until bubbles form at the bottom of the skillet. Dip a spoon into warm water and then into the meringue mixture. Take spoonfuls of the meringue and drop them into the skillet a few at a time. Lower the heat, as the water must not boil. Poach the meringues for 2 or 3 minutes on each side. Remove onto a tray lined with non-stick paper. You should have 24 1½-inch (4-cm) meringues.

4. Divide the custard into soup plates or deep bowls and place 4 meringues in each, to form a cross. Decorate with a few fresh raspberries. Purée the remaining raspberries with the icing sugar to make the sauce. Draw small hearts with the sauce, using a cocktail stick, between the meringues. Serve the rest of the raspberry sauce in a sauce boat.

Venison with pears, champignons du forêt and cranberry sauce

Yields 10 portions
Preparation time 24 hours
Cooking time 1 hour and 30 minutes
Degree of Difficulty ♥♥

- 1 large venison fillet (2 pounds or 1kg)
- 2 tablespoons green peppercorns
- 1 tablespoon pink peppercorns
- 1/4 teaspoon ground nutmeg and cloves
- 1/8 teaspoon ground allspice
- salt and freshly ground pepper
- 2 cups dry red wine
- 10 green onions, chopped
- 2/3 cup unsalted butter
- 1 cup canned whole cranberries with their juice
- 1/2 cup freshly squeezed orange juice
- 1oz (50g) dried mushrooms, cèpes, shiitake or chanterelles
- 10 small pears, peeled and cleaned, cut in half

1. Crush the peppercorns and mix with the spices and a little salt. Cover the fillet with this mixture, pour over the wine and stand in the refrigerator for 24 hours. Drain and keep the marinade.

2. Sauté the onions in half the butter, add half the marinade and simmer until half the liquid has evaporated. Add salt, pepper and the cranberries. Keep boiling until the sauce thickens. Transfer the remaining marinade to a bowl, mix with the orange juice and place the mushrooms in this mixture to swell.

3. Melt the remaining butter in a large non-stick pan with a heavy bottom. Sauté both sides of the fillet in the butter. Pour over the marinade with the mushrooms. Add the pears. Cover and simmer the meat for 25 to 30 minutes, until almost cooked. The inside must be pink.

4. Transfer the fillet and pears to a large ovenproof dish, pour over the sauce and keep warm at 300°F (150°C), covered with aluminum foil, until ready to serve. Serve the fillet carved in very thin slices. Serve the sauce in a sauce boat.

Stuffed quail with rose petals

Yields 8 portions
Preparation time 1 hour
Cooking time 2 hours
Degree of Difficulty ♥♥

- 8 quail, cleaned
- 4 tablespoons Dijon mustard
- 2/3 cup butter or margarine, in pieces
- 1 clove garlic, crushed
- 1 medium onion, grated
- salt, pepper, crushed thyme
- 1 bay leaf, crumbled
- 1/4 teaspoon each ground allspice, nutmeg, cinnamon
- 1/2 cup rosé wine
- 1½ cups chicken stock
- 1/2 recipe wild rice and cèpe stuffing (recipe on page 201)
- rose petals for garnishing

1. If you are using frozen quail, defrost and remove the giblets carefully. If you like, keep the heart and liver, chop finely, season, steam, and add to the filling. If you are using fresh quail, clean carefully, cut the birds open using scissors and cutting along the side, and remove the giblets carefully, taking care not to break the bile sac, because the meat will go bitter. Rinse carefully.

2. Fill the quail with 2 or 3 spoonfuls of stuffing, taking care not to use too much. Tie the legs together and arrange the birds in a buttered baking pan, with the stomach facing up. Place the rest of the stuffing in the pan about the birds.

3. Melt the margarine in a large pan. Sauté the onion and garlic. Add the spices and wine and stir over high heat for 2 minutes. Add the stock, salt and freshly ground pepper and simmer for 15 minutes. Pour the sauce into the pan, over the quail and stuffing.

4. Cover with aluminum foil and bake at 350°F (170°C) for 2 hours, until the meat is practically falling off the bones. Serve warm with the stuffing and decorate the plates with well-washed edible white rose petals.

Yields 16 thin slices, for a buffet
Preparation time 30 minutes
Cooking time 35 minutes
Degree of Difficulty ♥♥

- 1 large beef fillet
  (3 pounds or 1½kg)
- 1/3 cup butter
- 5oz (150g) foie gras
- 4-5 black truffles, sliced
- 12 bacon rashers

**For the béarnaise sauce
with green pepper**
- 1/2 cup white vinegar
- 1 cup dry white wine
- 1/3 cup finely chopped
  green onions
- 1 teaspoon crushed dried tarragon
  or thyme
- 2 tablespoons green and
  black peppercorns
- 8 egg yolks
- 2 cups unsalted butter, in pieces
- a little salt and pepper
- 1/4 cup coarsely ground
  green pepper

1. Prepare the sauce just before serving and keep warm in a double boiler. Place the vinegar, wine, green onions, tarragon or thyme and peppercorns in a pan and simmer uncovered, until half the liquid has evaporated. Strain and leave to cool. Beat the egg yolks in a small pan over a double boiler and add the liquid. Stir over low heat until the mixture thickens. Add the pieces of butter a few at a time, stirring constantly, until all the butter is absorbed and the sauce turns creamy. Remove from the heat and season with salt and pepper. Add and stir in the green pepper.

2. Cut the fillet open lengthways down the middle, without separating the two pieces. Open and beat lightly with a meat hammer, to form a thick oblong sheet. Spread the inside with foie gras, without covering the edges. Place the truffle slices along the center of the foie gras, one next to the other. Lift the sides of the meat and join them over the stuffing to form a roll.

3. Tie the roll with thread and cover with bacon slices. Tie again with thread. Bake at 425°F (220°C), just long enough for the meat to go golden brown but remain rare in the middle. Take out of the oven and remove the bacon and thread. Serve the fillet cut in slices on a réchaud platter, together with Anna potatoes with salmon. Serve the béarnaise sauce separately in a sauce boat.

Anna potatoes with smoked salmon

Yields 12 small soufflés
Preparation time 1 hour
Cooking time 45 to 50 minutes
Degree of Difficulty ♥♥

• 4 pounds (2kg) potatoes, very thinly sliced
• 1 cup clarified butter, cold
• 1 cup olive oil
• salt and black pepper
• 2 cups grated sweet kefalotyri cheese
• 1 pound 10oz (800g), finely chopped smoked salmon
• 4 cups double cream
• 1 cup finely chopped dill

1. Dry the potato slices well with absorbent kitchen paper. Heat half the butter with the oil and sauté the potatoes lightly, stirring constantly and separating the slices with a metal spatula.

2. Remove the potatoes from the heat and leave to cool so that you can handle them. Butter 12 soufflé dishes and line the bottoms and sides with non-stick paper. There should be about 1 inch (2cm) of paper lining left above the sides of each dish. Butter the paper.

3. Place one large potato slice at the bottom of each soufflé dish. Sprinkle with 1 teaspoon grated cheese and cover with a little smoked salmon. Sprinkle again with cheese and cover with another potato slice. Repeat the layers until you have almost reached the rim of the dish.

4. Melt the remaining butter and leave to cool. Mix with the cream and dill and pour the mixture over the soufflés, pushing the potatoes aside with a knife so that the sauce reaches the bottom. You will need about 1/3 cup cream for each soufflé.

5. Bake the soufflés in the oven at 425°F (220°C) for 10 minutes, lower the heat to 350°F (180°C) and keep cooking for another 35 to 40 minutes. Remove from the oven and stand for 10 minutes before unmolding onto a stainless steel serving platter. Can be reheated before serving or kept warm. Grill for 5 minutes, if you like, for a golden color.

Millefeuilles with phyllo pastry, frangipane cream and sugared baby roses

Yields 12 portions
Preparation time 1 hour
Degree of Difficulty ♥♥♥

- 4 thin sheets Beirut-type phyllo pastry
- 1/3 cup melted unsalted butter
- icing sugar for sprinkling
- 1 cup pomegranate seeds, for garnishing
- 12 sugared baby roses

For the syrup
- 1 cup sugar
- 1/2 cup water
- 1 tablespoon lemon juice

- a little vanilla essence

For the bitter almond cream
- 1/2 cup sugar
- 6 egg yolks
- 5 tablespoons corn-starch
- 2 cups milk
- 1 vanilla pod, split
- 1 tablespoon unsalted butter
- 1/2 teaspoon bitter almond essence
- 3 tablespoons Amaretto liqueur
- 2 cups whipped cream

1. Spread each pastry sheet in a buttered baking pan, and brush the surface with melted butter. Using a sharp knife, mark each sheet into 2-inch (5-cm) square pieces. Bake the pastry sheets at 400°F (200°C) for 10 minutes. Remove from the oven and leave to cool. Place in a cookie tin and keep until needed. Will keep in the freezer for several months. Before serving, drizzle each pastry piece with a little syrup, prepared by boiling all the ingredients together for 7 minutes. Stack the caramelized phyllo pieces together, three at a time.

2. Prepare the cream. In a large bowl, beat the egg yolks with the sugar, corn-starch and a pinch of salt, until thick and lemon-colored. Boil the milk and, stirring briskly, pour it into the egg yolk mixture, a spoonful at a time.

3. Remove the cream to a pan with a heavy bottom, add the opened vanilla pod and boil the mixture over very low heat until set, stirring constantly so that it doesn't stick to the bottom. It must simmer for 10 to 15 minutes, so that it doesn't smell of egg. Remove from the heat, add and mix in the butter, bitter almond essence and liqueur.

4. Cover the surface with cling film and refrigerate for up to 2 days. Just before using, mix in the whipped cream. Fill a piping bag using a No. 8B nozzle. Place 2 or 3 caramelized pastry sheets one on top of the other on a plate. Pipe out a cream rosette and cover with another 2 or 3 sheets. Repeat the layers ending with the pastry sheets. Sprinkle with icing sugar and garnish with sugared baby roses and pomegranate seeds.

Meringue hearts

Preparation time several hours
Degree of Difficulty ♥♥

- 2 recipes meringue (recipe on page 241)
- 1 recipe egg icing (recipe on page 182)
- good quality white cardboard

1. Draw and cut out 40 heart shapes on the cardboard, about 4 inches (10cm) each. Prepare the meringue and pipe out 40 meringue hearts using a #8B nozzle onto non-stick paper spread in baking pans. Bake the hearts at 200°F (90°C) for 2 hours, turn off the oven and leave to dry for 1 day in the oven.

2. Prepare the egg icing and coat the cardboard hearts with it, on one side. Stick a meringue heart onto each shape, handling with care so as not to break it and stand in a cool dry place for 1 or 2 days. Tie each heart with pink or dark red satin or velvet ribbons and hang them onto your guests' chairs as decorations, together with miniature bunches of roses prepared by your florist.

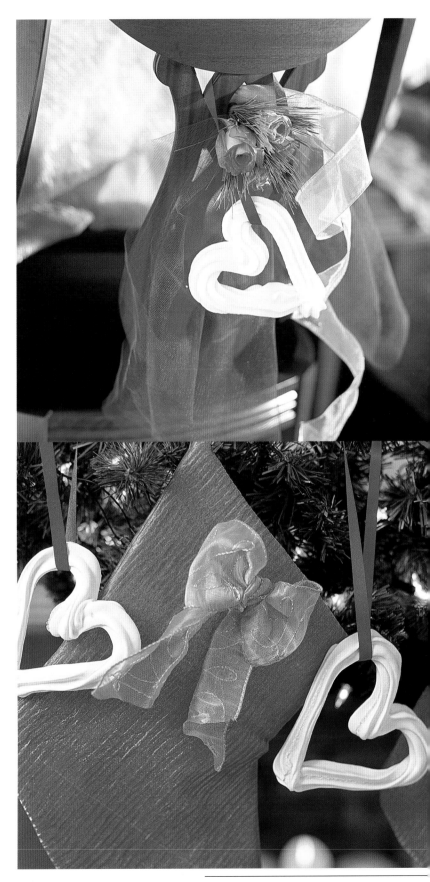

Wild rice, cèpe and chestnut stuffing

Will stuff a 14-pound (7kg) goose or turkey
Preparation time 30 minutes
Degree of Difficulty ♥

- 1 cup wild rice mixed with white long-grain rice
- 3 cups chicken stock
- 7oz (200g) bacon, finely chopped
- 7oz (200g) cleaned, boiled chestnuts
- 1oz (30g) dried cèpes (porcini)
- 1/2 cup dry white wine
- 1/4 cup butter
- 2 medium shallots, finely chopped
- 1 celery stick, finely chopped
- 1 tablespoon finely chopped garlic
- 1/2 teaspoon each crushed dried thyme, rosemary, sage
- 1/3 cup finely chopped parsley
- salt and freshly ground pepper

1. If you intend to bake the stuffing inside the bird, place the rice and stock in a large pan and simmer, until all the water is absorbed. If you are going to prepare the stuffing in a pan, add 1 more cup of stock and simmer as above.

2. Sauté the bacon in a small skillet, until crunchy. Add the chestnuts and stir over high heat for 2 minutes. Soak the mushrooms in the wine for 20 minutes. Drain and reserve the wine.

3. Melt the butter in a large pan and sauté the mushrooms, finely chopped, the onions, celery and garlic, until soft. Pour over the wine and stir for a few minutes over high heat. Remove from the heat, add and mix in the herbs, bacon and chestnuts. Mix the rice with all the sautéed ingredients in a large pan, and season to taste.

Croquembouche

Yields 60 large choux
Preparation time several hours
Degree of Difficulty ♥♥♥♥

- 4 recipes choux pastry (recipe on page 183)
- 2 recipes crème pâtissière (recipe on page 240)
- 2 cups whipped cream
- 2 recipes royal icing (recipe on page 183)
- 7 drops red food coloring,
  3 drops blue food coloring
- 30 large pink marzipan roses (recipe follows)

1. Prepare the choux pastry and fill a piping bag with a No. 1A or 1B nozzle. Spread non-stick paper in 4 cookie sheets and pipe our walnut-sized rosettes, at small distances from each other. Bake the choux at 425°F (220°C) for 15 minutes, reduce the temperature to 300°F (150°C), and keep baking for another 20 minutes, until golden brown.

2. Prepare the crème pâtissière, cover with cling film and stand in the refrigerator until cold. Mix with the whipped cream. To fill the choux, leave to cool and make a hole in the top with a wooden skewer. Put the cream in a piping bag and fill the choux. Refrigerate for 1 hour.

3. Prepare the royal icing and color with red and blue food coloring, so that it has a pinkish tint. Coat a glass dish with icing and stick the first layer of choux onto it, in a circle covering the entire surface. Pour over a little liquid icing and stick on another layer of choux. Repeat the process until you run out of choux. Pour the remaining icing over the choux cone. If you find it hard to get the layers to stick, refrigerate the dish for a while to stabilize the layers, and keep going.

4. Place the marzipan roses about the cone, using a little royal icing. The dessert will keep in the refrigerator for 1 day.

Marzipan roses

Yields 15 large or 30 small roses
Preparation time 1 hour
Degree of Difficulty ♥

- 8oz (250g) natural-colored marzipan
- 3 drops red food coloring
- 1 drop blue food coloring
- a little icing sugar
- round pastry cutters, 1 inch (2cm) and
  1½ inch (3cm)
- small rolling pin

1. Make a hole in the center of the marzipan and pour in the coloring. Knead the dough inwards with your hands, first in a bowl and then on a surface sprinkled with a little icing sugar, until the color is uniform. For chocolate dough, mix the marzipan with 1½oz (50g) melted chocolate.

2. Roll out pieces of marzipan on a surface sprinkled with icing sugar, using a mini rolling pin. Make very thin sheets of marzipan and cut out circles using both the pastry cutters.

3. Put a little water in a small bowl. Wet your fingers and roll up a small circle. Stick on another small circle to make a rosebud. Wet your fingers again and stick 4 small circles and 4 large ones about the bud, turning it every time you stick on a new circle. In this way you can make an open-petalled rose.

4. Leave the roses to harden on non-stick paper. Will keep for up to one month in a cookie tin.

Raspberry champagne sorbet

Yields 10 champagne sorbets
Preparation time 1 hour
Freezing time 12 hours
Degree of Difficulty ♥

- 1 cup sour cherry juice
- 2/3 cup sugar
- 1/3 cup frozen raspberries or strawberries
- 2 cups Champagne
- 1 egg white beaten with 1/4 teaspoon cream of tartar

1. Boil the cherry juice with the sugar for 10 minutes in a small pan, until a thick syrup is formed. Remove from the heat and leave to cool. Pour the syrup into the mixer bowl, together with the fruit and champagne, and beat to a uniform mixture. Pour the mixture into a metal ice-cream container and freeze for several hours.

2. Beat the egg white and cream of tartar to a stiff meringue. Remove the champagne sorbet from the freezer and defrost for 20 minutes. Pour into the mixer bowl, beat and then fold in the meringue. Freeze the mixture again for 2 hours. Take out, beat in the mixer and freeze once again. Serve scoops of the sorbet in champagne glasses between courses, to cleanse the palate.

Madeleines

Yields 36 madeleines
Preparation time 20 minutes
Cooking time 10 minutes
Degree of Difficulty ♥♥

- 4 eggs
- 1/4 teaspoon salt
- 1 cup castor sugar
- 1 cup soft cake flour (not self-raising)
- 1 teaspoon vanilla powder
- 1/4 cup melted butter

1. Beat the eggs with the salt and sugar for about 10 minutes, until double in volume. Sift the flour and vanilla into the mixture and stir in with gentle strokes. Finally, add the melted butter and mix lightly into the mixture, taking care not to deflate the eggs.

2. Butter and flour 3 12-case mini madeleine baking pans, and fill the cases with the mixture. Bake the cookies for 10 minutes at 350°F (180°C). Unmold, sprinkle with icing sugar and serve. Will keep fresh for a few days stored in a cookie tin.

Poached vanilla pears

Yields 24 portions
Preparation time 30 minutes
Cooking time 1 hour

- 24 well-shaped pears,
  not too large
- 2/3 cup freshly squeezed
  lemon juice
- 24 sprigs mint for decorating
- 1 recipe zabaglione,
  for serving

For the syrup
- 4 pounds (2kg) castor sugar
- 2 liters water
- 2 bottles good quality
  white wine
- 8 vanilla pods, split
- zest of 1 lemon

1. Peel the pears and coat with lemon juice so that they don't go black. Using a corer or sharp knife, remove the pips from the bottom.
2. Place all the syrup ingredients in a large deep pan and simmer for 30 minutes. Add the pears, as many as will fit in the pan at a time, and simmer for another 30 minutes, until half the syrup has been absorbed. Move the pears to a serving platter. Strain the syrup. Serve the pears decorated with a sprig of mint sprinkled with icing sugar and pour over some zabaglione, prepared just before serving.

Zabaglione

- 6 egg yolks
- 2/3 cup fine sugar
- 1 cup Champagne or Marsala or port or
  good quality semi-sweet wine
- a little vanilla powder

1. Beat the egg yolks and sugar in a double boiler, until the sugar melts and the mixture is thick and lemon-colored.
2. Add the wine little by little, beating constantly with a whisk, until the mixture is white, frothy and twice its original volume, about 5 minutes.
3. Add the vanilla and beat for another 5 to 10 minutes, until thick but light and airy. The mixture must be frothy, as its name originates from the Neapolitan "zapillare", which means to froth. Yields about 4 cups zabaglione.

Coeurs à la crème with raspberry sauce

Yields 6 hearts
Preparation time 15 minutes
Refrigeration time 6 hours
Degree of Difficulty ♥

- 8oz (250g) cream cheese
- 8oz (250g) ricotta or anthotyro cheese
- 2/3 cup icing sugar
- 1 cup Greek strained yogurt or 1/2 cup strained yogurt and 1/2 cup crème fraîche
- 1 teaspoon vanilla essence
- 1 tablespoon orange juice
- 2 teaspoons orange zest

For the sauce
- 2 cups fresh raspberries
- 1/2 cup icing sugar
- 2-3 tablespoons Grand Marnier

1. Cream both cheeses with the sugar in the mixer. Add the yogurt, vanilla essence, juice and orange zest, and beat until you obtain a homogeneous mixture.

2. Line a 6-heart baking pan with veiling, cheesecloth or thin gauze, leaving plenty of material at the sides. Divide the mixture between the 6 shapes, and cover with another piece of double veiling. Pull the material tight and fasten it at the back of the pan, so that, when overturned, the cheese mixture remains in the pan. Place the pan upside down in a tray, so that the liquid can drain out, and refrigerate this way for 4 to 6 hours. If you wish, use special heart-shaped French pottery for straining the coeurs à la crème.

3. Prepare the raspberry sauce. Mix 2/3 of the raspberries together with the sugar and liqueur in the blender. Mix the remaining whole raspberries in with the sauce.

4. Unmold the hearts onto a platter by carefully removing the veiling. Serve on dessert plates with the raspberry sauce.

Fondant tree

Yields 60 fondants
Preparation time 2 hours
Degree of Difficulty ♥♥

For the pink fondants
- 7oz (200g) unsweetened shredded coconut
- 7oz (200g) blanched almonds
- 1/2 cup sugar
- 1½ sachets powdered strawberry jelly (5oz or 150g)
- 1 tin condensed milk
- 2 teaspoons vanilla essence
- 5 drops red food coloring
- 2 teaspoons strawberry essence

For the colored sugar
- 1/2 cup fine sugar
- a few drops red food coloring

1. Place the coconut, almonds, sugar and jelly powder in the food processor bowl and pulse to a smooth powder. Transfer the mixture to a clean bowl, add the vanilla essence, food coloring and strawberry essence, and as much milk as necessary to blend the ingredients to a stiff mixture, which can be kneaded and is not too sticky.

2. Place the sugar in a clean bowl and color it pink with 1 or 2 drops red food coloring. Make small balls out of the dough, the size of a grape, and roll each in the sugar. To make the fondant trees you will need 2 Styrofoam cones, 12 inches (30cm) tall and 4 recipes each of red and green fondants. Cover the cones with silver or pink shiny paper and affix the fondants using small cocktail sticks. Will keep for a few days without being refrigerated. The longer they stand, the harder they get. Serve the fondant trees when welcoming your guests with a glass of champagne.

3. Alternatively, prepare the green fondants using lime jelly or gelatine instead of strawberry jelly (10 sachets or 10 tablespoons powdered gelatine), and replace the strawberry essence with lime zest or peppermint essence. Instead of red food coloring use green to color the mixture and prepare green sugar for coating the fondants.

THE EXOTIC WEDDING IV.

"What was I looking for when you arrived tinted by the sunrise
With the age of the sea in your eyes
And the health of the sun in your body – what was I looking for
Deep in the sea-caves, in the spacious dreams
Where the wind foamed with emotions
Unknown and deep blue, carving my chest with its
Ocean emblem"

Odisseas Elitis

Why marry anywhere, when you can marry in paradise? Choose one of Greece's magical beaches as a backdrop for the most beautiful and romantic day of your life.

The most romantic wedding imaginable is one where the sea breeze plays with your hair, the saltiness of the sea caresses your skin, and the sand forms the softest carpet for the most important steps you'll ever take. Modern and casual, a wedding on the beach can be as formal and luxurious as you want, without, of course, overstepping the limits of good taste. For modern brides who dream of soft sandals, and grooms who don't want to stick to the traditional rules of wedding attire, a wedding by the sea provides the freedom for original choices. Choose wreaths made of fresh flowers, and instead of a bouquet, hold a single flower, or a bunch of wildflowers growing on the seaside.

The wedding can take place in a chapel, not necessarily near to where you are holding the reception, and the bride and groom can be taken to the beach on a caique or a sailing boat. The young bridesmaids can wear floaty dresses in the colors of the sea – turquoise, sea green, violet or lilac, and hold baskets of rice and wildflower petals, just like little ethereal fairies.

In a scenery as rich in sensual pleasures as the sea, the beach, and the sunset, only minor decorations are needed in order to compose a Shakespearean evening, right out of A Midsummer Night's Dream. Tables set on the beach, with blue and white tablecloths, seafood delicacies, huge candlesticks lighting the tables and blue tulle on the buffet, give the evening a sensual note. Splendid vases filled with blue water and exotic flowers, a large white marquee for protection from the afternoon sun, and torches coloring the night, are just a few touches that can complete the magic of the scenery.

In the spirit of contradiction characterizing the reception, instead of a pastel and white cake reflecting the bride's virtue, you can have a huge chocolate cake dedicated entirely to the groom.

The choice of music can be anything from jazz, to melodious Greek music, ethnic rhythms or orchestrated classical music for the sunset and for cutting the cake. The fun can escalate with passionate Latin sounds. A pyramid of wine-glasses to be filled after cutting the wedding cake, adds a note of luxury. The champagne will flow like gold-dust in the iridescence of the sunset, and everyone will be enchanted by the spectacle. If you are a free spirit, and a lover of natural beauty, dare to make a difference on your wedding day, with an unforgettable reception.

Tomatillos with exotic guacamole

For a buffet
Preparation time 30 minutes
Degree of Difficulty ♥

For the exotic guacamole
- 4 large ripe avocados
- 1/3 cup lime juice
- 1 ripe mango, peeled and chopped
- 10 drops Tabasco sauce
- 1/3 cup finely chopped fresh cilantro
- 6 green onions, finely chopped
- salt and white pepper
- 50 tomatillos

1. Peel and stone the avocados and pour over the lime juice immediately. If you can't get limes, use lemon juice. Place the avocados in the mixer bowl, add the Tabasco and purée. Transfer to a clean bowl and combine with the green onions and cilantro. Season to taste.

2. Wash and dry the tomatillos. Cut a slice horizontally off the top and remove the insides with a spoon, taking care not to break the skin. Sprinkle the insides with a little salt, and place the tomatillos upside down on a grid to drain. Mash the tomato pieces you have removed, and mix them with the avocado mixture. Rinse the tomatillos and stuff them with the avocado mixture using a teaspoon. Serve on a platter.

3. Another easy idea for stuffed tomatillos is, once emptied, to fill them with a piece of mozzarella, 1/4 teaspoon pesto sauce, and garnish with sprigs of fresh basil, (photo on page 162).

Petits coeurs à la crème du saumon

For a buffet
Preparation time 30 minutes
Refrigeration time 4 hours
Degree of Difficulty ♥

• 14oz (400g) smoked salmon
• 1 small shallot, grated
• 1 pound 2oz (600g) ricotta or anthotyro or cream cheese
• 1 cup Greek strained yogurt
• 2 teaspoons gelatine, swollen in
  2 tablespoons water and heated until clear
• 1 teaspoon salt and
  1/4 teaspoon white pepper
• miniature round rice croquettes or cucumber slices for serving
• 1 jar red caviar for garnishing

1. Cream the salmon in the mixer. Add the onion, ricotta, yogurt, clear gelatine mixture, salt and pepper, and blend with the salmon cream. Place spoonfuls of the mixture into the cases of 6 mini heart or shell baking pans (12 cavities each), after having sprayed them with oil or brushed them with a little corn oil. Refrigerate the pans for several hours, or until the next day, to set.
2. For easy unmolding, place the blade of a knife between the cheese and the pan, to let the air in. Unmold and serve each mini cheese on a round miniature rice croquette. If you like, serve the hearts on slices of cucumber and garnish with a little red caviar.

Yields 25 miniature rolls
Preparation time 30 minutes
Frying time 20 minutes
Suitable for freezing
Degree of Difficulty ♥♥

- 25 square wonton wrappers (frozen)
- 2 tablespoons corn oil
- 2 cloves garlic, crushed
- 2 teaspoons freshly grated gingerroot
- 1/2 cup sliced fresh mushrooms
- 2 green onions, cut in julienne pieces
- 1/2 cup finely shredded white cabbage
- 1/3 cup blanched bean sprouts
- 1/3 cup finely chopped blanched leek
- 3 tablespoons soy sauce
- 1/2 teaspoon salt
- 1 tablespoon corn-starch diluted in 1 tablespoon water
- sweet and sour sauce or sweet chili sauce for serving

1. Heat the corn oil in a wok. Sauté the garlic and ginger. Add the mushrooms and onions and sauté for 2 minutes. Add the cabbage, bean sprouts and leek and sauté for another 3 minutes. Pour over the soy sauce, add and mix in the salt and corn-starch. Let the mixture simmer over low heat until it thickens.

2. Defrost the wonton wrappers. Place 1-2 teaspoons filling on one side of each square wrapper, and fold the edges right and left over the filling, so that it doesn't spill when frying. Roll up and seal by brushing the edges with a little water. Roll up all the wrappers in the same way.

3. Place the spring rolls on a plate sprinkled with corn-starch, so that they don't stick. At this stage, they can be stored in the freezer for 2 months. Fill 1/3 of the wok with corn or sunflower oil, and once sizzling, fry the spring rolls for 3 to 5 minutes, until golden brown. Serve with sweet and sour sauce or sweet chili sauce.

Prawn cocktail in crunchy nests

For a buffet
Preparation time 40 minutes
Degree of Difficulty ♥♥

For the prawn salad
• 1 pound (500g) Beirut-type (very thin) phyllo pastry
• a little olive oil, for brushing
• 24 large prawns, shelled and deveined
• 2 cups finely chopped lettuce
• 2 medium carrots, finely chopped
• 1/4 cup finely chopped gherkins
• 1/4 cup finely chopped cilantro or parsley

For the spicy cocktail sauce
• 1 cup mayonnaise
• 2 tablespoons ketchup
• 10 drops Tabasco sauce
• 3 tablespoons chili sauce
• 1 teaspoon grated fresh gingerroot
• 1 teaspoon horseradish sauce
• salt and freshly ground black pepper

1. Mix all the cocktail sauce ingredients together and stand in the refrigerator for 30 minutes. Boil the prawns, once you have cleaned them, together with the heads. Drain, discard the heads and chop the meat up. Mix with half the lettuce, the sauce and the remaining ingredients.

2. Join the pastry sheets in pairs, brushing with a little olive oil in between. Cut 4-inch (10-cm) squares out of the sheets. Place one square on top of another, to form 8-pointed stars. Join the two squares with a little water and place each star in the oiled grooves of a mini-muffin pan. Bake at 400°F (200°C) for 10 minutes, or until golden-brown.

3. Unmold the phyllo nests and leave to cool. Fill just before serving, so that they do not get soggy. Do not refrigerate. Place a little dry lettuce at the bottom and cover with one or two teaspoons of prawn cocktail. Garnish with cucumber cut in julienne pieces and halved olives stuffed with red pepper.

Thai rolls with roast duck

For a buffet
Preparation time 1 hour
Cooking time 50 minutes
Degree of Difficulty ♥♥

- 10 boned duck breasts (around 4 pounds – 2kg – lean meat)
- 1 teaspoon Chinese 5-spices
- 4 tablespoons grated fresh gingerroot
- 1/3 cup golden syrup or honey
- 1/4 cup soy sauce
- 12 green onions, cut in julienne pieces
- 4 medium cucumbers, cut in julienne pieces
- 20 Thai rice pancakes for spring rolls or crépes or Mandarina pancakes

For the sauce
- 3 tablespoons sugar
- 2 cups soy sauce
- 1/2 cup black bean sauce
- 1 tablespoon corn-starch, diluted in 3 tablespoons water

1. Season the duck breasts and rub them with the Chinese 5-spices mixture and the fresh ginger. Coat with the golden syrup or honey and the soy sauce. Make holes in the meat surface with a wooden skewer. If you like, remove the skin and only grill the duck fillets for 30 minutes.

2. Arrange the duck meat with the skin down on a grill and place a pan underneath to collect the meat juices. Grill the duck on the second shelf, not too close to the heat, for 30 to 35 minutes. Move the grill closer to the heat, overturn the meat and crisp the skin for another 15 minutes. Cut the duck meat into very thin strips. Place all the sauce ingredients in a small pan and stir for 5 minutes over low heat, until the sugar dissolves and the sauce thickens.

3. If you are using dry ready-made pancakes, place them in the bamboo steamer over a cabbage leaf, and steam over a wok of boiling water for a few minutes, until soft. Spread a soft pancake on the work surface and brush with a little sauce. Arrange a few pieces of duck, cucumber and onion on it, and roll up tightly. Seal the rolls by brushing the pancake with a little water at the join. Cut the roll in three and stand the pieces in a bamboo steamer lined with a cabbage leaf. When all the rolls are ready, steam them over a wok of boiling water. Serve with the remaining sauce.

Prawn fajitas

For a buffet
Preparation time 30 minutes
Cooking time 30 minutes
Degree of Difficulty ♥♥

- 2/3 cup olive oil
- 6 cloves garlic, crushed
- 2 large Vindalia onions, thinly sliced
- 8 medium peppers, red, green and yellow, cut in julienne pieces
- 20-40 drops Tabasco sauce
- 1/3 cup lime or lemon juice

- 1 teaspoon oregano
- 6 pounds (3kg) medium tiger prawns, shelled and deveined
- 1/2 cup finely chopped fresh cilantro or parsley
- 2 tablespoons sesame seeds

For garnishing
- 24 soft warm tortillas
- 4 medium avocados, peeled and cut in eighths
- 2 cups sweet chili sauce
- 2 cups sour cream

1. Heat the oil in a wok. Add the garlic, onions and peppers and sauté for 8 to 10 minutes, until very soft. Add and mix in the Tabasco, juice, oregano and prawns and simmer for 5 to 6 minutes, until the prawns are cooked. Blend in the cilantro and sesame seeds, and remove from the heat. To fit all the ingredients in the wok, prepare the dish in two doses.

2. Serve the prawns and peppers in an oven-proof dish, set over small candles to keep warm. Accompany with warm tortillas, avocado slices, sour cream and sweet chili sauce. Alternatively, use Greek strained yogurt mixed with a little garlic and finely chopped mint, instead of sour cream.

Chinese 5-flavor chicken

For a buffet
Preparation time 20 minutes
Cooking time 40 minutes
Degree of Difficulty ♥

- 3 pounds (1½ kg) chicken fillet, no skin or bones
- 1 teaspoon salt
- 1 teaspoon freshly ground black pepper
- 1/4 cup corn oil
- 2 teaspoons freshly grated gingerroot
- 1 green chili pepper, finely chopped
- 1 red bell pepper, finely chopped
- 4 green onions, finely chopped
- 1 tablespoon orange zest
- 2 tablespoons sesame seeds

For the sauce
- 1/4 cup soy sauce
- 1/4 cup rice wine or sherry
- 1/2 teaspoon sugar
- 1/4 cup orange juice
- 1/2 cup chicken stock
- 1 teaspoon Chinese 5-spices mixture
- 1 teaspoon sesame oil

1. Wash the chicken well, chop up and season. Heat the oil in a wok and sauté the ginger for 1 minute. Add the chicken and sauté for 8 to 10 minutes. Add the peppers, onions, orange zest and sesame seeds, and stir for 3 minutes.

2. Add all the sauce ingredients except for the sesame oil and mix well. Simmer the chicken in the sauce for 30 minutes, until there is only a little liquid left. Lastly, pour in the sesame oil and remove from the heat. Garnish, if you like, with pieces of orange rind rolled into rosettes. Serve the chicken in a crispy tortilla nest.

Tortilla nest

For the tortilla dough
- 1/2 cup all purpose flour
- 1/2 cup corn-flour (polenta)
- 1/2 teaspoon salt
- 1/4 cup vegetable shortening
- 1/3 cup warm water

1. Sift all the flour and salt into a bowl. Add the butter and knead with your fingers, to make dry crumbles. Add as much water as necessary, to make the dough soft and elastic. Remove to a floured surface, and knead for 3 minutes. Place in a food bag and stand for 15 minutes.

2. Divide the dough into 6 equal parts and roll out into 8-inch

(20-cm) circles. For smaller, 4-inch (10-cm) tortillas, divide the dough into 12 parts. Use the smaller-sized tortillas for the enchilladas.

3. Heat a large non-stick skillet. Do not use butter or oil. Cook the tortillas one by one, turning once, when bubbles start to form on the surface. Once cooked and while still soft, spread two tortillas on the back of two round metal bowls. Brush with a little corn oil and bake at 400°F (200°C) for 15 minutes, or until crisp. Use the two tortilla nests to serve the chicken and cut the rest into triangles while still soft. Deep-fry to make tasty fresh nachos.

Salmon with wild greens

For a buffet
Preparation time 30 minutes
Cooking time 1 hour
Degree of Difficulty ♥

• 2 pounds (1kg) white beets, fennel, Italian greens, blite and other greens
• 1 pound (500g) fresh spinach
• 1 cup olive oil
• salt and freshly ground pepper
• 1 cup finely chopped green onions
• 1/4 cup finely chopped dill
• 6 pounds (3kg) salmon fillet, no skin or bones, chopped in 5-cm pieces
• 1 small clove garlic, crushed
• 1 tablespoon freshly grated gingerroot
• 1/3 cup freshly squeezed lemon juice
• 1 cup finely chopped tomatoes
• 1/3 cup soy sauce

1. Clean the greens and discard all the hard bits. Wash thoroughly, chop up, blanch and drain off all the water. Heat half the oil in a pan and sauté the onions lightly. Add the greens, dill, salt and freshly ground pepper and mix in with the onion. Take spoonfuls of the mixture and arrange them on a large baking pan.
2. Top each stack with a piece of salmon. Heat the remaining oil in a small pan and sauté the garlic and ginger. Add the lemon juice, the tomatoes and soy sauce, a little salt and plenty of pepper. Boil the sauce until quite thick and pour over the fish and greens, a spoonful at a time. Bake at 350°F (180°C) for 1 hour, until there is only a little liquid left. Serve warm or cold.

Neptune Risotto

For a buffet
Preparation time 30 minutes
Cooking time 30 minutes
Degree of Difficulty ♥♥

- 2 cups Thai or Basmati rice
- 1 pound (500g) cleaned mussels
- 14oz (400g) shelled chopped prawns
- 1/2 cup olive oil
- 2 tablespoons grated fresh gingerroot
- 2 cloves garlic, crushed
- 1 red bell pepper, cut in julienne pieces

- 1 cup grated carrot
- 1 cup shredded cabbage
- 1 cup bean sprouts
- 8 green onions, cut in julienne pieces
- 1 teaspoon red chili pepper flakes
- 1/3 cup soy sauce
- 1/4 cup tinned pineapple juice
- 2 tablespoons oyster sauce
- 4 pineapple slices, chopped

1. Place the rice in a pan with 3½ cups water and bring to the boil. Lower the heat and simmer with the lid on, until all the water has been absorbed. Leave to cool. It is better to boil the rice on the previous day and store it in the refrigerator.

2. Wash the mussels thoroughly. Soak in a bowl of water for a while, discard the water, and repeat the process until the water remains clear. Place the mussels and prawns in a saucepan with 1/4 cup water or white wine, over high heat and boil for 4 minutes. Remove to a bowl using a slotted spoon. Wash and drain the sprouts thoroughly.

3. Heat half the oil in a large pan or wok and sauté the ginger, garlic, peppers, carrots, cabbage, sprouts and onions until soft. Transfer to the bowl with the seafood. Pour the remaining oil into the wok and sauté the rice, stirring briskly to heat up. Add and mix in the chili peppers, pineapple juice and sauces.

4. Remove from the heat and combine the rice with the other sautéed ingredients. Add the pineapple pieces and stir. Transfer the mixture to an oiled heart-shaped cake mold. If necessary, reheat the risotto in the mold before serving. Unmold onto a platter. Garnish, if you like, with whole boiled prawns. Equally delicious warm or cold.

Crab Enchilladas

Yields 48 mini enchilladas
Preparation time 30 minutes
Cooking time 20 minutes
Degree of Difficulty ♥♥

For the filling
- 1 tablespoon butter
- 4 green onions, finely chopped
- 14oz (400g) crabmeat
  from boiled crabs,
  or chopped frozen crab substitute
- 1½ cups grated yellow cheddar
- 1 cup finely chopped
  canned mushrooms
- 1/4 cup finely chopped cilantro
  or parsley
- 16 soft tortillas or crépes

For the sauce
- 1 large red bell pepper
- 14oz (400g) canned tomatoes
  with their juice, finely chopped
- 2 tablespoons olive oil
- 3 cloves garlic, crushed
- 1 large onion, finely chopped
- 1/4 cup ketchup
- 20 drops Tabasco sauce
- 1/4 teaspoon ground cumin
- 1 teaspoon coriander powder
- 2 tablespoons white vinegar
- 1 teaspoon sugar or honey
- salt and freshly ground pepper

1. Prepare the enchilladas with fresh crabmeat or frozen crab substitute. Melt the butter in a small skillet and sauté the green onion for the filling. Transfer to a large bowl, add and stir in the crabmeat, 1 cup cheese, the mushrooms and half the herbs.

2. Prepare the sauce. Purée the pepper and tomatoes in the blender. Heat the oil in a small pan and sauté the garlic and onion until golden. Add the tomato purée, ketchup, Tabasco, cumin, coriander, vinegar and sugar. Season to taste. Cover and simmer the sauce for 20 minutes.

3. Brush each tortilla or crépe with two tablespoons sauce. Divide the filling between the tortillas or crépes. Roll up and arrange in a buttered oblong or round ovenproof dish. Pour over the remaining sauce and sprinkle with the rest of the grated cheese. Bake for 20 minutes at 400°F (200°C). Cut each enchilada into three pieces with a sharp knife. Garnish with the remaining fresh cilantro or parsley. Serve warm.

Seared baby lobsters or yabbies

For a buffet
Preparation time 2 hours
Cooking time 20 minutes
Degree of Difficulty ♥♥♥

• 24 live baby lobsters, 2 pounds (1kg) each, or 48 yabbies

For the sauce
• 2 tablespoons corn-starch, diluted in 2 cups soy sauce
• 1/2 cup oyster sauce
• 3 tablespoons dark brown sugar
• 3 tablespoons freshly squeezed lemon juice
• 1 tablespoon freshly grated gingerroot
• 1/2 cup finely chopped green onions
• sprigs of fresh cilantro, to garnish

1. Bring water to the boil in a large pan. Dip in the baby lobsters, a few at a time, head-first, cover, and boil for 10 minutes. The lobster must be half-cooked. Transfer to a colander to drain and cool. At this stage, cut and remove the heads. Break open the pincers, and use the meat for the lobster nachos, as described below. Cut open the tails lengthways using kitchen scissors. Leave the lobster meat in the shells.
2. Prepare the lobsters to this point on the previous day, cover and refrigerate. Prepare the sauce. Place the ingredients in a small pan and simmer, until you have a clear thin sauce. Reserve half the sauce for basting the lobsters while cooking.
3. Grill the opened lobster tails on a double grid over hot charcoal just before serving. Use a special brush to baste them with the reserved sauce. Cook for 4 or 5 minutes on each side, making sure they don't dry out. If you are using yabbies, they will need less cooking. Do not overcook, otherwise the meat will be dry.

Nachos with yabbies or crabmeat and exotic guacamole

Prepare the yabbies and the exotic guacamole according to the recipes in this chapter. Clean the cooked lobster or yabbie pincers, and chop their meat finely. You may add 1 pound (500g) canned crabmeat for extra flavor. Mix with the exotic guacamole. Cut small triangles out of soft tortillas, brush with a little olive oil and toast in the oven. Serve spoonfuls of the guacamole mixture on the toasted nachos as a starter, and garnish with a teaspoon of chili sauce and a little fresh cilantro.

Steamed Pearls

Yields 40 ground meat pearls

Preparation time 30 minutes
Cooking time 40 minutes
Degree of Difficulty ♥

- 1 cup Basmati rice
- 6 green onions, finely chopped
- 2 tablespoons freshly grated gingerroot
- 1 large clove of garlic, crushed
- 14oz (400g) pork or chicken ground meat
- 3 tablespoons oyster sauce
- 1/4 cup finely chopped currants
- 1 teaspoon ground chili peppers
- 1/4 teaspoon salt and white pepper
- 2 tablespoons rice flour
- 2 tablespoons soy sauce
- 2 tablespoons rice wine or medium-dry sherry
- 1 egg
- salt, pepper
- 3 large cabbage leaves and a few sprigs of celery

1. Soak the rice in cold water for 20 minutes. Place the meat in a large bowl, add all remaining ingredients except the cabbage and rice and knead well until blended. Refrigerate for 20 minutes. Then shape the mixture into small pearls, the size of a grape.

2. Spread the rice onto a large shallow plate, and roll the pearls in the rice until covered on all sides. Fill a wok with water and place the bamboo steamer inside. Line the three tiers of the steamer with large cabbage leaves and a few celery sprigs, for flavor, and then arrange the meat pearls on the leaves. Cover and steam the pearls for 40 minutes, until the rice swells.

3. Discard the celery leaves and serve warm, inside the bamboo steamer. This dish can be prepared several hours in advance and stored in the refrigerator for one day. Reheat in the steamer for a few minutes, so that the pearls soften. This Chinese delicacy is named after the precious jewels of the sea, and is served on formal occasions.

Coconut Cream and Raspberry Tartlets

Yields 30 tartlets
Preparation time 2 hours
Degree of Difficulty ♥♥♥

For the pâte brisée
- 1 cup unsalted butter
- 1/3 cup sugar
- 2 egg yolks
- 2 tablespoons Cognac
- 1/2 teaspoon vanilla essence
- 3 cups all-purpose flour
- 1 teaspoon baking powder

For the filling
- 2 cups whipped cream
- 2 teaspoons coconut essence
- 30 large fresh raspberries
- raspberry jam

1. Prepare the tartlets. Beat the butter and sugar together until white and creamy. While beating, add the egg yolks one by one, and then the Cognac and vanilla essence. Stop beating, add the flour in 2 or 3 parts and then mix in for 1 more minute, until the dough has formed a ball around the dough hook.

2. Roll out the pastry in 2 sheets, about 3 mm thick, and cut out 24 round shapes with a pastry cutter. These should be big enough to cover the bottom and the sides of twenty-four 2-inch (5-cm) tartlet molds. Prick the pastry cases all over using a fork and bake the tartlets for 15-20 minutes in a 400°F (200°C) oven, until the surface is golden. Remove from the oven, unmold and arrange on a serving dish.

3. Mix the whipped cream with the coconut essence. With a piping bag, fill the tartlets with the mixture, and pipe a border around each tartlet. Decorate with a raspberry and brush with a little melted jam. Serve cold.

Tiramisu Cake

- 1 cup whipping cream
- 3 tablespoons icing sugar and a little vanilla essence
- 1 pound (500g) mascarpone or cream cheese
- 4 egg yolks and 2 egg whites
- 1/3 cup icing sugar
- 2/3 cup ready-made espresso coffee
- 2/3 cup Amaretto liqueur

1. Whip the cream with the icing sugar, adding a little vanilla essence. Whip the cheese separately until soft and creamy. While beating, add the egg yolks one at a time. Beat the egg whites separately in a clean bowl with clean beaters and add the sugar little by little, to form a stiff meringue. Gently fold the whipped cream into the cheese mixture, and then fold in the meringue again very gently.

2. Mix the coffee and liqueur in a bowl. Dip half the ladyfingers in the liquid for a few seconds to soften, and arrange in a round 9-inch (22-cm) deep pan, about 6 inches (15cm) tall, covered with cling film. Cover with half the cream. Make a layer of the remaining ladyfingers and cover with the rest of the cream. Refrigerate the cake. Once set, unmold onto the top cake tier and remove the cling film.

The recipe continues on page 239.

White Chocolate Cake

- 4 eggs
- 1 cup castor sugar
- 1 teaspoon vanilla essence
- 1 cup self-raising flour
- 1 pound (500g) white chocolate
- 2 tablespoons glucose
- 2 egg yolks
- 2 cups whipping cream
- 1 cup slivered almonds, roasted

1. Prepare the sponge cake. Beat the eggs, sugar and vanilla at the mixer's top speed for about 15 minutes, until fluffy. Sift the flour and add to the egg mixture little by little, continuing to beat at a very low speed. Take care not to deflate the eggs. Place the mixture in a round 11-inch (28-cm) baking pan and bake the cake at 350°F (175°C) for 35 minutes.

2. Melt the chocolate with the glucose in a double boiler or over very low heat. Blend in the egg yolks, stirring a few minutes over the heat, to incorporate into the chocolate mixture. Remove from the heat and let the chocolate mixture cool. Whip the cream in a clean bowl. Pour the melted chocolate into the whipped cream and stir the mixture gently. Add and mix in the almonds.

3. Remove the sponge cake from the oven and unmold onto a platter lined with oven paper sprinkled with icing sugar. Leave to cool and divide into two layers. Join the two layers with the chocolate cream and place the cake onto the middle cake tier. Refrigerate the cake until set.

"Mousse au Chocolat" Cake

- 2 recipes sponge cake (as in white chocolate cake)
- 1 tablespoon gelatine powder
- 1/3 cup milk
- 1/2 cup unsalted butter
- 1/2 cup unsweetened cocoa powder
- 10oz (300g) fine-quality dark chocolate, in pieces
- 2 tablespoons Kahlua
- 2 egg whites
- 1/3 cup castor sugar
- 1 cup whipping cream

1. Prepare the sponge cake as in the white chocolate cake, using 1 1/3 cups flour and 2/3 cup cocoa for a chocolate sponge cake. Divide the mixture into two round 10-inch (25-cm) baking pans, buttered and lined with oven paper. Bake the cakes at 350°F (180°C) for about 30 minutes. Unmold onto oven paper sprinkled with icing sugar and remove the paper from the cakes carefully. Place one of the cakes on the bottom cake tier and enclose it with a metal flan ring.

2. Dilute the gelatine in the milk and leave to swell. Melt the butter and mix with the cocoa. Add and mix in the gelatine and stir until it dissolves. Then add the chocolate and stir until it melts. Remove from the heat, mix in the liqueur and leave to cool.

3. Beat the egg whites with the sugar to a soft meringue. Whip the cream. Fold the whipped cream and then the meringue into the chocolate mixture. Pour the cream over the first sponge cake encased with the ring. Cover with the second cake and refrigerate for 4 hours, until set. Remove from the refrigerator, open and carefully remove the ring.

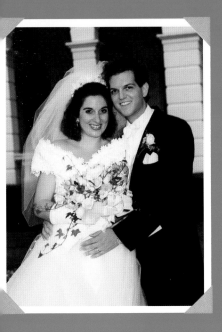

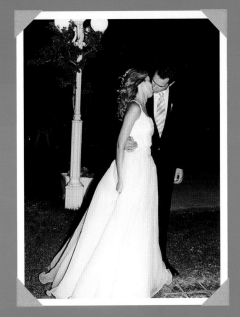

4

WEDDING CAKES

Let them eat cake !
Qu'ils se mangent de la brioche!

Marie-Antoinette

(Although the above statement is attributed to Marie-Antoinette, wife of Louis XVI,
it has actually been recorded by Jean Jacques Rousseau,
in his book Confessions, in 1768, as having been made by Marie-Thérèse, wife of Louis XIV).

Instructions and Recipes for Wedding Cakes

Choose the cake you want to use as the base of your wedding cake, and accompany it with the appropriate filling. Consult the table below for the quantity of cake mix to use in each baking tin, and the cooking time required. The following quantities yield cakes that are about 2 inches (5cm) high. For taller cakes, repeat the process. You should have two $2^1/_4$-inches (5.5cm) high cakes, made using each size of pan. Cut each into two layers and join the cake bases with your favorite filling. When placing one cake on top of another, use 3 or 4 wooden skewers to stabilize the structure.

For baking pans larger than 10 inches (28cm) it is a good idea, before pouring in the cake batter, to place a metal baking rod in the center of the pan, so that the heat is distributed evenly throughout the cake. If you don't have a baking rod, when the cooking time is up, open the oven and pierce the center of the cake with a wooden skewer. If it comes out wet, lower the temperature and keep cooking until the skewer comes out of the center dry. To avoid the surface drying out, you can place the cake on the bottom rack and cover the surface with non-stick oven paper. Make a 2-inch (5-cm) hole in the center of the paper so that you can pass the skewer through to check the cake. Consult the following table for cake and cream filling combinations.

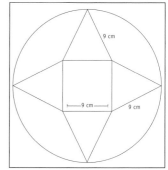

ROUND OR HEART-SHAPED PAN

DIMENSIONS ∅	QUANTITY OF FILLING	COOKING TIME/°F & °C	QUANTITY OF CAKE BATTER
22cm/ 8-inch	1 cup	45 min. at 350°F (175°C)	1 cup
28cm/ 10-inch	2½ cups	1 hour at 350°F (175°C)	2 cups
34cm/ 12-inch	3 cups	50 min. at 330°F (170°C)	3 cups
40cm/ 14-inch	3½ cups	1 hour and 10 min.	4 cups

SQUARE OR HEXAGONAL PAN

DIMENSIONS ∅	QUANTITY OF FILLING	COOKING TIME/°F & °C	QUANTITY OF CAKE BATTER
22cm/ 8-inch	1 cup	45 min. at 350°F (175°C)	1 cup
28cm/ 10-inch	2 cups	50 min. at 350°F (175°C)	2 cups
34cm/ 12-inch	2½ cups	50 min. at 330°F (170°C)	3 cups
40cm/ 14-inch	3½ cups	1 hour at 330°F (170°C)	4 cups

 ♥ cream fillings

cakes	Chocolate	White Chocolate	Bitter Almond	Caramel	Vanilla	Strawberry Rasberry	Mocha	Orange	Lemon	Tangerine	Coconut	Passion Fruit	Praline
Vanilla / Yogurt / Sponge Cake	♥♥	♥♥♥	♥♥♥	♥♥♥	♥♥♥	♥♥♥	♥♥	♥♥	♥♥	♥♥	♥♥	♥♥♥	♥♥♥
Hazelnut	♥♥♥	♥		♥♥	♥♥		♥♥♥						♥
Lemon					♥♥	♥♥		♥♥	♥♥♥	♥♥♥			
Orange	♥♥				♥		♥	♥♥♥	♥♥♥	♥♥♥			♥
Mocha	♥♥	♥♥	♥♥♥	♥♥	♥♥♥		♥♥♥	♥					♥♥
Mastic	♥♥	♥♥♥		♥♥♥	♥♥♥		♥♥						
White Chocolate				♥	♥	♥♥♥	♥♥				♥♥♥		♥♥
White Sponge Cake	♥♥♥	♥♥♥	♥♥♥	♥♥	♥♥♥	♥♥♥	♥♥♥	♥♥	♥♥	♥♥	♥	♥♥♥	♥♥♥
Rich Chocolate Cake	♥♥♥	♥♥	♥♥	♥♥♥	♥♥			♥♥♥	♥♥♥		♥		

Simple Vanilla Cake

- 1 cup soft unsalted butter
- 2 cups sugar
- 1 teaspoon vanilla essence
- 4 large eggs
- 3 cups self-raising flour
- 1 cup milk

1. Cream the butter, sugar and vanilla together at the mixer's medium speed. While beating, add the eggs one at a time. Stop beating and add the flour and milk gradually, beating well between each addition.
2. Butter a round 10-inch (28-cm) baking pan. Line the bottom with buttered non-stick paper and pour in the cake batter. Bake at 350°F (175°C) for 1 hour. Remove from the oven, overturn onto a rack and leave to cool. Divide in layers and fill according to your preference.

Hazelnut cake: replace 1/2 cup flour with 1 cup finely ground hazelnuts.

Mastic-scented cake: mix 1/4 cup of the sugar with 1/4oz (10g) mastic and add to the mixture with the rest of the sugar.

Lemon or orange cake: Replace the vanilla with 1 tablespoon lemon or orange zest. Add 2 tablespoons Grand Marnier to the orange cake.

Fluffy Yogurt Cake

- 1 cup unsalted butter or soft margarine
- 1³⁄₄ cups sugar
- 4 large eggs
- 3½ cups self-raising flour
- 1/2 teaspoon baking powder
- 1/2 teaspoon salt
- 1 cup yogurt
- 1/2 cup milk
- 2 teaspoons vanilla essence

1. Place all the ingredients in the mixer bowl. Beat slowly for 1 minute to blend the ingredients and then for 3 minutes at medium speed, until fluffy and double in volume.
2. Butter a round 10-inch (28-cm) baking tin well, line the bottom with buttered non-stick paper and pour in the cake batter. Bake at 350°F (175°C) for 1 hour. Remove from the oven, overturn onto a rack and leave to cool. Divide in layers and fill according to your preference.

White Chocolate Coconut Cake

- 1 cup fine-quality white chocolate chips
- 1 cup milk
- 2½ cups self-raising flour
- 1¼ cups sugar
- 1 cup unsalted soft butter or soft margarine
- 3 eggs
- 1 teaspoon vanilla essence
- 1/2 cup roasted ground almonds
- 1/2 cup unsweetened shredded coconut

1. Melt the chocolate with 1/4 cup of the milk over low heat. Remove from the heat and leave to cool.
2. Place the flour, sugar, butter and the remaining milk in the mixer bowl. Beat at high speed for 2 minutes. Add the eggs, vanilla and melted chocolate and beat at high speed for another 2 minutes. Add the almonds and coconut and mix in well.
3. Butter a round 10-inch (28-cm) baking pan, line the bottom with buttered non-stick paper and pour in the cake batter. Bake at 350°F (175°C) for 1 hour. Remove from the oven, overturn onto a grid and leave to cool.

Almond Sponge Cake

See "Rose engagement cake" on page 156.

White Spongecake for Wedding Cakes

- 3 cups self-raising flour
- 1/4 teaspoon salt
- 1¹⁄₃ cups milk
- 1 teaspoon vanilla essence
- 1/4 teaspoon bitter almond essence
- 1 cup soft unsalted butter
- 2 cups castor sugar
- 8 egg whites
- 1/2 teaspoon cream of tartar
- 1/3 cup sugar

1. Place all the ingredients except the last three in the mixer bowl and beat for 2 minutes, until fluffy. Beat the egg whites in a clean bowl with clean beaters, together with the cream of tartar and sugar, until soft peaks form. Fold the mixture gently into the cake batter, so as not to deflate the egg whites.
2. Divide the mixture evenly between three well-buttered round baking pans (8 inches or 20cm) lined with oven paper and bake for 25 minutes at 350°F (175°C). When done, overturn each onto a cloth sprinkled with icing sugar and leave to cool. Join with the filling you prefer to make a tall wedding cake.

Vanilla Sponge Cake

See "Vanilla Lemingtons" recipe on page 156.

Butter Sponge Cake

See "Pyramid Cake" recipe on p.156.

Chocolate Sponge Cake

See "Ring Pillow Cake" recipe on p. 131..

Engagement China-cakes

1. Prepare 1 recipe white sponge cake for wedding cakes. Butter and line 2 jelly roll pans with oven paper. Divide the cake mixture between the pans, and smooth the surface with a spatula. Bake the cakes separately, in the oven center for 25 minutes at 350°F (175°C).
2. Remove the cakes and overturn onto tea-towels spread with icing sugar. Cut 12 3-inch (8-cm) circles out of the first cake, and 12 2-inch (5-cm) circles out of the other.
3. Prepare 1 recipe hazelnut mousseline cream. Cut each small and large circle in two horizontally, using a sharp knife. Join the two halves with the cream. Brush the surface (central part) of the 12 joined large circles with a little jam, and stick the 12 smaller circles on top, so as to make 12 two-tier cakes. Brush with a little jam or buttercream icing (you will need 1½ recipes).
4. You will also need 2 pounds (1kg) Regalice. Roll out pieces of the icing on a surface sprinkled with icing sugar and cut out thin discs, about 9 inches (26cm) in diameter. Spread the icing carefully to cover the two-tier cake surface. Color a piece of the remaining icing lilac and cut out small leaves with a pastry cutter. Stick these onto the iced cakes using a little water. Color another piece of icing gold and use this to make ribbons for decorating the bottom of each mini-cake. Color a little buttercream icing lilac and use this to pipe pretty shapes onto the cakes. Store in the freezer or refrigerator until serving. (Photo on page 80).

Strawberry Cream with Cream Cheese

- 1/2 pound (250g) cream cheese
- 1/2 cup unsalted butter
- 1/3 cup icing sugar
- 1 sachet (60g) instant strawberry-flavored pudding
- 2 cups milk

1. Prepare according to the recipe for mocha cream. Yields 3 cups strawberry cream filling.

Continued from p.231: "Groom's Chocolate Surprise Cake"

Chocolate Icing

- 1 pound (500g) fine-quality cooking chocolate
- 6 egg yolks
- 1/4 cup Cognac or Amaretto liqueur
- 1/3 cup evaporated milk
- 3 cups icing sugar

For decorating
- 14oz (400g) fine-quality white chocolate
- 14oz (400g) fine-quality dark chocolate

1. Melt the cooking chocolate over very low heat, stirring constantly. Beat the egg yolks gently with the Cognac and milk, and add to the melted chocolate, stirring constantly. Sift the icing sugar into the melted chocolate and stir the mixture well. Cover all three cakes with the icing, pouring it over the center of the surface of the cakes, and letting it flow to the sides.
2. Prepare the two-toned strips for decorating. Melt the two types of chocolate separately. Line two small oblong baking pans with cling film, and brush with corn oil. Divide the dark chocolate between the two pans and refrigerate until almost hard. Pour over the melted white chocolate. Refrigerate again for 3 hours. Remove the two-toned chocolate bars by overturning the pans, remove the cling film carefully and leave to soften. Using a vegetable peeler, shave off two-toned chocolate strips and use to decorate the cakes. Keep the cakes refrigerated until serving.

Mocha Filling with Cream Cheese

See "Lace meringues with mocha cream", recipe on page 107

Bitter Almond Cream

See "Millefeuilles with frangipane cream", recipe on page 200.

Chocolate Cream Filling

Yields 1 cup
Preparation time 20 minutes

- 7oz (200g) fine-quality dark chocolate
- 3 egg yolks

- 1 teaspoon vanilla or bitter almond essence
- 5 tablespoons milk
- 3 tablespoons unsalted butter
- 1½ cups icing sugar

1. 1Place the chocolate in a double boiler and leave to melt. Mix the egg yolks with the essence and milk in a small bowl and add the butter chopped in pieces. Pour this mixture together with the icing sugar into the melted chocolate, stirring briskly with a wooden spoon, until you obtain a smooth and shiny chocolate mixture. Remove from the double boiler and leave to cool.
Alternatively, replace the essence with 2 tablespoons Cognac.

Fluffy chocolate filling: mix the chocolate cream with 1 cup whipped cream. (Yields 2 cups cream).

Chocolate mousse filling: beat 2 egg whites to a soft meringue and fold gently into the fluffy chocolate filling. (Yields 4 cups cream).

White Chocolate Buttercream

Yields 2 cups icing
Preparation time 30 minutes

- 1 cup sugar
- 1/3 cup water
- 1/3 teaspoon cream of tartar
- 1 egg
- 1 cup cold unsalted butter, cut in small pieces
- 8oz (250g) fine-quality white chocolate
- 1/4 cup milk
- 1 tablespoon glucose

1. Boil the sugar with the water and cream of tartar, to make a thick syrup.
2. Beat the egg in the mixer bowl and add the syrup a little at a time, beating constantly. Keep beating until the mixture is cold and fluffy.
3. Chop up the butter and add it to the mixture gradually while beating. The whole process should take about 7 minutes. The mixture will become thin at first, but as you keep adding more butter it will thicken as it cools down.
4. Melt the white chocolate in a double boiler with the milk and glucose. When the mixture has cooled down, add and stir into the butter mixture.

Fruit Cream Filling

Yields 2 cups
Preparation time 30 minutes

- 6 tablespoons corn-starch
- 2 cups fruit juice (orange, tangerine, strawberry)
- 1/8 teaspoon salt
- 1/2 cup sugar
- 4 egg yolks, slightly beaten
- 2 teaspoons zest or 1 teaspoon fruit essence
- 2 tablespoons butter (optional)
- 2 cups whipped cream (optional)

1. Dissolve the corn-starch in 1/2 cup orange juice. Place the rest of the juice with the salt in a small pan over medium heat and bring to boiling point.
2. In the meantime, whisk the egg yolks with the sugar to form a frothy pale yellow mixture. When the juice comes to the boil, add the beaten eggs together with the dissolved corn-starch and keep whisking briskly, until you obtain a smooth thick custard.
3. Remove from the heat, and stir in the butter to melt. Leave the custard to cool. Add and mix in the zest.
4. If you are using whipped cream, at this stage fold it into the mixture with gentle strokes. Keep the orange cream in the refrigerator, covered with cling film.

Lemon cream: use 1/3 cup lemon juice and the rest orange juice or milk. If using lemon juice and milk, you will need 1 cup sugar.

Coconut cream: omit the corn-starch and make the cream with 5 egg yolks, 2/3 cup sugar, 1 cup canned coconut milk and 1 teaspoon coconut essence.

Vanilla-scented crème pâtissière

Yields 2 cups cream
Preparation time 40 minutes

- 2/3 cup sugar
- 5-6 egg yolks
- 5 tablespoons corn-starch
- a little salt
- 2 cups milk
- a little vanilla powder or essence
- 2 cups whipped cream (optional)

1. Beat the egg yolks and sugar in a large bowl until thick and lemon-colored. Sift the flour and a pinch of salt over the mixture and stir.
2. Boil the milk and, stirring briskly, add to the egg yolk mixture a spoonful at a time.
3. Transfer the mixture to a small heavy-bottomed pan and boil over low heat, stirring constantly so that it doesn't stick to the bottom, until you obtain a thick custard. The custard must simmer for 10 to 15 minutes to eliminate the floury smell.
4. Cover the surface with cling film and refrigerate for up to 2 days. Before using, mix with 2 cups whipped cream to make it lighter.

Chocolate cream: add 4oz (125g) melted cooking chocolate to the cream. You must mix the cream with 2 cups whipped cream, otherwise it will be too thick when the chocolate cools. Yields 4 cups cream.

White chocolate cream: add 6oz (180g) pieces of white chocolate to the warm cream, and stir until melted and incorporated. After it cools down, mix the cream with 2 cups whipped cream. Yields 4 cups cream.

Fluffy White Vanilla Icing

- 1 cup white vegetable shortening or butter
- 2 teaspoons vanilla essence
- 4 cups icing sugar
- 1/4 cup milk

1. All the ingredients must be at room temperature. Beat the butter with the sugar and vanilla at medium speed, until the mixture is fluffy and creamy soft. Do not beat at high speed because the butter will curdle. Add as much milk as necessary to obtain a thick, fluffy, smooth, stiff, snow-white icing.

2. For chocolate icing add 1/2 cup cocoa to the icing sugar, and more milk until you obtain the right consistency. If you want colored icing, add a few drops of food coloring and a few drops of you favorite essence (e.g. bitter almond, coconut, strawberry or lemon essence) and beat the icing in the mixer until the color is uniform. Fill a piping bag and use to decorate your cakes. One recipe will cover 1 round 9-inch (24-cm) cake.

Miroir Passion [Passion Fruit Filling]

Filling for 3 layers of 8-inch (20-cm) cakes

- 1 cup milk
- 6 egg yolks
- 2/3 cup castor sugar
- 1 tablespoon gelatine
- 2/3 cup passion fruit seed and juice pulp
- 2 cups whipping cream

1. Heat but don't boil the milk. Place the egg yolks in a heavy-bottomed saucepan with the sugar and beat until you have a thick yellow mixture. Add a few spoonfuls of the warm milk to the egg mixture and stir. Then pour in the remaining milk all at once and stir over medium heat until thick.

2. Mix the gelatine with 2 tablespoons water and leave to swell. Add to the hot custard and stir in until dissolved. Remove from the heat, leave to cool slightly and add and stir in the fruit pulp. Cover the surface of the cream with cling film and leave to cool. Whip the whipping cream and fold into the passion fruit mixture.

3. Place 3 sponge cake layers, 8 inches (20cm), in a metal flan ring, with the cream spread in between the layers. Cover the last layer with cream and refrigerate the cake until set. Decorate with fresh clean rosebuds.

Praline Mousseline Filling

Will fill 12 6-inch (15-cm) round cakes

- 1/2 cup sugar for the praline
- 2 tablespoons water
- 3oz (100g) blanched roasted almonds
- 2 cups milk
- 4 egg yolks
- 1/4 cup sugar for the custard
- 3 tablespoons corn-starch
- 1/2 tablespon gelatine
- 4 cups (1 liter) whipped cream

1. Melt the sugar with the water for the praline in a heavy-bottomed pan, add the almonds and simmer until you have a brown caramel. Pour the caramel onto a marble surface, lightly oiled, or a baking pan spread with non-stick paper, also oiled. Let the praline cool and harden. Chop up and powder in the food processor.

2. Prepare the custard. Heat the milk to boiling point. In a large saucepan beat the egg yolks with the rest of the sugar and the corn-starch until you obtain a thick yellow mixture. Dilute with a few spoonfuls of the hot milk and then pour in the rest of the milk all at once. Mix over medium heat until thick enough to cover the back of a spoon

3. Mix the gelatine with 2 tablespoons water and leave to swell. Add to the custard and stir until it dissolves. Blend in the powdered praline. Remove the custard from the heat and leave to cool. Once cold, fold in the whipped cream.

4. To make individual wedding cakes, bake 2 recipes "White sponge cake for Wedding Cakes" in jelly roll pans. Cut 12 5-inch (12-cm) circles from each cake. Place half the circles in small flan rings, divide the praline filling between them, and cover with the remaining circles. Refrigerate for 4 to 5 hours, until the filling sets. Remove the rings and brush the surface of the cakes with a little warmed raspberry jam. Roll pieces of Regalice out into 9-inch (25-cm) sheets and cover the individual cakes, spreading and smoothing the icing with your palms. Draw ribbons, dainty flowers or other bridal themes on the surface with icing, using a piping bag and white or gold or silver-tinted royal icing.

5. Hazelnut mousseline cream: use roasted unsalted hazelnuts instead of almonds.

Meringues

Yields 2 meringue layers, 8 inches (22cm) each.

- 4 egg whites (from extra large eggs)
- 1/4 teaspoon cream of tartar or a few drops lemon juice
- 1 cup fine sugar
- 1/4 teaspoon vanilla powder or 1 teaspoon vanilla essence

1. Beat the egg whites with the cream of tartar in the mixer, until thick and fluffy. While beating, gradually add half the sugar. Lower the mixer speed. Add the remaining sugar and vanilla and beat for 1 second, just a couple of turns.

2. Draw two 8-inch (22-cm) circles on two sheets of non-stick paper. Spread the paper on two oven grids. Place the meringue mixture in a piping bag with a large nozzle and use to cover the circles on the paper, making spirals from the center outwards.

3. Bake the meringues at 180°F (90°C) for 2 hours, in a fan oven. Turn off the heat and let the meringue layers cool inside the oven. Will keep for 5 to 6 months in boxes, protected from humidity.

Wedding Planner

From "yes"... to "I do"

12 to 6 months before the big event	Deadline	✍	
Family Meeting			Organize an evening at your house, if you have already moved into your new home, and invite both families so they can meet each other. It's a good idea to include siblings or the best man or maid of honor in the invitation, so that the atmosphere is not tense and the evening flows more easily for the new couple.
Ordering the Rings			The names and the date of the engagement or wedding are engraved on the rings.
Engagement Announcement in the Press			This is not compulsory, but if you wish, you can do it on the day of the engagement.
Official Engagement Party			If you decide to have an official engagement, remember that it is a small rehearsal for the wedding. You can arrange to have it in a tight family circle, with relatives or only your friends. Such moments are unforgettable, so enjoy them and save the memories for your future common life. Print invitations, choose a dress, organize an unforgettable evening, pay as much attention to detail as if it was your wedding.
Set a Date			Make a note of the date that suits you, and choose a few alternative dates, in case there are problems with the church, the contributors or the reception hall.
Choose the best man and maid of honor			Once you have selected the best man and maid of honor, remember that their availability is absolutely essential for the final setting of a date.
Reserve the church			Make sure that the church and reception hall are not too far away from each other. Contact in time the right person at the house of worship of your choice in order to discuss details if you are having a mixed faith ceremony
Reserve the reception hall			
Choose the caterers			In order to save time and avoid extra expense, contact a wedding planning agency. Good organization might be a life-saver, and might also cost less than you think. If you prefer to do the organizing yourself, start looking for the right place now. Remember that many reception halls provide catering, although not necessarily up to standards, and many caterers will provide you with halls to choose from. It's a good idea to choose a place where the

	Deadline	✍	
			quality of the food is equal to the quality of the surroundings.
Choosing a wedding dress			Rent or buy; now is the time to begin your market research, so that soon you can decide at least who is going to make the dress. Fittings may take several months. Remember that if you intend to go on a diet, your weight should be stable for at least 2 weeks before the wedding, so that the final fitting for your dress doesn't require drastic changes.
Dressing the groom			Rent or buy, act now as both will need numerous fittings.
Draft a first guest list			Make a draft list of the people you and your future husband want to invite to the wedding. Planning ahead will help you not forget anyone, and have time for any amendments to the list. To avoid family disputes, consult both families on their guests. The best man and maid of honor are also entitled to invitations for their personal friends or families. Ask them to give you the names of their guests, so you have a complete guest list.
Select and order the invitations			Contact a company as soon as possible, who can prepare the wedding invitations, visiting cards with your new address, monogrammed envelopes and thank-you cards with matching envelopes.
Choose a florist for: • Decorating the church • The bride's bouquet • The bride's crown of flowers • Decorating the reception hall • Crowns and bouquets for the bridesmaids • The groom's and best man's boutonniéres • Decorating the car			If you choose one florist for everything, you will definitely get a better offer. Don't choose anyone before you have done some extensive market research. A basic principle is to go to a serious company, having first compared both prices and quality. You may choose for the church flowers to be carried to the reception area straight after the ceremony. Make appropriate appointments with florist and/or event decorator on location.

6 to 4 months before	Deadline	👍	
Choose a photographer and a cameraman for the video			Ask to see some recent work, so that you get an idea of the quality beforehand. Also ask for how long they will stay at the wedding. A good idea is to ask them to stay for the entire reception and prepare a beautiful photo album for you.
Choose a band or a DJ for the reception			Do some market research before you decide, and discuss the type of music you want.
Plan your honeymoon			If you choose to leave right after the wedding, now is the time to make reservations. If you choose somewhere tropical, be sure you are aware of the weather conditions there, as well as of any shots you may need to have before you go.
Choose your sugared almond cases or wedding favors, candles and wedding wreaths together with the maid of honor			In Greece, the best man and maid of honor pay for these, but the final decision on the type and quality of the above must be yours.
Choose your bridesmaids			*Greek custom:* young boys and girls dressed in white or ivory, to match the wedding dress; they follow the bride and hold the train of her dress. *English custom:* a little girl holding a basket of rose petals, and a little boy holding the rings on a cushion. 2-3 single young women and an equal number of bachelors, so that they make pairs, make up the bride's entourage, all dressed in dark colours, dark red, dark blue, silver-grey. They walk ahead of the bride. *American custom:* a little girl holding a basket of rose petals, and a little boy holding the rings on a cushion. 4-6 girlfriends of the bride dressed in pastel-coloured dresses, holding bouquets like the bride's form the bridesmaids' entourage, and an equal number of male friends of the groom in light-coloured suits make up the ushers' entourage. They walk ahead of the bride.

4 to 2 months before	Deadline	👍	
Choose and order the wedding cake			You can select a theme to match the wedding dress, the season, the sugared almond cases, the flowers, or the specific theme of the whole wedding.
Reserve the place where you plan to spend your wedding night			
Arrange transport to and from the church			Some companies rent luxury cars, limousines, helicopters or horse-drawn carriages – depending on your finances.
Arrange all the documents necessary for the wedding			Check with the bride's parish (Greece) or the Town Hall and house of worship according to your nationality and religion.
Buy the bride's accessories: • the lingerie, pantyhose, garter • the petticoat (if separate from the gown) • the veil • the gloves • the shoes (pumps, sandals or sling-backs to match the style or color or fabric of the dress) • the handbag • the jewelry • the headpiece (tiara or satin wreath)			
Decide on the final guest list			
Arrange for the scripting of the invitations			

2 to 1 month before

	Deadline	👍	
Register at one or more stores for your wedding list			Get wedding list cards from the stores to send with your wedding invitations or with your "shower" invitations.
Book rooms and arrange transport for guests arriving especially for the wedding from other towns			
Discuss the final menu with the caterer			Pay attention to detail. Include lighter dishes for the elderly, and dishes for vegetarians. Also make sure that the menu agrees with the style of the whole wedding.
Reach an agreement with the church if you want a carpet, a choir, the entire ceremony, and anything else it can offer. Choose the decoration of the aisle and altar.			The wedding ceremony is a unique, moving and once-in-a-lifetime experience. If you have the choice, arrange the whole ceremony, lasting around one hour.

	Deadline	👍	
Announce the wedding in a local newspaper one month in advance			
Try out your hair-do and make-up, and let the professionals know what day and time you will be needing them			Arrange for the trial to coincide with a party or special event so that it is not wasted.
Send the invitations			The invitations must be delivered personally, or by courier, except in cases where such a delivery is not possible.
Make a Guest List			Make note of the answers you receive from now until shortly before the wedding day, so you know who is coming and who is not.

2 weeks before

	Deadline	👍	
Order the "Maid of Honor's Bombonnière"			Sugared almonds are offered to the maid of honor in a crystal or silver container, which can be a gift for her home.
Choose and buy gifts for the best man and maid of honor			You can give them your gifts now, or after the wedding when they visit you at your new home.
Organize the "making of the bed" or your "bridal shower'			Invite single women and a mother with a small child for the old Greek tradition of "making the bed".
Final wedding dress fitting with shoes and accessories			At the final fitting, offer sweets to everyone and bring your best friends with you.
Check all details with the following: • Church • Maid of honor – Best man • Bridesmaids - Ushers • Caterers • Reception hall • Florists • Confectioner for the cake • Photographer • Cameraman (video) • DJ or Orchestra • Hair stylist • Make-up artist • Transport • Travel agent			
Write thank-you notes, as you receive gifts at your new house			
Choose a song for the first dance			Traditionally, the new couple starts the dancing at the reception with a romantic

	Deadline	👍	
			song. Choose your favorite. The first dance of the rest of your life as a married couple should impress the guests. Tango or waltz lessons make a good impression.

1 week before

	Deadline	👍	
Have a final rehearsal with the bridesmaids and ushers in the church			
Meet with the caterer			Discuss the table arrangement and where everyone is going to sit. The caterer should prepare a design of the space and the arrangement of the tables for you. Remember that the groom's parents, the bride's parents, the best man and the maid of honor should sit at the bride's table. If there is space left over, this should be kept for honored guests.
Make sure the wedding cake is delivered directly to the reception hall on time			
Receive: • The bonbonnières • The candles • The wedding wreaths • The wedding dress • The groom's suit • Shoes and accessories • Bridesmaids' clothes			Wear your shoes often inside the house, so that they get soft and don't hurt you on the big day. Try on the dress (bride), the suit (groom); despite the final fitting, you might still discover something wrong, which will have to be fixed before the ceremony. Make sure your attendants have received their clothes.
Prepare an overnight bag with everything you will need on your wedding night			
Prepare your luggage for the honeymoon in advance if you are planning to leave right after the wedding			
Bride and groom: • Have some beauty treatments • Manicure • Pedicure • Facial • Massage			
On the last Thursday: Making the Bed or Bridal Shower			Organize and have your bridal shower as glamorous as you like it.

2-3 days before	Deadline	☙	
Have your bachelor party			Don't leave this until the last day before the wedding. You'll have more fun if you have it a few days earlier, as you'll have time to rest before the big day.
Buy a gift for your parents and parents-in-law			Do not forget to show your gratitude to those who stood by you during the whole organization period

1 day before

Confirm:

	Deadline	☙	
Transport			The bride is accompanied to the church by her father and the bridesmaids.
Hair stylist Make-up artist			Make sure they arrive at your home several hours before the ceremony, so that you are rested for the photo shoot that takes place before the beginning of the ceremony.
Florist			Have the hair-piece delivered fresh to your home, while the hair stylist is there, so that you can have it adjusted or be shown how to do it just before the ceremony. Keep it in a cool place in the shade until you are on your way to the church, because the flowers are very delicate.

on the Wedding Day

	Deadline	☙	
Play wedding songs loudly at your house			
Follow the traditions:			• The groom must not see the wedding dress before the ceremony. • The groom must not sleep in the same house as the bride on the night before the wedding. • The groom must not see the bride at all on the wedding day, until she steps to the altar. • The bride's friends come to the house a few hours early and help her to dress. • Write the names of single guests on the

	Deadline	☙	
			soles of your wedding shoes. The ones whose names are rubbed off, will soon get married. • Don't forget, on your way out of the church, to toss your bouquet to the single women. The groom throws the bride's garter at his bachelor friends. • Make sure two or three of your friends have decorated baskets containing rice and rose-petals to be shared out among the guests and tossed when the best man is exchanging the wreaths in the church or when the couple exits. • Be traditionally late – about fifteen minutes. Step on the groom's foot when the priest says "The woman shall respect and fear the man", provided the groom's sense of humor allows it. • Save the last tier of the wedding cake and store it in the freezer to share with your husband on your first anniversary. • The groom lifts the bride over the threshold of their new house on their wedding night. • The couple breaks a pomegranate on the doorstep of their new home, for luck and fertility. Traditions always have a logical explanation. The bride is definitely stressed about her dress and her appearance before the wedding. If someone close to her, and especially her husband-to-be makes a negative, in her opinion, comment, about anything that is stressing her, a row is inevitable. Remember Murphy's law without worrying too much, and face it with a sense of humor: "Nothing is as easy as it seems, everything takes longer than you expect, and if something is about to go wrong, it will at the worst possible moment". Now get organized, relax, and enjoy THE MOST BEAUTIFUL DAY OF YOUR LIFE.

Index

CATERING
• Elena's Gourmet Cake House, Elena Georgitziki, Reception Catering, 31, Kolokotroni St., Thermi, Thessaloniki, tel: 2310-465 570, mobile: 0944 91 48 66, www.elenasgourmet.gr
• Big Deals Catering, 50, Char. Trikoupi St. & Diligianni, Kifissia, Kefalari, tel: 210-6230 860
• Giannis Anthimos, Marquees and reception settings, Athens, tel: 210-9845 651, Thessaloniki, tel: 2310-420 019, e-mail: anthimos@otenet.gr, www.anthimos-i.com
• Platis Gestronomie, (Winter Reception wedding cake and preparation of Pyramid wedding cake – created by Alexia Alexiadou), 310, Kifissias Avenue, Kifissia, tel: 210-6251 588

JEWELRY
• BVLGARI, 8, Voukourestiou St., Athens, tel: 210-3247 118 (-9)
• Kaisaris, 7, Panepistimiou St., Athens, tel: 210-3310 600
• Alexis Alexopoulos, 127, Char. Trikoupi St., N. Erithrea, tel: 210-8071 268 (Title diamond ring, p. 49, and diamond cross, p. 7)

CHINA – WEDDING LIST
• Vefa's House, 1, Kressnas St., Likovrissi, tel: 210-2846 984
• Costa Boda, 19, Stadiou St., Athens, tel: 210-3252 814
• Happyland, 21, Stadiou St., Athens, tel: 210-3252 814
• Herrend (Engagement), 1, Valaoritou St., Athens, tel: 210-3627 007

WEDDING CAKES
• Donna Chalas, The Bridal Sweet, 425, Vouliagmenis Ave., Ilioupoli, tel: 210-9957 093, www.weddings.gr
Many thanks to Donna Chalas for all the unique cakes photographed for the Wedding Cakes chapter. Confectionary lessons on how to make your own wedding cake are given at Donna's workshop.
The sugar paste roses on page 7 and the cakes on pages 11 and 179 are also Donna's creations.

COSMETICS
• L'occitane, 7, Kolokotroni St., Kifissia, tel: 210-8089 454

FLOWERS – CHURCH/RECEPTION FLORAL DECORATIONS
• Giorgos Harmandas, 1, Irinis Ave., Pefki, Athens, tel: 210-6120 325
• Greenpiece – I. Nanos, G. Hatzopoulos, 5, Ilia Pilidi St., Panorama, Thessaloniki, tel: 2310-341 725

WEDDING GOWNS AND HAUTE COUTURE CLOTHING
• Nikolas Mavropoulos, Haute Couture, 5, Loukianou St., Kolonaki, tel: 210-7222 692
• Denise Eleftheriou, Designer (Wedding by the Sea wedding dresses, and wedding dresses on pp. 12, 13, 150-51, 175), 6, Karolou Deal St., 2nd floor, Thessaloniki, tel: 2310-272 477
• Aslanis Boutique, 16, Anagnostopoulou St., Kolonaki, tel: 210-3600 049, (evening wear, p. 82)
• Stolidis, Wedding, Baptism accessories, Krioneriou Ave., Ag. Stefanos, tel: 210-8141 518 (-9), (bridesmaids, pp. 176,177,179)
• Demetrios, Weddings, Baptisms, 7, Kornarou St., Athens, tel: 210-3222 503, (bridesmaid in white dress, p. 208, 227, 229)
Many thanks to Nikolas Mavropoulos designs for providing his atelier for the photographs taken for the Wedding Dress Fittings chapter.

HOME APPLIANCES
• Vefa's House, www.vefashouse.gr, Central distribution, Athens, tel: 210-2846 984, e-mail: info@vefashouse.gr
• Sandra, Athens, tel: 210-9480 198
• La taste, 359, Kifissias Ave., N. Erithrea, tel: 210-6202 319
• Past and Present, 1, Kolokotroni St., Kifissia, tel: 210-6231 299
• Utopia, 26, Skoufa St., Kolonaki, tel: 210-3612 987

SPECIAL WEDDING ACCESSORIES
• Vefa's House, 1, Kressnas St., Likovrissi, tel: 210-2846 984

WEDDING FAVORS – WREATHS – CANDLES
• L'arte di Artemide, 22, Karneadou St., Kolonaki, Athens, tel: 210-7227 772
• Antigoni Danou, (church decorations, sugared almonds and candles, p. 13), 11, Proxenou Koromila St., Thessaloniki, tel: 2310-270 024

FURNITURE
• Andreas Kritikos, Interior Decoration, Furniture, 338, Kifissias Ave., Kifissia, Athens, tel: 210-6208 542
Many thanks to our friend Andreas for lending us his store for the photoshoots for chapters: Diamonds for Breakfast and Family Meeting.

LINEN
• Kyros Interiors, 16, Levidou St. & Argiropoulou, Kifissia, tel: 210-8085 540

MODELS
Valentini Daskaloudi
Eleni Moundrea
(At the Christmas Reception, Eleni is wearing her own wedding dress, made by "Loukia" Haute Couture).

FRIENDLY PARTICIPATION
Steve Kanaris, Agis Drakopoulos

BRIDESMAIDS
Chara Kitsaki, Marina Siati, Anastasia Siati, Eftichia Zaragga, Adrianna Bouzaki, Maria Chanou

BRIDE'S GIRLFRIENDS
Lena Siati, Sofia Daniil, Georgia Psomiadi, Eleni Giamarellou, Vasso Kitsaki, Aphrodite Kozomboli, Laura Venizelou, Anna Maria Barouch, Emmanuella Tsaggari, Zozefina Drakopoulou, Elena Kontopoulou, Sofia Argyriadou – Bouzaki

PHOTOGRAPHY– VILLAS
Many thanks to the following families for providing their villas: Vefa and Kostas Alexiades – Chalkidiki, Katerina Ladaki and Lefteris Gripaios – Politeia, Angie Alexiadou and Giannis Dodoros – Dionysos, Lena and Christos Siatis – Drosia.

WEDDING PHOTOGRAPHS
Many thanks to my friends for sharing their wedding moments; page 134 (starting from left page): Katerina Gamiliari and Andreas Athanasopoulos, bride; Sofia Daniil (married to Takis Daniil), Alexia Alexiadou and Vaggelis Kitsakis, bridesmaids: Elina Anastasiadi. Maid of Honor: Elena Kontopoulou; page 135: Bridesmaids: Katerina Kiousi, Victoria Kioussi, bride: Angie Alexiadou, Vefa and Kostas Alexiades, bride: Eleni Giamarellou, Angie Alexiadou and Giannis Dodoros, Voula and George Georgitzikis, Eleni and George Giamarellos, bride: Aphrodite Kozomboli, Chara and Charalambos Kitsakis, Dimitris Andreadakis and Aphrodite Kozomboli, best man and maid of honor: Vaggelis Kitsakis and Alexia Alexiadou.

Wedding photos on page 232, bride: Joyce Tabbal, bride: Galateia Traganou, Galateia Traganou and Marios Efstathiou, Joyce and Steven Rogers, Heather Kanost and Maurizio Cartone, bridesmaid: Hara Kitsaki, Doris and Gary Christelis; page 233: Doris and Gary Christelis, Maria and Panagis Voutsinas, Emmanuella and Giannis Kassimatis, Angela and Giorgos Doukas, bride: Emmanuella Tsaggari, Aggeliki and Spyros Chronaios, Fotini Softi and Kosmas Giakoumatos, bride: Elena Kontopoulou (married to Lazaros Bachtsevanos), Emmanuella and Giannis Kassimatis.

Many thanks to my good friends, without their priceless help this book would not be complete: Takis Daniil, Elena Georgitziki, Antonis Stamoulis, Lena Siati, Sofia Daniil, Elena Kontopoulou, Katerina Ladaki, Ada Kassimati, Achilleas Bouzakis, Aris Kokorakis, Pepi Stogia, Smaro Drakopoulou, Doris Chistelis, Giota Tsanaxi, Giota Nitsou, Svetlana Sidorkaya.

CAR PHOTOGRAPHS
The white Rolls Royce is taking Doris and Gary Christelis from the church to the reception, at cosmopolitan Newport, Rhode Island.

COVER PHOTOGRAPH
The silver tray bearing the sugar-coated almonds and rice is placed on a table covered with a snow-white tablecloth. On the day of the engagement, the groom places the rings on the tray, to make his proposal official. On the wedding day, the priest places the wedding rings and the wreaths on the tray and blesses them.

The silver tray on the cover is a wedding gift to the author from her aunt, Voula Georgitziki.

"Wedding Days" is dedicated with much love to all couples married for more than seven years. To my mother and father, who are in the 43rd year of their marriage, yet my father still sends her flowers. To my sister who has spent 20 happy years with her husband, and with whom she still celebrates each anniversary like the very first time. To my parents-in-law, whose love has remained undying for 42 years of marriage.

It is also dedicated with much love to all my girlfriends, the newly-married ones still in their honeymoon period, the married ones supporting the family institution, and the single ones dreaming of their wedding day and of a happy life.

Everything you have read is ONLY the beginning, what you need for a successful wedding ceremony and reception. A successful marriage needs many more ingredients, such as dedication, patience, understanding, care, and love.

My wish to newlyweds: May you live united like butter and sugar in hot caramel, suit each other like meringue and whipped cream, and may your life flow softly and smoothly like velvety melted chocolate.